V for Vendetta
as Cultural Pastiche

V for Vendetta
as Cultural Pastiche

A Critical Study of
the Graphic Novel and Film

JAMES R. KELLER

McFarland & Company, Inc., Publishers
Jefferson, North Carolina, and London

LIBRARY OF CONGRESS CATALOGUING-IN-PUBLICATION DATA

Keller, James R., 1960–
    V for vendetta as cultural pastiche : a critical study of the
graphic novel and film / James R. Keller.
      p.   cm.
    Includes bibliographical references and index.

    ISBN 978-0-7864-3467-1
    softcover : 50# alkaline paper ∞

    1. V for vendetta (Motion picture)   2. Moore, Alan, 1953–
V for vendetta.   I. Title.
PN1997.2.V24K45   2008
791.43'72 — dc22   2008000031

British Library cataloguing data are available

On the cover: *Guy Fawkes Mask,* Brian Chan, paper origami, November
2006; background ©2008 Shutterstock

Manufactured in the United States of America

*McFarland & Company, Inc., Publishers
  Box 611, Jefferson, North Carolina 28640
   www.mcfarlandpub.com*

Contents

Introduction

Shadow Texts, Superstrings, and Parallel Universes

Allow me to begin with a metaphorical digression, with a layman's description of a theoretical model from physics, one that attempts to account for all energy and matter within the universe — a "Theory of Everything." In this way, I hope to elucidate the abstruse concepts surrounding intertextual theory, thus, ironically, illuminating the seemingly incomprehensible by explicating the merely esoteric. The latter, at least, has a provisional form that can help one to visualize the conceptual and linguistic subject matter pertinent to this study of the varied cultural productions surrounding *V for Vendetta*, originally a graphic novel written by Alan Moore and David Lloyd in the 1980s, but more pertinently the cinematic production (2005) by James McTeigue and the Wachowski Brothers, of *Matrix Trilogy* fame. The very rudimentary model of M-Theory or String Theory will allow us to conceptualize the interrelations between multiple textual productions in the present, between those of the past and the present, and between those of the present, past, and future. Thus we will open up a portal on the interplay or interpenetration of language, concepts, and images within the various *V for Vendetta* texts and more broadly within artifacts of both high and low cultures.

M-Theory

For a time, efforts to create a "Theory of Everything," to explain all of the observable phenomena of the universe with the known laws of

1

physics, were hindered by a theoretical schism within the field, a breach between Einstein's law of "Special Relativity," which explained the macrocosmic or the grand structures of the universe, and "Quantum Dynamics," which addressed the microcosmic, the physics of the atomic and subatomic levels. These two very useful laws were functionally incompatible until the introduction of "String Theory" (Greene, *Elegant* 3, 13). The new model actually necessitated the existence of both Special Relativity and Quantum Dynamics in order to be coherent (Greene, *Elegant* 16). Yet it became mired for a time in wrangling over the exact number of additional dimensions that existed beyond the observable four — three of direction (forward/backward, up/down, and right/left) and one of time. "String Theory," based upon the image of trembling fibers (billions of times smaller than an atom), each of which vibrates at a separate frequency, for a time hypothesized ten requisite dimensions. However, there were five competing and viable theories attempting to explain these strings. The resolution to the impasse came with the introduction of an eleventh dimension — a postulate that resulted in the genesis of "M-Theory," the brainchild of renowned physicist Edward Witten (Kaku 211–214).

With the addition of an eleventh dimension, the competing elucidations of "String Theory" were reconciled, and a new and refined hypothesis of the structure of "Everything" evolved — "M-Theory." While the "M" in "M-Theory" is the slipping signifier, suggesting "Mother," "Mystical," "Magical," or "Model," depending on the interpreter, it is the signifier "Membrane" that momentarily fits our purposes, and we might even consider adding "Metaphorical" to the burgeoning list of descriptive "M's." Via some inaccessible (to the layman) mathematical and theoretical acrobatics, M-Theorists have gleaned that the strings postulate the existence of "parallel universes," in one visual model, dangling, bending, warping, and rippling side by side, not so much like strings as corresponding sheets or membranes, each of which constitutes an alternate universe (Greene, *Fabric* 391–394). Within this framework, physicists have conceptualized "Black Holes" as portals or "wormholes" linking the corresponding membranes or even as the points of inception for newly created universes (Greene, *Elegant* 264–265, 369). The "Big Bang" (which created all matter and energy in our known universe, a process which continues even now, the structure continually flying apart in every direction) is thus conceived as the simultaneously creative and cataclysmic result of the membranes smashing into each other (Kaku 222). In the "inflationary model" of the cosmic expansion, the black hole is conceived as a puncture in the fabric of space/time that initiates the "big bang" and rapid inflation of a new universe in an alternate dimension, each branching from another like interlocking and interdependent balloons. These newborn universes may explain what has been termed "dark matter," which attempts to account for the missing 70 percent of the matter in our own cosmological vista (Kaku 221). The parallel membranes also account for the weakness of gravity within our universe — an idea postulated by Harvard physicist Lisa Randall — which holds that gravity is not native to or does not originate within, so much as permeate, our universe; it is a particle — a graviton — that penetrates all of the dimensions, and, therefore, is diluted. It may be a residual effect emanating from outside our observable dimensions. In other words, we experience only the remainder or the filtrate of the full gravitational force (Kaku 216–221).

By now the reader has probably begun to wonder, "What possible application could such a subject have to the study of film, literature, and intertextual theory?" And the answer is "Much, but all metaphorical." While there are indisputably more problems with and omissions in the above description of string theory than can be briefly listed in twice as much space, that need not concern us since the purpose of this discussion is to construct metaphors for esoteric literary theory — to track the intertextual footprints crisscrossing the porous and constantly interpenetrated terrain of James McTeigue's and the Wachowski Brothers' film *V for Vendetta* (2005). We deal in art, not objective observation and experimentation. Since it is based upon a graphic novel, the film is at its very inception intertextual, paralleling the text from which it was derived, the details of the corresponding narratives constantly interpreting and reinterpreting each other as they intersect and diverge for a variety of pragmatic, conceptual, aesthetic, and inadvertent purposes. The respective narratives dangle like parallel membranes or strings, waving or vibrating (because they are not stable) at similar yet separate frequencies, and occasionally slide against or crash into each other, generating particularly evocative interpretive structures, not in the text, but in the mind of the reader, and there are as many texts as there are readers and viewers. Each subject (re)creates the text within the "workshop of filthy creation," fashioning Adam and/or monster out of his or her own experiences and predispositions (Allen 7).

The collision between parallel textual universes generates meaning in accordance with linguistic theory, dating back to the work of Ferdinand de Saussure, whose revolutionary lectures, collected under the title *A Course in General Linguistics*, taught us that signifiers have no inherent meaning because they are arbitrary and that meaning is generated through the interplay of binary signs, all meaning relational (J. Culler 33, 61). All language refers only to other language, never to a material reality; thus meaning exists exclusively in the cognitive processes, in the apprehension of the text, not in a material reality, not even in books or films (Allen 65). The ideas of Saussure and the subsequent structuralist and post-structuralist movements in language, literature, philosophy, and anthropology also generate the theory of "intertextuality"—a word coined by French Feminist Theorist Julia Kristeva (*Desire in Language* 36)—which argues that other cultural artifacts and processes resemble language insofar as they refer only to other cultural products. Thus an individual film is not at all individual but plural, constantly interpenetrated by other aesthetic, social, historical, political, cultural, and other types of productions; "The text is not an individual isolate object but, rather, a compilation of cultural textuality" (Allen 36), as Roland Barthes states in *S/Z*, "the text is a galaxy of signifiers, not a structure of signifieds" (*S/Z* 6). Thus a film such as *V for Vendetta* is every bit as derivative of or interdependent upon other texts as, for instance, Gus Van Zant's 1998 frame by frame remake of Hitchcock's *Psycho* (1960), yet *VfV* is not dependent upon the graphic novel exclusively, but mirrors and quotes a wide variety of texts and mediums—literature, cinema, history, medicine (epidemiology/immunology), painting, music, sculpture, politics, and sociology. Like Eliot's *Waste Land*, *VfV* evokes, in fragmentary fashion, the history of Western culture and beyond, here suggesting a cyclic chronical of repression and liberation, each replacing the other at regular intervals. It simultaneously exposes the historical continuum of artistic reactions to the varied recurring socio-political hegemonies or *epistemes*.

The parallel textual universes ostensibly appear independent even as they "shadow" each other, but there are many theoretical connections, interdependencies that can be accounted for within our model. For example, the originating text, in this case Moore and Lloyd's graphic novel, exerts a consistently weak gravitational pull upon the film/screenplay, the latter persistently trying to break free while being pulled back to the presumed origin; however, if one examines the Moore and Lloyd text, one finds that it too is, as Yeats puts it, but a "spume, that plays/Upon a ghostly paradigm of things," it too pulled toward antecedent and even subsequent texts, foundation or meaning in any merely a chimera. Black holes or wormholes between textual universes suggest that the intertext is not limited by simple chronology. The Black Hole that may empty into another dimension, or perhaps another place in the same, may be unidirectional, but may also be complemented by other sites flowing in the opposite direction, an idea which elucidates the seemingly illogical element of inertextual theory that conceptualizes the most recently created cultural production (in this case a film narrative) in a chronological sequence as implicated in the (re)production of its own source material. Borges observed the illogic in the reciprocal flow of signifiers between past and present: "Each writer creates his or her precursors ... evolution is constituted by each new artistic phenomenon, moving not from past to present but from present to past" (qtd. in Iampolski 55). The creation of each new aesthetic object changes the meaning or reinvents precedent texts. The simple explanation for this is that meaning is entirely confined to the perceiving and analyzing agent, not to a supposed compendium of transhistorical knowledge; the reinvention of each work of art takes place in the conceptualizing subject; thus the introduction of a new product colors the subject's perception of those prior, (re)constructing them. Barthes describes the process of generating transitory and unlimited meanings within the text:

> To read is to find meanings, and to find meanings is to name them;
> but these named meanings are swept toward other names; names call
> to each other, reassemble, and their grouping calls for further meaning: I name, I unname, I rename: so the text passes: it is a nomination
> in the course of becoming, a tireless approximation [*S/Z* 11].

Here, he describes reading as a kind of linguistic vorticism, a textual black hole that draws whatever is near inexorably into the spin of signifiers and signifieds, a chaos of apprehension and comprehension, perhaps the process even delivers the reader to an unknown intellectual dimension, removing them forever from the place of origin. The dimension in which the source exists is losing and supplying its energy to other textual or aesthetic dimensions subsequent and antecedent. The "playfulness" and liberation of authorial restraints that Roland Barthes observed in the intertext (*S/Z* 16) can be understood within the M-Theory model as the link between multiple membranes, which are as numerous as the stars, the network of wormholes linking text to text in an endless interplay of signs and forms.

The "Black Holes" can also be conceived as those points of the narrative or the cultural artifact in which the mass of references and implications are too great for the current interpretive structure to support; the text collapses and is drawn to its sources and referents. Mikhail Iampolski, in his book length study, *The Memory of Tiresias: Intertextuality and Film*, argues that the intertext is observable when the known laws or structures of the subject matter can no longer be reconciled by those details present within the text, thus compelling the reader/audience/observer to travel outside of the text for answers (30). This conceptual vortex exerts a gravitational pull so strong that the reader is drawn out of his or her singular and closed reading and forced to consider the interrelation of the present texts with its "shadows" in order to construct what is now a broader and sometimes seemingly endless structure of interrelated products. These points of critical mass, like Black Holes, cannot be discerned by the naked eye; they can only be hypothesized via the behavior of surrounding points of light. The revolution of ideas represented by the surrounding stars (circling the drain, if you will) constitutes a revolution in textual exegesis. The old structure falls apart and a new one is created, thus the (celestial) objects swallowed by the Black Hole may emerge in another part of the same conceptual universe, or they may resurface in an entirely separate domain. In other words, the textual ruptures transport the reader/audience to another text; once there, they may return to the former altered by the journey or follow the play of signifiers across the multidimensional fabric hypothesized by intertextual, String, or M-Theory.

The waving textual membranes occasionally and unexpectedly collide, creating a "Big Bang" which can be understood as a theoretical restructuring of the fragmentary narrative in relationship to those, both before and after. The collision can be either a place where the texts diverge so suddenly that they create an exegetical crisis, an interpretive rupture that leads to a reinvention of a particular textual focus, or a moment of convergence that allows for a revolutionary restructuring or understanding of the textual potential within the context created by that convergence. The idea that the shadowing text does not create a uniform influence upon the narrative membrane, but strikes and misses periodically, suggests their interdependence. When the texts diverge, they create a relational meaning;

they become foils, defining each other through opposition. Perhaps these deviations define the trajectory of the narrative most completely. The membrane is a universe because it appears to be self-contained, independent, but M-Theory suggests that the text has a multiplicity of shadows, which have their own shadows in a process that encompasses the entire conceptual spectrum. In other words, the interpretive framework of a cultural artifact has no bottom, being pulled inevitably into the "event horizon," elongated, and bisected into infinity.

Film and Intertext

The indebtedness of *VfV* is not limited to textual allusion, quotation, appropriation, or influence as figured in the "Membrane" trope. In the memorable words of Roland Barthes, the "Author is dead"; the text of any cultural production signifies beyond the (un)specified intentions of even the most meticulous, eloquent, and concise writer/creator. Language is bound up in a lengthy history of significations and associations none of which can be completely eradicated: "Every text depends on a language within which is inscribed vast histories of meaning" (Allen 66–67). Barthes describes the text as "woven entirely with citations, references, echoes, cultural languages ... antecedent or contemporary, which cut across it through and through in a vast stereophony" (Barthes, *Image* 160). The visual image as captured on film has its own shared history. The structures, genres, techniques, and so forth of a particular cinematic text (even the most innovative) are indebted to a historical evolution of cinema and narrative. Each camera angle and each cut or visual sequence has an antecedent that is or can be drawn by the appropriate subjectivity into the subsequent text, thus scattering, conferring and/or enhancing ephemeral meanings. Even when the content or imagery of a production seems unprecedented, the means by which the ideas are conveyed are over-determined, recognizable cinematic patterns that carry a history of their own, stretching back even beyond the genesis of cinema into poetry and fiction. Film innovator D.W. Griffith borrowed from Dickens, Tennyson, Whitman, Emerson and others in the development of his filmic techniques (Iampolski 51–83). Moreover, there are few or no artistic endeavors (with the possible exception of architecture) that are as fully collaborative as film, which may be a definitive example of the intertext since it is the product of many minds even in the process of its initial formation; even the presumed controlling intellect of the director is plural, made so by the slippery or indeterminate nature of language. The director, as *auteur,* is at best an effort to assign credit for the production, the singular ascription of the aesthetic object to his intellect merely pragmatic, serving only to reduce the number of creditors for the purposes of brevity. The director is not the singular *auteur* of the cinematic text; there is also the producer(s), screenwriter(s), art director(s), or writers of antecedent and subsequent materials. This seems to be particularly vexing question in *VfV*, which is often referred to as a Wachowski Brothers film, perhaps exclusively for marketing purposes since they are the much acclaimed directors of *The Matrix Trilogy* and because they wrote the screenplay for *VfV* and obviously initiated the project. But it is difficult to assign full credit for the film to either McTeigue, the director, or the Wachowski Brothers since the film is based upon a graphic novel by Moore and Lloyd, and to leave them out seems invalid and irresponsible. I have been tempted to write the following at various times in the composition of this study, "The McTeigue, Wachowski, Moore and Lloyd film *V for Vendetta* ...," or perhaps just "McTeigue's et al...." I will spend a great deal of time discussing the selection of art for V's "Shadow Gallery," artifacts that Gerard Genette would refer to as "Metatextual," those that interpret or expostulate with another text (Allen 102); Iampolski calls this practice *la construction en abime*—"the text within the text," "a painterly and graphic form of representation ... a small scale model" of ideas in the film, a technique that (mis)directs or (re)directs and compounds the pursuit of meaning (37). The paintings in the gallery were not selected by McTeigue, although he gave direction and probably final approval; thus the art director and his or her crew made aesthetic decisions about the text, adding their own interpretive dimensions to the porous and ungrounded visual and auditory texts.

One might ask, as many have already, "Why *V for Vendetta*?" Perhaps because, as I sought to exhaust the meaning of the text, more and more vistas opened up, drawing me into separate dimensions, and those subsequent textual realms contained their own ruptures, vortices, or wormholes. The work began as a single essay about the Gun Powder Treason and progressively compounded until the process had to be abandoned due to considerations of length. The continuous deferral of meaning in the

V/V text is even embodied in the metaphorical dimension of the central character. V's name, or lack thereof, constitutes the slipping signifier whose referent cannot be finalized. The title *V for Vendetta* suggests that "Vendetta" is only one of a multitude of significations that can be associated with the enigmatic appellation "V." The film title's effort to delimit has the effect of reminding the audience that there are other concepts to stand in for the letter. The syntax of the title might conversely suggest that V is simply committed to a vendetta and not that he personifies the same. Close study of the two primary *V/V* productions — film and graphic novel — divulges a series of potential referents for the letter, most prominently "Victory," an allusion to Churchill's trademark hand gesture during World War II and perhaps to the mid-twentieth century counterculture's sign for peace, one revived in response to the second Iraq war and one that in the context of the film might serve as a reminder of the necessity of curbing militarism and aggression in the interests of avoiding the apocalyptic cataclysm that devastated the civilization of the narrative. The large red V that is the trademark of the *V/V* texts is also a visual quotation of Michael Radford's cinematic version of Orwell's *1984* (also starring John Hurt), where V stands for "Victory" as well. This signification evokes a history of resistance to war and the respective tyrannies originating from the political right and left. "V" derives more than one signification from the Guy Fawkes and Powder Treason historical text of the film. Guy Fawkes Day is November 5 (V), and the pontiff who initiated Elizabeth I's persecution of English Catholics was Pope Pius V, who excommunicated the Queen, deposed her in absentia, and, in principle, released her Catholic subjects from their duty to the Crown. Other significations include "Villain" — V is, after all, the progeny of the villain hero of Shakespearean drama, the Vice; "Virus" — film and novel comment upon the ongoing AIDS pandemic, merging it with the more immediate fear of biological terrorism; "Valerie" — the person whom V chooses to vindicate via his revenge, the former screen actress Valerie Page; prison cell number "V" — the place of V's incarceration at the Larkhill Internment Camp, the room where he lost his former identity and became only V; "Vexatious," "Variable," "Verbose," "Vain," "Valorous," "Violent," "Vanquished," "Virtuous," "Validate," "Vaudeville," "Venerate," "Vitriolic," "Virtue," "Virulence," "Vow," "Victim," and "Visage" — a case can be made for any of the preceding and more. V reveals his fascination with the unfettered play of the pertinent letter in his first speech of the film where he introduces himself to Evey with a vaudevillian flair, creating a verbose alliteration of V's.

As a result of the fires at Larkhill, V has no face or, at least, no face that he is willing to reveal to the world, and certainly his unseen visage is without character or definition, as is common among those with extensive facial burns. His visage embodies the slipping signifier to which no stable meaning can be attached. He is without identity save for the several masks he puts on for the world and for the ghostly command that "all alone" lives within the "book and table of …[his] memory." The other characters do not know how to interpret his intentions or his actions and frequently misconceive him. At the beginning of the film, no one is sympathetic toward his cause, including Evey, but by the conclusion, he has converted the masses by demonstrating the deceptiveness of appearances; those who appear virtuous are full of vice and visa versa. The movement of V's undefined character through a variety of *tableaux vivants* once again foregrounds the role of the signifier. V embodies the shadow text, disguised, lurking in dark corners, mirroring and foiling those whom he stalks; he remains both villain and victim. V's blank face is the intertext; he leaps into and out of a variety of narratives, deriving and lending a meaning only briefly before he moves on to the next meta–cultural reference. He plays Edmund Dantes in the cell at Chateau D'If, Winston Smith and Sam Lowry battling their respective bureaucratic hegemonies, and Ivanhoe returning from the Crusades to liberate his country from a tyrannical usurper. He plays Frankenstein's monster in pursuit of his unprincipled creator and a malign pathogen assaulting the Bastille of the immune system. He is the devil to Lilliman's Faust, Bergman's Death confronting plagued humanity, the confidential informant in an espionage narrative, the hero in an action thriller, the holocaust survivor confronting the Nazi Death Camp commander, and the male romantic lead in love's tragedy. V's shape shifting confers meaning, insofar as it invokes a particular narrative genre, and defers the same because the multiplicity of roles that he plays undermines the authenticity of any single gesture.

The Shadow Text

With the phrase "shadow text" I only partially invoke Derrida's definition and repudiation of the "metaphysics of presence," the belief that the system of signifiers is rooted by a "transcendental signified," which precedes all signifiers, a meaning that exists outside of the text or outside of language — the belief that the soul or meaning of the signifier is stable (*Grammatology* 49). The "shadow text," like the alternate universes, informs, parallels, animates, and enervates the textual body, masquerading as a foundational narrative. However, the "shadow text" has its own shadow, which has its own in its turn in endless succession backward and forward, an incoherent mass of the howling damned, pleading for substance, increase, and remission, or an endless train of puppets carried in front of the fire to cast deceptive shadows on the wall in the theatre of dementia. Within this context, the term "shadow" can suggest "actor" (in the early modern sense) or "the ghost in the machine," the soul bound within the physical body. Like the actor, the "shadow text" only postures, briefly performing the part of source and influence, but just as quickly doffing its disguise and quietly slipping away into another role. The shadow has illimitable faces, potentially as many as there are cultural artifacts within human production and experience. The "ghost in the machine" brings consciousness and understanding to the subject and sutures the fissure between the written word and the historical compendium of concepts in language. However, those concepts are only more words that have their respective "ghostly paradigms" — still more words. Each time the reader believes that she or he has attained the cynosure of the text, the occupying shadow, the probative subject passes through the object, revealing its transparency — its absent presence. Indeed, potentially all shadows simultaneously occupy the same space, which from one perspective appears singular and from another legion.

The shifting signification of V (both word and person) and the contextual details of the narrative will be traced within the chapters that follow, and many of the same textual details recur in alternate contexts. From another critical perspective, we might call this a highly complex allegory, obviating multiple layers of meaning that operate concurrently, and while this description is ostensibly accurate, "allegory" may be too readily associated with didacticism and the metaphysics of presence in language. The repetition of details illustrates the plurality of the text or the endless interplay of the intertext without any particular meaning prioritized or finalized. The shadow in its traditional signification creates an appropriate metaphor as it suggests context or perspective, the shade cast in opposition to the angle of light, the lower the angle, the longer the shadow. But the darkness shifts and/or disappears with an alteration in perspective and the passage of time.

What remains then is to observe that play of shadows on the walls or the plasticity and multidimensionality of the *V for Vendetta* text(s). The individual chapters within this discussion attempt localized readings of specific intertextual dimensions. Through the accumulation of readings or chapters, the plenitude of *VfV* is released. The various readings sometimes appropriate textual details employed previously, sometimes in contradiction to their usage in other segments of the same critical analysis. The purpose is to delimit the potential referents and antecedents. As discussed above, the personified focus of the narrative wears multiple masks at any given point in the narrative. While all of the readings that follow are textual, some focus on the historical shadows, others on the social and still others on the cultural.

The first chapter, "Tyranny and the Powder Treason," excavates the fragments of early modern textuality within the film imagery and dialogue, obviating the historical, cyclical, and rhetorical struggle of the British against the tyranny of nationalism from without and within. The traces of the 1605 Gunpowder Plot and the antecedent persecution of Catholics by the English Crown are linked to the 20th century struggle against the national socialists or fascism and to the potential introduction of English nationalism along with the accompanying loss of civil liberties.

Chapter Two, "V's Terrorism: Power and Performance," strives to problematize the contemporary conception of terrorism, demonstrating that Western governments tend to define the activity in order to exclude "state terrorism" (the mechanisms by which power intimidates and restrains the masses) and to elide the terrorist activities mythologized and sanctioned in the formation of those governments that now decry the practice elsewhere, refusing to acknowledge that terrorism could signal the genesis of liberal democracy emerging from a repressive state. The discussion also addresses the performative dimension of terrorism, which requires an audience to witness the desperation and bloody resolution of the politically activated, and relates this practice to the thespian flair of V's revolution.

The third chapter, "'Half Sick of Shadows': Tennyson, Waterhouse, and 'The Lady of Shalott,'" examines the conspicuous placement of John

William Waterhouse's canvas within V's home — The Shadow Gallery. The painting operates as a shadow or meta-text, commenting upon and constructing an alternative dimension of the cinematic narrative. The dynamic moment depicted in the painting, in which the Lady, having broken from fixation with the mirror, embraces her mortality, enters her boat, and begins her journey to Camelot, summarizes the pattern of liberation that can be detected/constructed within varied narrative arcs of the dramatis personae. The painting creates a micro-universe, a window on a hidden, yet accessible, dimension of the text, one structured upon the paradoxical binary of life in death and creation in destruction. The Lady's life embracing gesture in the Shalott narrative simultaneously ensures her own destruction and death, but the brief moments of liberation from fear transcend considerations of safety and longevity.

Chapters Four through Seven examine the circulation of ideas within the intertext. "V and *The Count of Monte Cristo*" tracks the ponderous footprints of the antecedent Dumas text across the *VfV* narrative; however, the discussion problematizes the one to one correspondence of traditional source or influence scholarship, revealing that the intertext is not limited to individual pairs of binary texts. Both texts are the sites of many multifarious pressures, precedent, current, and subsequent. The appropriation of the antecedent Dumas narrative is cluttered by the plethora of *Monte Cristo* cinematic texts. *V for Vendetta* repeatedly cites Rowland V. Lee's 1934 film version, selected from no fewer than twenty cinematic productions of the story. Moreover, *VfV* exists in no fewer than three versions — the graphic novel, the McTeigue film, and the novel based upon the film. For instance, the Dumas antecedent is far less prominent (and arguably non-existent) in the Moore and Lloyd version. In addition, neither the *VfV* nor *CMC* text is limited to a single impactful relationship within the intertext; the latter borrows from Dante and Machiavelli and the former from the legion of cultural influences that are examined in this text, including, but not limited to, those discussed in the Chapter Five, "*1984* and the Dystopian Genre." Orwell's classic novel of a leftist ideology gone mad in the pursuit and practice of population control shadows the *VfV* narrative and drags along with it the attendant dystopian genre, in both ink and image. Chapter Five surveys the pocked surface of the McTeigue film, isolating the impact craters of antecedent narratives, including Terry Gilliam's *Brazil*, Huxley's *Brave New World*, Bradbury's *Fahrenheit 451*, and Alex Cox's *Revengers Tragedy*.

Chapter Six, "Knight, Death, and Devil," explores an eclectic selection of shadow texts that crisscross the *VfV* narrative. Walter Scott's *Ivanhoe*, Goethe's *Faust,* and Bergman's *The Seventh Seal* share a preoccupation with medievalism — the appropriation of the medieval aesthetic and worldview within a more contemporary context. Scott's *Ivanhoe* shares with *VfV* a usurped government, a protagonist bent on liberation and vindication, a society vexed by internecine conflict, and a strident persecution of minorities. Goethe's *Faust* informs the relationship between Evey and V, reenacting Gretchen's dilemma on the eve of her execution — to accept Faust's assistance and thus align herself with the Devil or to embrace death, a terrifying but ultimately preferable choice. Finally, allusions to Bergman's cinematic classic *The Seventh Seal* create an analogue between V and the *Danse Macabre* (Dance of Death). V leads his merry chain of victims in an inexorable dance toward the grave. The plague fraught land to which Antonius Block returns after years in the Holy Land necessitates a restoration and renewal just as V brings revolution, deliverance, and restoration.

Chapter Seven, "'Odds and Ends Stolen Forth of Holy Writ': Shakespeare and the Invention of V," succumbs to the prodigious gravitational pull of Shakespeare within the English canon of texts. Shakespeare's work is of such immense weight that subsequent English literary history is trapped within his spatial warp unable to extricate itself from his graceful revolutions, an observation that may ultimately lead to a revised version of the Derridean and post-structuralist mantra: "There is nothing outside of the [Shakespearean] text." This portion of the discussion probes the multiple Shakespearean quotations and allusions within the *VfV* cinematic text, many of which are not included in the graphic novel, and reveals that the Shakespearean paradigm structures not only the narrative but also the person of V, a revenger with a theatrical flair.

"'Monuments of Unaging Intellect': The Shadows in V's Gallery" studies the interactive relationship between the artifacts in V's home and the events and characters of the narrative. The paintings, films, sculptures, and music within the Shadow Gallery are meta-textual, a multiverse commenting on the broader movements of the *VfV* storyline, offering insights into characterization and context. As in Yeats' "Sailing to Byzantium," the fragments of a once great civilization are preserved by the appropriations and solicitations of the villain hero V. His aestheticism distinguishes him from his antagonists, and his cultural treasures constitute the phoenix egg from which the (re)emergent, reconstituted, and rehabilitated culture will emerge.

Chapter Nine, "V for Virus: The Spectacle of the AIDS Avenger and the Biomedical Military Trope," examines *VfV*'s not so subtle allusions to the AIDS panic of the 1980s, the period in which Moore and Lloyd conceived and composed their viral avenger, yet the most pointed allusions to the AIDS pandemic are not found in the graphic novel but in the screenplay, which describes the St. Mary's virus as an impetus for various "immune pathologies." In this construction of the narrative, V becomes a literalization or personification of AIDS conspiracy theories, specifically the AIDS avenger of urban legend, one so enraged and/or addled by his illness that he willfully infects others in order to share his burden and force change in the institutional perception and treatment of the disease and those suffering from it. The chapter also examines the frequency of military or security metaphors in the rhetoric of immunology and generates a reading of the *VfV* text that involves an extensive bio-medical military trope in its portrait of V's role within England's political system.

One

·⟨⟨⟨⟨·

Tyranny and
the Powder Treason

To identify the importance of the 1605 Gunpowder Plot in the construction of James McTeigue's film *V for Vendetta* (2005) seems at first unnecessary since the film opens with a brief narrative of the audacious conspiracy, including Guy Fawkes' intrigue, his capture, and his execution. The film also includes a villain hero who wears a Fawkesian Halloween mask and actually succeeds in blowing up Parliament in order to ignite revolutionary change. However, *V for Vendetta* allows the idea of the Powder Treason (as it was known in the 17th century) to stand generically for the revolutionary ambitions of a populace combating tyranny. The allusions to contemporary politics — specifically to the increased security, xenophobia, and intrusiveness of government in the U.K. and U.S.A. following the terrorist bombings of September 11 and the London tube stations — abound within the narrative, operating as a warning against the evolution of a national security state and a fascist abridgment of expression and other civil liberties. Less apparent are the subtle analogies between V's post-apocalyptic London and the religious and political milieu of Elizabethan and Jacobean England, the same that produced the Gunpowder Treason.

Tyranny and Gunpowder

When Elizabeth I was proclaimed Queen of England in November of 1558, she sought to manage the country's deepening religious rifts and animosities by adopting a conservative Protestant creed while advocating toleration for English Catholics who remained quiet and loyal. Thus unlike her two half-siblings who enjoyed the throne before her, Elizabeth did not want the country to endure another bloody shift in religious orientation, one that would result in burning heretics or hanging and drawing traitors. Edward the VI had continued the Reformation begun by his father, Henry VIII, who wanted a divorce from his first wife, Catherine of Aragon, and who had been rigorous in the persecution of anyone opposed to his split with Rome. Upon Edward's early death, Mary I drew the country back to Catholicism amid a multitude of burning heretics and prominent Protestants fleeing for the Continent. While there was some anticipation and uncertainty in the popular mind regarding the religious orientation of the new Queen Elizabeth when she followed her half-sister to the throne, in retrospect her choice seems almost inevitable. She was the daughter of the Reformation, her mother marrying Henry while, in the view of Catholics, he was still wed to Catherine. Thus the Catholic Church regarded Elizabeth as illegitimate, a bastard who could not be named in the succession (Fraser 6). Her retention of power may have necessitated her Protestantism, yet Protestantism simultaneously endangered that power from within and from without.

Elizabeth's well intentioned toleration of Catholicism did not endure. The Northern Rebellion led by the Duke of Norfolk that threatened a Spanish invasion, coupled with the support of English Catholics, was defeated and savagely rebuked by the Queen's army. The seemingly tireless machinations of her cousin Mary Queen of Scots — an unwanted visitor to the realm, the presumptive heir to English throne, and the preferred choice of Catholics at home and abroad — eroded the patience with religious diversity that had characterized the Elizabethan Settlement. While Mary was held prisoner by Elizabeth for almost two decades, a variety of intrigues and treasons aimed at freeing the former and placing her on the throne were periodically interdicted and repressed by the growing spy service of Elizabeth's government, the network managed primarily by her "rank puritan" Francis Walsingham (Budiansky 83–99). The Ridolfi, Throckmorton, and Babington plots served to harden Elizabeth's government against Catholics (Hogge 126). However, Pius V's ill-considered Papal Bull *Regnans in Excelsis* (1570) officially excommunicated Elizabeth and released her subjects from allegiance to her, thus effectively equating Catholicism in England to treason, and inflamed Elizabeth and her council against her Catholic subjects (Fraser 6). Fines were leveled for non-attendance at Anglican services, and in the year 1581, the same were greatly increased, reflecting the growing paranoia of the government following the previous year's introduction of covert Jesuit priests to the realm (Hogge 106). *God's Secret Agents,* Alice Hogge's history of the Jesuit mission in England, offers a rich account of the measures adopted by priests to minister to the spiritually neglected Catholics of the age as well as the countermeasures adopted by Elizabeth's government to interdict this mission. Although the Jesuit charge explicitly forbade the involvement of its priests in politics (Hogge 81–82), Elizabeth's government was never convinced that these hidden priests had no further objective than to minister to the souls of the spiritually neglected. The Treason Act of 1581 made it punishable by death to withdraw English subjects from their loyalty to the Queen (Hogge 86) and further legislation in 1585 made it treason for any Englishman to be ordained a Catholic priest and for any subject to offer a priest assistance (Hogge 114–115). On both sides of the religious divide, networks of secret operatives formed, either to conceal the offending Jesuits or to capture, interrogate, torture, and execute them.

The year 1588 saw the long awaited Spanish threat materialize in the form of the Armada, which was to be aided by a seasoned army from the Spanish Netherlands. The anti–Spanish and the anti–Catholic hysteria in England peaked as the country mobilized for war. Internment camps for prominent Catholics were created so that the religious apostates could not aid the Spanish fleet (Hogge 110). However, many or even most English Catholics were determined to prove their national loyalty and for a time became as vehemently anti–Spanish as their Protestant countrymen. After the fleet was defeated by fire ships and foul weather, the English remained in a state of readiness and anticipation for many months before they felt sufficiently safe to celebrate their victory. In spite of the failure of the invasion and public demonstrations of patriotism from Catholics, the judicial and legislative reprisals against English recusants did not relent. Nevertheless, the hope of Catholics in an English Counter-Reformation began to increase as the aging and childless Queen refused to name her heir. Throughout the 1590s speculation regarding the new monarchy increased even though Elizabeth had officially forbade discussion of the succession. The hopes of many Catholics were riveted on James VI of Scotland; even though he was raised a strict Presbyterian, he was the son of Mary Queen of Scots, who had once been the principal hope of Catholics for a new and sympathetic monarch. When it became apparent that Elizabeth would not live much longer, Robert Cecil, the Queen's principal council member and statesman, initiated secret negotiations with James. The Queen had refused to name her successor even in her final days, although it is reported that just before her death, she made a sign of a crown over her head at the mention of her Scottish cousin's name (C. Lee 97–104).

In the negotiations with the English, James repeatedly implied that he would be tolerant of religious diversity, but most promising was the report that the Monarch's wife, Queen Anne, converted to Catholicism just before the royal couple departed for their English coronation (Fraser 15). James forgave the fines previously levied against recusants and suspended further penalties for one year (Fraser 65). Moreover, he had employed many Catholic ministers in his previous government and had immediately sworn into his English Privy Council two members of the formerly disgraced Percy and Howard clans, both of whose progenitors had been implicated in and executed for conspiracies to liberate Mary Queen of Scots from her English captivity (Fraser 38–40). James also initiated an evacuation of priests from English prisons, including the release and banishment of the former head of the Jesuit mission, William Weston (Hogge 303). James sent a counselor secretly to the Vatican to inform the Pope that he was considering a return to the church (Hogge 304), and he initiated efforts to end England's twenty years of hostility with Spain. It is in the peace with Spain and the 1604 renewal of Elizabeth's law against priests and recusants (Hogge 322) that the Gunpowder Treason was engendered. The hopes of Catholics for a relief from fines, imprisonments, and executions were dashed by the publication of the *Act for the due execution of the Statutes against Jesuits, Seminary Priests and Recusants* (1604) and by the peace with Spain. English Catholics could no longer even hope for an invasion to liberate them from the Protestant persecution.

Although it is Guy Fawkes who has retained the notoriety and most of the culpability for the Powder Treason, the stratagem was actually the brainchild of Robert Catesby who, following the peace with Spain, remarked that "The English Catholics were now in a worse situation than slaves, despised by their enemies as God's Lunatics" (qtd. in Fraser 130). He assembled an initial collection of four additional conspirators, who met at The Duck and Drake Inn, 1604. This initial group included Catesby,

Fawkes, Tom Wintour, Jack Wright, and Thomas Percy (Fraser 97). The plan itself is notorious. They sought to place gunpowder in the storage areas beneath the Houses of Parliament, and on November 5, when all of the statesmen as well as the King and most of his family were present for the opening of the new legislative session, the conspirators would "blow them at the moon." The King's daughter Princess Elizabeth would be abducted and placed on the throne to rule in a puppet government that embraced Roman Catholicism as its official faith (Frazier 116–118). Of course, the plot was eventually betrayed by an unknown confederate, and the conspirators (now numbering 13) who could be captured were either killed in apprehension or rounded up, tried, and hanged, drawn, and quartered for high treason.

The revelation of the Gunpowder Plot shocked the kingdom, generating another period of intense paranoia and persecution like that which preceded and followed the Armada. The exasperation of crypto–Catholics over the repressive policies of the English government against its own citizens — most of whom were yet loyal to the Crown — was embodied in the desperate and doomed scheme to destroy the entire government, Catholics and all. However, in the years that followed, the true threat to the Stuart monarchy revealed itself in the Puritan opposition, who sought greater reforms within the Anglican Church itself, an institution which in the view of the Protestant radicals was — ironically — still all too Catholic.

V for Vendetta

The circumstances of the Gunpowder treason that inform the *V for Vendetta* text evoke the contemporary apprehension and rage of the English and American people over the increasingly repressive policies created to interdict terrorism in the years since 9/11. Similarly, the graphic novel *V for Vendetta*, written in the 1980s, sought to interrogate the conservative Thatcherite government's policies on AIDS, homosexuality, and public surveillance (Moore and Lloyd 6). Eliciting a portion of the novel's apparent social agenda, the cinematic *V for Vendetta*, nevertheless, updates many of the references, including evocations of the more contemporary threat of Islamic terrorism. The film warns against the willful sacrifice of civil liberties in pursuit of safety from terrorism, suggesting that such concessions may ultimately necessitate protection from the protectors. Alan Moore loudly objected to McTeigue's treatment of the graphic novel because he felt that the original subjects of "fascism and anarchism" had been replaced by "American neo-conservatism" and "American liberalism" (*V for Vendetta*, Wikipedia.com 3). While the allusions to American politics following 9/11 are heavy-handed in the film — including actual footage of the war in Iraq — the fictive Adam Sutler's fascist government is certainly more extreme in its anti-terrorist measures than is the Bush or Blair administration. The film rather creates a dire prediction that both England and America are flirting with fascism through their intrusions upon liberty in the interests of national security. Popular polls among many Americans immediately following the 9/11 catastrophe indicated that most would be content to sacrifice some civil rights in order to feel safe from terrorism, and certainly the Bush administration has proceeded as though it has a mandate on that priority, introducing torture (the secret CIA prisons and Abu Ghraib), spying (FBI phone tapping), internment camps (Gitmo), unwarranted search and seizure, and lengthy incarceration without due process, all explicitly retrograde to our Bill of Rights and, in some cases, our international treaties. In the UK, the film was scheduled for release on the weekend of the 400th anniversary of Gunpowder Plot (November 5, 2005), but the film's debut was pushed back to November 17. Some argued that the delay was due to the London Tube bombings of the previous summer; however, the filmmakers insist that the production was not finished in time for the original release date (*V for Vendetta*, Wikipedia.com 5).

    V for Vendetta does seem to condone terrorism or at least make some terrorism seem a justifiable expression of outrage from the powerless against the tyranny of the majority and/or the establishment. Invoking the Gunpowder Plot reminds the British and their former colonies that they established their own liberties through means that today might be considered terrorism. Within the first few minutes of the film, a television commentator alludes to the Boston Tea Party as well as events that in the fictional present of the film have driven the U.S to civil war and the UK to fascism. The England of *VfV* is one in which liberty is already lost, the setting dystopic. A fascist regime has been established to restore order following widespread civil unrest and a catastrophic outbreak of a lethal pathogen. The leader of the government, Adam Sutler (John Hurt), is associated with that most notorious of German Chancellors in both name and title. He is maniacal in his behavior, Hitlerian in his appearance, and intolerant of all resistance to his will. The cinematic imagery of his flashy storm troopers is indicative of the black clad SS, parading through the streets in a grotesque pageant of pride and dominion. The compliant multitudes are repeatedly depicted anesthetized by television propaganda and beer, the images revolving back and forth between the living room couch and the pub, as the people are harangued by the mouthpiece of government propaganda, former Commander Lewis Prothero (Roger Allam).

In its consolidation of power, Sutler's government has first demanded religious uniformity, violently suppressing diversity of faith. The governmental slogans plastered on walls throughout the city argue for the necessity of religious unanimity: "Strength through Unity, Unity through Faith." This formula equating uniformity with security is reminiscent of Bishop Edwin Sandys's speech opening Parliament in 1571 in which he argued that diversity of religion is inconsistent with monarchy: "One God, one king, one faith, one profession is fit for one Monarchy and Commonwealth. Division Weakeneth" (qtd. in Hogge 47). McTeigue's slogan here has been altered from Moore and Lloyd's original, which holds "Purity" as the bridge between "Strength" and "Faith" (11). The modification alludes to a more contemporary threat to the security of the realm — Islamic terrorism — thus supplementing the film's cultural and political references from those of the Thatcherite era — AIDS and governmental surveillance (closed-circuit TV, or CCTV) — when the graphic novel was created (Moore and Lloyd 6). In his fiery rightwing condemnation of the anarchy within which America has foundered and which Britain has transcended, Lewis Prothero reminds his audience that it is divine grace that restored order to the UK, while it simultaneously punished America for its "Godlessness." He lists the undesirables who had to be eliminated in the reestablishment of uniformity: "I saw it all — immigrants, Muslims, homosexuals, terrorists. Disease ridden degenerates. They had to go. Strength through Unity, Unity through Faith." The speech elicits Percy Shelly's "Ode to the West Wind," which visualizes the autumnal winds as the spirit of revolutionary and/or apocalyptic change that sweeps the "pestilent stricken multitude" into the grave to be resurrected and rejuvenated:

O Wild West Wind, thou breath of Autumn's being —
Thou from whose unseen presence the leaves dead
Are driven, like ghosts from an enchanter fleeing,

Yellow, and black, and pale, and hectic red,
Pestilence-stricken multitudes! — O thou
Who chariotest to their dark wintry bed

The wingèd seeds, where they lie cold and low,
Each like a corpse within its grave, until
Thine azure sister of the Spring shall blow

Her clarion o'er the dreaming earth...

The "yellow, and black, and pale, and hectic red" refer simultaneously to the races of humanity, the colors of the Galenic four humors, and the color of dead leaves — thus evoking the society, the individual, and the natural world, all impacted by the revolutionary impulse. While humanity may be driven underground or into its grave, there it awaits the trumpets of the spring that signal the moment of rebirth, emergence, rejuvenation, and/or revolution. While the phrase "disease ridden degenerates" (or the "pestilence stricken multitude") of Prothero's speech refers ostensibly to the groups singled out for repression and expulsion by the Sutler regime, it also encompasses the generalized English population whose liberties and expressions have been stifled by the national security apparatus of the Norsefire regime. The film gives the increasing Islamic threat the primary role in the narrative. Gordon Deitrich (Stephen Fry), the heroine Evey's (Natalie Portman) employer and confidant, is summarily executed when the secret police find that he is in possession of a 14th century copy of the Koran. It does not matter that he is not Muslim or a terrorist; simple possession of interdicted materials warrants the immediate death of a well known and popular television personality.

The allusion to the predicament of Catholics during the reigns of Elizabeth I, her predecessors, and her successors is represented clearly in the uniformity of religion in the film's fascist England. Historically, the boy King Edward VI had imposed a *Book of Common Prayer* in 1549, repealing heresy legislation, and opening the way for priests to marry (Mac-Culloch 81). In the brief period of Mary Tudor's reign, the Catholic liturgy was restored and heresy laws reactivated. However, upon Mary's death, Elizabeth restored Edward's *Book of Common Prayer* and in 1559, her government imposed the *Act of Uniformity* which empowered the secular law in the maintenance of piety, granting it authority to enforce attendance at Anglican services (Collinson 178). Despite the seeming permissiveness of the Elizabethan Settlement, efforts to eradicate Roman Catholicism in England grew increasingly more ferocious over the four and a half decades of Elizabeth's reign. Among the comparatively minor penalties for persevering in Catholicism were (in addition to the imposition of fines for failing to attend the state sanctioned services) bans upon receiving university degrees, holding public office, serving in the Army, practicing law, carrying weapons, and voting (Fraser 283). The more severe consequences included the loss of property and/or life, the latter reserved for priests and those who succored them.

Because the consequences for a priest of being apprehended on English soil were so grim, an elaborate but by no means foolproof system for their maintenance and security was created, including a series of safe houses, which contained "hides" or hidden chambers in which the priests as well as the articles of the mass could be secreted when the house was being searched by government agents (Hogge 117–119). The builder of many of the most successful hides was Nicholas Owen, whose secret chambers were so well constructed that they were able to conceal priests for days while the house was searched by scores of priest hunters (Hogge 119). Father John Gerard was concealed beneath a fireplace for four days while the Broadoaks estate was thoroughly searched (Hogge 217–221); and at Badesley Clinton in 1591, a total of nine people, including priests Henry Garnet, John Gerard, and Robert Southwell, hid in a sewage tunnel underneath the residence while the house above was ransacked (Hogge 150–155). This network for the concealment of priests constitutes a desperate effort to salvage the vestiges of an increasingly abrogated faith that represented for its enemies an overly ornate, mystical, and decadent tradition.

Similarly, the apostates of *V for Vendetta* have created safe spaces for the preservation of a past represented by various cultural artifacts that have been systematically banned and eradicated. Like the crypto–Catholics of the 16th century, the malcontents of Sutler's London combat the philistinism of the present fascism, preserving the cultural heritage of England in their own version of the early modern "hides." Gordon Deitrich's residence includes a large hidden chamber in which he secretes various forbidden artifacts, the very same that eventually warrant his summary execution. The content of this chamber is a reflection of the disguise that he wears for the world. Gordon is "passing" as heterosexual, the Sutler government having driven him "underground" in a matter of speaking. In addition to the Koran, he conceals gay erotic photos and a camp, Warholesque depiction of Chancellor Sutler as Elizabeth II, carrying the legend, "Long Live the Queen." The items hidden in Gordan's chamber reveal not only his refusal to conform to the censorship imposed by the Norsefire regime, but also his homosexuality, and in a gesture all too real for gays and lesbians of the 20th and 21st centuries, Gordon must conceal his alternative sexual identity in order to preserve his job and prosperity.

V's residence, which he refers to as his "Shadow Gallery," literalizes the expression "underground" insofar as it refers to a counter-culture that opposes conventionality, uniformity, and/or tyranny. It is a multitextual parallel to the predominant ideological framework of the Sutler government. While it defines through opposition, it is in itself plural, offering glimpses of a multiplicity of world views and intellectual, cultural, and aesthetic *epistemes*, shadowed and shadowing others. V literally lives in the long abandoned London Underground or "tube" system. The closure of the underground by the Sutler government inadvertently alludes to the terrorist attacks on the London tube system in 2005, despite the fact that V's residence in Moore and Lloyd's graphic novel from the mid–'80s was also an abandoned subway station, probably because the underground has previously been targeted by radicalized groups such as the Irish Republican Army. V's residence evokes the vast covert network that smuggled and succored Catholic priests seeking to minister to the spiritually neglected Catholic populace of England in the 16th century, an "underground railroad" not for those escaping tyranny and bondage but for those attempting live discretely within it. At least according to the paranoid speculations of Elizabeth and James' governments, this system was the fountainhead of rebellion and treachery within the realm. The image of V lurking in his subterranean chambers is visually parallel to Guy Fawkes on the day of his capture. Dressed in black boots, hat, and cape, he was discovered on November 5 prowling in the chambers beneath the Parliament.

Within his Shadow Gallery, V displays cultural artifacts rescued from the "Ministry of Objectionable Materials"; these include paintings, sculptures, and films, primarily but not exclusively Western, and previously on display in the various London galleries such as the Nationals and Tates.

Prominently featured in the center of the room is John William Water-house's painting *The Lady of Shalott*, based upon Tennyson's poem of the same name, Titian's *Bacchus and Ariadne*, Jan van Eyck's *Portrait of Giovanni Arnolfini*, and Andrea Mantegna's *St. Sebastian*. V and Gordon's salvaging of the artifacts from those ages that are anathema to the contemporary ideological configuration reveals the heavy hand of censorship that has become a foundation of the Sutler government. The cinematic narrative reveals the arbitrary selection of items added to the blacklist. V plays the *1812 Overture* on the public address system to draw the public's attention just before he blows up the Old Bailey. In his rage following the bombing, Sutler bans the unoffending piece of music simply because it reminds him of the challenge to his hegemony. Moreover, television programming scripts must be approved by government agents. When Sutler is parodied on Gordon's variety show, the latter explains that he substituted the officially sanctioned script with another just before shooting the episode. The swiftness with which the government agents descend upon Gordon's house after the transmission demonstrates that the Sutler government will brook no criticism. Unflattering characterizations of the Chancellor and his council are regarded as sedition, as Inspector Finch (Stephen Rea) discovers when he attempts to investigate important party members.

The role of censorship in the monarchies of the early modern age is notorious, and as with Sutler's government, the apparatus for the suppression of information was employed in the maintenance of the leader's vanity. In her latter years, Elizabeth disdained the creation of paintings that were faithful to her actual aged appearance. Painters were obliged to represent her in her prime, perhaps the early modern analogue to plastic surgery. In addition, speaking freely in Elizabeth I's England could lead directly to the gibbets or the quartering table. John Stubbs had his hand chopped off by the executioner for his authorship of "The Discovery of a Gaping Gulf...," a tract critical of the Queen's marriage plans to the French Duke of Alencon, and Bishop Grindal was imprisoned when he presumed to criticize Elizabeth's effort to suppress "prophesying," conferences intended to school ministers in interpretation of scripture (Somerset 299–301). The first laws for the censorship of public performances date to 1535 when Henry VIII forbade the dramatization of scriptural topics (Asquith 23–27), and by the end of the century, all play scripts required approval of the Stationer's Register, which would freely prohibit entire plays or scenes. Most notoriously, staging the deposition scene from Shakespeare's *Richard II* was forbidden during the Queen's lifetime because she believed that the portrayal of Richard was a subtle criticism of her rule.

The terminology employed in *VfV* evokes the religious controversies of the 16th century. Several characters refer to the "Reclamation" as a time of great upheaval and revolution in the recent past, an upheaval that was the genesis of the present regime. In one of the meetings with his cabinet, Sutler is reassured by Creedy that the Fingermen, covert government agents, are still very active in the interdiction of crime and dissent: "Arrests have been as high as they have been since the Reclamation." The final term creates an analogue to the "Reformation," the process initiated by Henry VIII whereby the English severed their Church from the authority and control of the Papacy. Henry became the supreme authority over the Church of England. The property of the very wealthy religious houses became the property of the crown and was sold to enrich the royal coffers. Those who opposed the transformation were brutally suppressed as is evident in the treatment of Sir Thomas More, Henry's Lord Chancellor, who was led to the block because he would not consent to the King's split with his wife and with Rome (Weir 384). The "reclamation" suggests the usurpation of the country from undesirables, most likely the same cited at the beginning of the film — "immigrants, Muslims, homosexuals, [and] terrorists." As with its 16th century predecessor, the Reclamation constitutes an effort to wrestle ownership of and influence within the country from seemingly external influences, to restore the country to indigenous Englishmen and establish uniformity of faith, ethnicity, and sexuality. The Reclamation is the seminal period in the past when Sutler assumed absolute authority over the realm.

While upbraiding Finch for his investigation of influential party members as well as events that occurred during the Reclamation at St. Mary's and the Larkhill detention facility, Sutler alludes to the inspector's violation of the "Articles of Allegiance." While the phrase remains undefined within the film, its content can be gleaned from the context. The "Articles of Allegiance" constitute an oath in which citizens — or perhaps only government employees — vow not to compromise the security of the nation by engaging in activities that tend to undermine the authority of the ruling party. The "Articles" shadow the "Oath of Allegiance" sought by Robert Cecil as a solution to the conflicted loyalties of English

Catholics in the late 16th and early 17th centuries, a piece of legislation that he finally achieved in the wake of the Gunpowder Treason. English Catholics could retain their faith if they acknowledged that the English Monarch was the legitimate ruler, that the Pope had no authority to depose a sovereign monarch, and that they would never aid an invading foreign power or participate in any contrivance intended to harm the sovereign (Hogge 379–384). The "Oath" and the "Articles" reveal respective administrations under assault within their own realms (at least ideologically); they are governments that look to be washed away at the next tide. In both cases, the government's own paranoia is its worst enemy, justifying ever greater repression under a veil of security, consolidating power by constantly invoking the enemy at the gate.

In the graphic novel, V blows up Parliament first and later attacks the Old Bailey, while in the film the destruction of Parliament is saved for the denouement, a final desperate act to bring about fundamental change. Obviously the destruction of or at least the attempt to destroy Parliament is requisite to the Guy Fawkes motif; however, as an assault upon Sutler's government, the act is incoherent since it seems clear that Sutler permits no popular representation in his government; he rules absolutely with the assistance of a small cadre who obey him unquestioningly. Thus the destruction of Parliament can only signify the damage that has already been done to representative government. More importantly, the destruction of the Parliament is an event for the contemporary age in which the legislative body is perceived to be complicit in the increasing infringement upon civil liberties. V's attack upon the Old Bailey has a similar significance, constituting an indictment of injustice within the Sutler government. The Old Bailey is the Crown Court for central London, built on the location of Newgate Gaol, its façade constructed with the very bricks that composed the worst of the twelve prisons in early modern London. Jesuit priest and poet Robert Southwell was interred in Newgate just before his execution. Indeed, Newgate was considered "a staging post for the scaffold, a waiting room for death" (Hogge 184–185). V's attack upon the Old Bailey, however, is mostly directed at the statue of justice that stands astride the building's central dome. The figure of justice is blindfolded, holding a sword in one hand and a scale in the other, suggesting the balancing of justice and mercy. V's violent repudiation of the figure signifies his challenge to the hypocrisy of the Norsefire regime.

In Sutler's government, Lewis Prothero's scaremongering incites a perpetual state of emergency, evoking the chaos and anarchy elsewhere that threatens to engulf the country. In the mythology of its power, only the Sutler government can keep the people safe from invasion and sedition. Prothero, on his nightly television address, reminds his audience of the social unrest that preceded the Norsefire regime and the civil war that presently rages among England's former allies. The reports of ongoing conflict in the U.S., where disunity has split the country into contending factions, serve to legitimize the crackdown in the U.K., where a compulsory unity ostensibly ensures peace. Unless Sutler imposes martial law on his country, a similar pandemonium will ensue. The contemporary allusions to the Blair and Bush administrations' efforts to legitimize governmental encroachments upon civil liberties and to compel the populace to endorse their own loss of freedom in the interests of interdicting terrorism are heavy-handed, but the siege mentality that has so much contemporary social relevance also has a 16th century analogue, and one directly relevant to the Powder Treason.

The state of alarm in Elizabeth I's government was inspired partially by the wars of religion that had engulfed many of the Continental states, particularly in France and the Lowlands, both regions which had tried to practice toleration toward religious diversity. Despite opposition from the Pope and her son-in-law, Philip II of Spain, Queen Mother Catherine de Medici, in the interests of peace, had tried to achieve toleration for French Huguenots, but the St. Bartholomew's Day Massacre demonstrated that neither side of the religious divide was willing to compromise with its contentious countrymen (Frieda 248–272). The Lowlands were burdened with civil war in an effort to eject the invading Spaniards. The potential for comparable civil turmoil in England kept the court increasingly rigorous in its suppression of religious variance. However, ironically, it is the peace treaty between England and Spain — legitimized without a clause guaranteeing toleration for Catholics — that led to the Gunpowder Plot (Hogge 331), the ferocity of which was calculated to reveal decades of pent-up rage, the accumulated exasperation of those all too familiar with persecution. The conditions that gave rise to the Gunpowder Treason create a rich analogue to contemporary terrorism, which speaks the language of exasperation of a perpetually disempowered people and one that speaks to a defensive religious posturing.

Andrea Mantegna's painting of St. Sebastian's martyrdom hangs prominently within V's shadow gallery, reminding the audience of the canon of Catholic martyrs. V is indicative not only of 17th century religious terrorism, but also of the more peaceful agenda of Jesuit missionaries in England, and V's willingness to martyr himself creates this parallel. It was an automatic sentence of hanging, drawing, and quartering for any priest to be caught ministering to Catholics in England during the last two decades of the 16th century and the beginning of the 17th. Thus Jesuits had to prepare themselves for the eventuality of torture and execution before they were free to minister to the neglected English flock. In the climax of the film, Creedy wonders aloud why his antagonist will not die in spite of being shot several times, and V responds, "Beneath this mask there is more than flesh. Beneath this mask there is an idea, Mr. Creedy, and ideas are bullet proof." Here V signifies a fanatical commitment to principle, and a principle can inhabit a multitude of bodies. Immediately after killing Creedy, V, wounded, drops his bullet proof plate and, in a gesture that would seem to contradict his boast, slowly dies. However, even as he passes, the narrative reveals that he has won a multitude of converts to his cause, the street above crowded with citizens in Fawkesian masks, violating curfew and confronting a line of armed troops before Parliament. The emergence of the multitude of fledgling V's validates the axiom that one martyr creates a mass of converts. The master of Elizabeth I's spy service and the man responsible for interdicting threats against the monarch's person and power, Francis Walsingham, warned that the martyring of priests increased the devotion of English Catholics to their faith (Budiansky 104). Regardless of the most rigorous punishments and increasing harassment, Elizabeth I's government was never able to eradicate English Catholicism or even to curtail the flow of clergymen into the country, priests willing to die in order to keep their "idea" alive.

The fate of captured missionary priests in England was not limited to the scaffold. The clergyman could expect to endure prolonged imprisonment and torture in the government's effort to compel the revelation of their confederates and sponsors. A variety of inducements were used, the most fearful of which was the rack, an instrument so horrific that often detainees needed only to be shown the apparatus in order to induce complete cooperation. While the government officials found it difficult to coerce confession and betrayal from interdicted priests, their co-religionist laymen proved more ready to inform upon their charges. Elizabeth's chief priest hunter, Richard Topcliffe, compelled the confession of Anne Bellamy by raping and impregnating her. Her subsequent assistance led to the capture of Robert Southwell at Uxendon Manor in 1592 (Hogge 178–180). Catesby's servant, Thomas Bates, who falsely implicated Father Garnet in the Gunpowder Treason, did so after being threatened with the rack (Fraser 206–207).

Torture is of course a prominent subject in *VfV*, where Creedy's Fingermen are charged with compelling information from captives, where there is an expectation of torture for anyone who runs afoul of the law, and where all extreme measures are justified in the interests of deterring terrorism and counter revolution. When V's reticent accomplice Evey Hammond reveals her desire to be free of the fear that has pursued her throughout her life, V secretly abducts her and subjects her to incarceration and torture in an effort to relieve her of fear; those who are out of fear of pain and death are free from trepidation and apprehension. Government no longer has the power to compel her obedience by eliciting fear if she is prepared for death. This particular topic reveals a potential historical origin for Evey's name. When she first reveals her identity, V seems amused and unsurprised, implying that her name has some unstated significance for him, a significance that he does not share with her. Aside from the biblical implication of the name "Evey," which suggests that she will defy the power structure and restore freedom of choice to her people (in Miltonic terms, the "mother of science" and apostasy), Evey also signifies within the context of the Gunpowder Treason, her name a homonym for the initials of a high profile participant in the concealment of priests. In the redoubled efforts to interdict Catholic priests in the days and weeks following the revelation of Catesby and Fawkes' conspiracy, one family of recusants became the focus of sustained interest by government officials. The Vaux family had successfully concealed Father Gerard, a Jesuit, from the general roundup of known priests and recusants following the revelation of the plot. Eliza Vaux, whose initials create a homonym of the name Evey, distinguished herself for her bravery and cleverness. The search of Harrowden, her home, had gone on around the clock for days. In order to bring the search to an end so that she could succor the hidden (and now starving) priests, Eliza revealed a hide which contained many objects of the Catholic Mass but no concealed persons; searchers significantly relented in their efforts following this misleading disclosure, allowing the Vauxs to bring Father Gerard out of hiding for brief periods. When Eliza was later questioned as to the whereabouts of Gerard she refused to acknowledge that he had ever been at her residence or even that she knew he was a priest. When one of her questioners attempted to coerce her into exposing the priest, threatening her with death if she did not confess, she balked, "Then I would rather die, my Lord" (Fraser 197–199). Eliza's proud rejoinder shadows the rectitude of Evey Hammond, who, given the option to reveal V or die, chooses the latter: She would prefer to be taken behind the "chemical shed" and "shot" than divulge anything to her torturers/interrogators. Both Eliza and her namesake are subsequently freed. As with Vaux, Evey, in the eyes of the power structure, is guilty by virtue of association; even the appearance of harboring V is sedition, an automatic death sentence.

The destruction of the Houses of Parliament in the final scene of *V/V* is justified by Evey's statement that the "country needs more than a building right now. It needs hope." As with the attack upon the Old Bailey, the destruction of Parliament does not seem to be a repudiation of the institution that it represents (at least not within the narrative context) but instead a recognition that representative government has been displaced and nullified by tyranny and dictatorship. The destruction of Parliament is accompanied by the image of the legion of Fawkesian rebels peacefully breaching the military lines that impede their passage to the capitol. Evey's desperate act constitutes a "counter-reclamation": the people taking back control of their lives and their government. In Lloyd and Moore's graphic novel, the final target for the explosive-laden train is not Parliament, but 10 Downing St., the home of the Prime Minister. Thus the final act of terrorism is more clearly directed against dictatorship. However, in the film, the act is more complex. The Houses of Parliament have come to symbolize the loss of representative government, and ironically the annihilation of that building suggests its restoration or a renewal of what it represents. This final paradox is resolved within the social context of the film's creation where contemporary historical events bleed through the well-wrought narrative fiction. The Parliament of Sutler's government may not be guilty, but the Parliament of contemporary England is, as it has acquiesced in the affront to civil liberties and in the Blair administration's hawkish policies in Iraq. Here are parallel textual dimensions operating simultaneously, each aiding and subverting the other(s).

Conclusion

The destruction of the Parliament within the film signifies at least twice: once for the citizens of post-apocalyptic London in the film, and once for the movie audience who see their future reflected in the mirror of art, who may one day need to restore their once coveted freedoms by reclaiming their own government. Thus the film signifies outside of its own context, serving as a caution to the actual governments of post–9/11 America and Britain that the overly enthusiastic effort to interdict terrorism will only create more terrorists, not from without but from within. The surrender of civil liberties in the interests of national security is an ill-founded enterprise. The enemy that the people must combat will rapidly become their own government grown increasingly intrusive and controlling. An open society must brook disorder in the maintenance of freedom; it must countenance multiple competing political, social, and historical texts. The paranoid and restrictive measures adopted by a government that perceives itself under siege will progressively come to legitimize further consolidations of power, power no longer designed for the safety of the masses but for the defense of itself. Then revolution must reassert the people's rights to determine their own good, to define their own threats.

The unpopular measures adopted by both the British and American governments in the wake of 9/11 and the London tube bombings are a thinly veiled subject of the film. The war in Iraq that was condemned by a wide majority of the population in Britain from the very beginning has not become more popular in the intervening years. The civil war that consumes America in the film is attributed, in the words of Lewis Prothero, to the "war they [America] started." The repressive measures adopted by the Sutler government reflect the desperate and unpopular procedures implemented by the American and British governments to interdict terrorists. In America, the list of encroachments reads like a point by point nullification of the Bill of Rights, the Bush government violating constitutional guarantees against torture, unwarranted intrusions upon personal privacy, freedom of expression, and incarceration without representation and due process.

By linking future, past, and present in *V for Vendetta*, the film constructs a history of resistance to tyranny, one that exposes the slippery slope any people tread when they sacrifice hard won civil liberties for the Delilah of an illusory and ill-defined national security. When governments declare war on terrorists who could be anywhere at anytime, even within the indigenous population, they in effect declare war upon themselves, upon their own freedoms. The residual reminders of the Gunpowder Treason operate as historical lessons. The British have experienced absolutism formerly and struggled for centuries to be free of it. They must not now reinstitute it through popular consent or indifference and expect to claim a more beneficial outcome. In her final statement, Evey recognizes that Guy Fawkes and those who carry on his traditions are progenitors of the contemporary free and open society and that people must remember their sacrifices in the present in order to avoid in the future the [re]installation of a similarly abhorred cultural hegemony. The film script repeatedly quotes Shakespeare's *Macbeth*, yet one of the most appropriate Shakespearean axioms is conspicuously absent:

> Nought's had, all's spent,
> When our desire is got without content.
> 'Tis safer to be that which we destroy
> Than by destruction dwell in doubtful joy [III.ii.6–9].

Two

❧

V's Terrorism

Power and Performance

In the days immediately following the 9/11 attacks, while the country was still reeling from the incomprehensible events, George W. Bush demanded from the rest of the world that they choose sides in the ensuing conflict: "You're either with us, or you're with the terrorists." The simple-mindedness of the ultimatum was stunning, but in eliciting support for the action in Afghanistan, the President's imperative had the desired effect: Much of the world endorsed America's newly invigorated crusade against terrorism. Every country in the world — except Iraq — expressed sympathy for the events in lower Manhattan, Washington, DC, and the skies above Pennsylvania, and the coalition for the invasion of Afghanistan was unprecedented in its comprehensiveness; however, when the Bush administration broadened their objectives to encompass the conquest of Iraq the global consensus on his campaign collapsed into a "coalition of the willing." Most of the countries who could grasp the connection between Osama Bin Laden and the Taliban regime that harbored him balked at the suggestion that Iraq posed a similar threat, that Saddam Hussein was preparing to attack the West — specifically America — with poison gas and nuclear weapons. Those who resisted were accurate in their assessment of the transparent tissue of lies and misconstructions that led to America's debacle in Iraq. However, neither the American administration nor those who opposed the policy of "regime change" seem willing to acknowledge that terrorism has a state component. Terrorism is not exclusively the practice of rogue groups and individuals, not exclusively the weapon of the weak against the strong, but is practiced by governments around the world in the control of their own populations.

In his thought-provoking book *The Culture of Fear*, Barry Glassner argues that Americans have been conditioned by the media and other social institutions to fear all of the wrong dangers. Instead of being outraged over the thousands of people a day who die from the effects of prolonged consumption of alcohol and cigarettes, Americans become hysterical over the necrotizing staph infection or flesh eating bacteria. Instead of becoming alarmed over the number of people who die on our highways each day, we dread the prospect of terrorism. It would seem that in our public imaginations, novelty prevails, as illustrated in the journalistic axiom, "Dog bites man is not news worthy; man bites dog is." The more unusual the fate, the more frightening it is. Perhaps the traditional differentiation between "horror" and "terror" can assist us in understanding this phenomenon. "Horror" is inspired when the ghastly object actually appears and can be processed and evaluated by the audience, while "terror" results when the monster is still lurking in the shadows preparing to leap out at any moment. We develop a tolerance to the horror that we can see, but the unrevealed threat is embellished by apprehension and made far more frightening.

The horror/terror binary can also account for the difference between governmental and individual/group terrorism. The latter is that which we frequently associate with religious extremism abroad, or in this country, with right wing survivalists and separatists; the former is a more insidious kind of terrorism insofar as it is hiding in plain sight. Governmental terrorism is near kin to horror because it is constant, mechanical in its operation, used as a means to subdue — through fear — a population that might otherwise revolt against domination. Governmental terrorism is social control employed in the repression of a population through the manipulation of public and private anxieties. It is less terrifying because it retains an element of inevitability and predictability. The population believes that the avoidance of particular behaviors or ideological beliefs will ensure a respite from governmental intrusion and persecution. In contrast, it is the randomness of individual, group, or revolutionary terrorism that strikes fear into the hearts of the populace, as a reminder of our vulnerability (Townshend 1, 7); the population can glean no rationale in the selection of targets, and thus they can practice no avoidance behaviors; everyone is a potential victim.

The ill-defined linguistic category "terrorism" can even be understood as exclusive of governmental actions. Weber argues that the state is "that human community, which, within a given territory claims for itself the legitimate monopoly of physical violence" (qtd. in Duvall and Stohl 232). According to this definition, the state can be construed as legitimate in its application of violence and intimidation and remain outside the definitional parameters of "terrorism." However, many descriptions of terrorism include a governmental dimension. A case in point would be the definition adopted by the U.S State Department: "Terrorism means premeditated, politically motivated violence perpetrated against non-combatant targets" (qtd. in Nacos 22). If one considers that most or even all institutional brutality can be understood as "premeditated and politically motivated," then the propriety of including governmental violence within the parameters of terrorism seems defensible even by our Department of State's own definitions. The FBI's designation for terrorism, however, is more problematic: "Unlawful use of force or violence against persons and property to intimidate or coerce a government, the civilian population" (Nacos 21). The inclusion of the term "unlawful" would seem to exclude the state's violence against its own people, as government determines legality within its borders. Yet those state actions which cannot be justified within the preexisting law, according to the FBI terminology, may nevertheless be understood as terroristic. I strive here also to differentiate between "governmental" and "state sponsored" terrorism; the latter can be understood as a policy of support (whether it be financial, logistical, territorial, or material) for terrorist activity against foreign or perhaps, in some circumstances, local populations. Governmental terrorism applies violence and intimidation uniformly in the effort to pacify its own people. In the words of Duvall and Stohl, it is "an official policy designed to govern through the creation of intense fear in the population" (251). Governmental terror may also include the sponsoring of nominally independent organizations within the state that practice intimidation and coercion upon poorly integrated segments of the same society, as was the case with Mississippi's Ku Klux Klan, whose activities intimidating African Americans and those who support integration and civil rights legislation were unofficially sanctioned by the state government and were operating in a much larger conspiracy to arrest inevitable social change.

The problem of definition in the question of terrorism continues to plague the study of the phenomenon, each interested party seeking to the define the term exclusive of its own activities or of those perpetrated by groups whose complaints and tactics it considers legitimate (Nacos 24), thus leading to the relativist cliché, "one man's terrorist is another man's freedom fighter." In the months of near hysteria following the 9/11 attacks of 2001, the term "terrorist" itself became a weapon of terror, used by supporters of the Bush administration to stigmatize and coerce those who opposed rigorous and intrusive policies; the term was employed to impose conformity of opinion in the lead-up to war. Protesters were designated terrorists, and those who opposed the actions in Iraq were called "treasonous" by rightwing demagogues. Indeed, George Bush's blunt demand for unity ("You're either with us or [else]....") effectively compelled conformity by designating anyone a "terrorist" who does not agree with his policies.

Revolutionary Terror

The problems and questions surrounding the concept of terror are fundamental to the narrative of McTeigue's cinematic *V for Vendetta*. Indeed the ideological content of the film might be understood as a negotiation between "governmental" and "revolutionary" terrorism, the former calculated to maintain power, the latter to overturn it. Thus the film evokes the historical intertext — the rhetoric of contemporary politics — the seemingly rigid boundary between fiction and reality and/or between art and politics become permeable, and the grave consequences of international conflict merge with millennial or apocalyptic fantasy. The film operates as a reminder that some forms of terrorism are not only acceptable, but also desirable, or even necessary. V's coercive and violent actions are calculated to reveal a greater hypocrisy and violence than that of the Sutler regime. This chapter addresses the performativity of terrorist violence, the idea of power on display, a power advertised through public spectacle, combining the dire consequences of politics with the seemingly inconsequential practices of theater. Indeed the contest between V and his opponents can be understood as metadramatic metaphor, a single show with dueling directors, a primary trajectory being to problematize the concept of terrorism, to propose that surrendering to a rightwing fundamentalist ideology in the effort to interdict nuisance terror may lead to a far more insidious form of the same, one that impacts every facet of the people's lives — government through "cruelty and injustice, intolerance and oppression."

Harry R. Targ in *Societal Structure and Revolutionary Terrorism: A Preliminary Investigation* defines revolutionary terrorism as

> one form of behavior by individuals or groups in support of fundamental change in a given society. It is the threat and use of violence against individuals selected by the terrorists for their symbolic value to galvanize a population through fear or respect [128].

Targ identifies the preconditions for "revolutionary terror against repressive regimes," which includes an atmosphere of "oppression," "a political party with direct action tactics," and individuals with militant character traits (128). The precursors for revolutionary terrorism "against democratic institutions" include "a weakening of democratic values," "a party with tactics of direct violence," a period of "defamation" against the targeted "institutions," and a collection of activist "personality types" (129).

Targ concludes that revolutionary terrorism is "less common" in liberal democracies that have "broad based movements for revolutionary change" (130). Thus, if we apply these principles to the *VfV* narrative, it becomes clear that the Sutler government's efforts to eliminate terrorism as well as political opposition and to simultaneously impose order upon the British people make revolution and terrorism more likely. Foucault, in *Discipline and Punish*, has taught us that the exercise of power generates its own opposition (73), and this political axiom seems to be particularly accurate in describing the genesis of V, who was created by the fiendish experiments of future Norsefire Party members seeking to develop a devastating virus in order to consolidate power through fear. V, the avenger, generated in the laboratories of the Larkhill Internment Facility, responded to the virus by growing stronger while all of the other subjects died, and it is out of his blood that the antidote for the virus was created. V laments that the crimes against him were "monstrous," to which Evey adds, "And they created a monster." V sees his origins as an inevitable response to the inhuman violence perpetrated against him, a genesis that follows Newton's third law: "For every action there is an equal and opposite reaction." Thus by implication, the narrative rebuts some common misconstructions in the public mind regarding the motivations for terror. The terrorist is not necessarily mad or fundamentally criminal nor is she or he moved solely by the desire to create mayhem (Stohl 8–13, 15–17);

his or her actions can often be traced to social and political conditions, and this is particularly true for the revolutionary terrorist who seeks to replace the existing power structure with one that is more sympathetic to the needs of an oppressed segment of the population.

V for Vendetta struggles mightily to make V and his objectives sympathetic. The revenger is portrayed as a gentle aesthete even when he is destroying buildings. He is an example of those George H.W. Bush disparagingly termed the "cultured elite" in his 1992 presidential campaign. V surrounds himself with objects of beauty rescued from the vault of the Ministry of Objectionable Materials, his living room a gallery, recital hall, and theater, his bedroom a library piled high with books. He spends his time at home cooking, practicing his fencing, listening to music on his jukebox, and watching old movies on video. He is gentle and considerate in his interaction with Evey, his overblown gestures of formality, cordiality, and deference reminiscent of the early modern courtier or the suitor in an eighteenth century romance. He cooks breakfast for his guest/abductee while he dons a frilly apron that a middle-aged provincial housewife from the 1950s might have worn. He is always soft-spoken and rational in his discourse, even when he confronts those upon whom he has longed to exact revenge.

His honesty when admitting his crimes to Evey suggests that he acts without compunction, not because he is a sociopath, but because he is confident that his actions are just. He carefully avoids civilian casualties in his extravagant demolitions, save in the Jordan Tower incident, but here the newsmen are actually shot by the SWAT team endeavoring to neutralize the terrorist threat. The single instance of potential civilian loss of life is the bomb that he leaves in the control booth of the British Television Network (BTN). However, the fact that Mr. Dascomb, the director of the facility, is able to defuse the device without any training or assistance suggests that either the bomb was not real or it was not rigged to explode when someone tampered with it. While there is always the possibility that the explosive was live and that Dascomb was only lucky in defusing it, there had been an abundance of time to evacuate the building of civilian personnel. The idea that V would have put so many civilian lives at risk is undermined by the content of the speech that he delivers at the station, one that sides with the oppressed population of the country. Moreover, he must know that Evey Hammond works at the station, and having saved her life the night before, it would be incoherent for him to kill her with a bomb the next day. In addition, if the bomb exploded while he was in the building, which seems highly probable since he could not be certain of how long it would take him to exit a building filled with policemen, then his plans for revenge against those who victimized him and his countrymen would be foiled since not a single one of the principal perpetrators of the viral conspiracy was in the building at the time. The subsequent state-sanctioned news broadcast so utterly misrepresents the events at Jordan Tower that the film audience is left believing there was never any danger to civilians:

> A psychotic terrorist identified only as the letter V attacked the control booth with high powered explosives and weapons that he used against unarmed civilians in order to broadcast his message of hate.... During this heroic raid, the terrorist was shot and killed.... The danger is now over. The terrorist is dead.

The false commentary is accompanied by a video reel that shows a member of the crew dressed like V being shot by police, the presumed evidence of the terrorist's death.

V's character is constructed as a counterpoint to Sutler and his government, and many of the myths about terrorists that are not descriptive of V are instead indicative of the power structure. V's veracity, integrity, and compassion operate in sharp contrast to the disposition of the sitting regime. While V, who is described as "psychotic," remains resolute, focused, rational, and considerate throughout the narrative, Sutler's wrath and inhumanity are unrelenting. He roars many lines of dialogue, hurling insults, threats, and accusations at his closest councilors, creating the impression of a man unhinged, so willful and narcissistic that he cannot brook resistance or failure. His cabinet members receive only recriminations for their efforts at interdiction. While V is willing to patiently endure criticism and alternative points of view, the Sutler government inters, tortures, and kills all opposition to its power.

Evey progressively realizes that the true threat to the peace, happiness, and prosperity of the English people is not V, but the very institutions that have been constructed ostensibly to guarantee order and security. Under Sutler, England has become a national security or police state whose primary objective remains the consolidation of power and the maintenance of national secrets, not the facilitation of prosperity, and the transformation of Evey's perception of V serves as a guide to the complexity of terrorist issues. While initially Evey condemns him as a murderer, a thief, a madman, a "monster," and, in her most charitable moments, a misguided idealist, she nevertheless comes to understand that desperate measures and grand gestures are necessary to shock the population out of its complacency so that it will openly oppose the repressive and tyrannical tactics of the real madman and his paranoid regime. Of course, the event that leads to Evey's understanding is in and of itself paradoxical. V must incarcerate and torture her in order to expose the despotism of the sitting government. By the end of the film, Evey and the movie audience have concluded that the Parliament must be destroyed in order to facilitate social and political change. Thus the film audience has embraced a terrorist agenda, emotionally and ideologically complicit with Evey in her grand act of destruction. The film version of Finch — the representative of law and order — even quietly acquiesces in the demolition, allowing Evey to send the explosive-laden train under the Parliament building.

The vehicle for the conversion of the masses in *V for Vendetta* is not the destruction of the Old Bailey or the Parliament, but the mass media. In the words of Margaret Thatcher, "publicity is the oxygen of terrorism" (Nacos 208). The violent and destructive acts of terrorists are less important to the perpetrators than is the media coverage that ensues, because media permits the terrorists to advertise their motivating political or social cause(s), and V certainly knows how to work the media to his advantage. His destruction of the Old Bailey is an advertisement, a spectacle that acts as prelude to his revolutionary manifesto articulated during his broadcast via the BTN. Even the explosion had its prelude in the form of a symphony aired over the public broadcast system, a performance intended to bring people out of their houses in spite of curfews so that they can witness the main event, the destruction of London's enduring symbol of justice. Moreover, the piece of music that V selects — Tchaikovsky's *1812 Overture*— constitutes a reminder of America's own national origin in terrorism against the British crown. Tchaikovsky's symphony is a traditional piece of music in the celebration of our national independence on the 4th of July, and in this context a reminder of the guerilla tactics deemed requisite to that struggle, the same that have been subsequently lionized.

Following his initial appearance on the BTN news, V does not need to offer any more public orations; he only needs to continue to create mayhem. Because the governmental propaganda initially refused to acknowledge his act as terrorism, calling it instead an unplanned demolition, V was obliged to contradict the official party line in order to advertise his cause and to demonstrate simultaneously that the government is controlling and manufacturing the news, an act no doubt calculated to undermine its credibility with the populace. Once V's agenda is common knowledge, the Sutler government and state controlled media have to cover his subsequent acts and make public efforts to interdict his activities, each effort another example of their inability to neutralize him and of the extravagantly oppressive tactics perpetrated by the Sutler government in the interests of order.

Stohl argues that "political terrorism is theater" with "the world" as its "stage" (1), and the performativity of V's violence is foregrounded within the text. In the opening scenes, V prepares his costume in a space reminiscent of an actor's dressing room, and his subsequent activities are conducted with an affected dramatic flair. He quotes Shakespeare's *Macbeth* and *Hamlet* as he liberates Evey from the Fingermen who have detained her for their own lascivious designs. Identifying himself as a musician, he then cordially invites her to attend a performance which turns out to be the destruction of the Old Bailey, bringing her to a nearby rooftop for an advantageous view. When the *1812 Overture* begins on the public address system, he imitates a conductor, waving his hands to the music to indicate that he controls every facet of the performance. At the point in Tchaikovsky's composition that the canons traditionally fire, he initiates the demolition of the court house as well as a fireworks display with a finale that features his signature logo — V circumscribed. The careful coordination of events suggests the musician's or dramatist's attention to aesthetic detail. Indeed the orchestral conductor becomes a paradigm for V's long planned project. The careful attention to each note and phrase of the musical piece, the effort to guide each musician's contribution to the performance, and the endeavor to bring the composition to an appropriately stunning crescendo are shared with the villain hero of *V for Vendetta*, who has labored for years to fashion and arrange the performance of his great revenge. The orchestral trope prefigures the domino metaphor at the climax of the film, both of which demonstrate that every placement has been calculated in advance to bring about his desired conclusion. The dominos fall creating a circle intersected by a V, once again the terrorist's logo. As they fall, the narrative runs through a series of rapid cuts revealing the chain of events that V has set into motion within the public realm and setting the stage for the final confrontation and revenge. As the dominoes fall, all the faux musicians play their parts, contributing to the orchestral design of the terrorist's project.

The purpose of the terrorist's "violent theater" (a phrase borrowed from Duvall and Stohl 236) is to impact the audience of the piece in an advantageous way, by inspiring fear that may in turn force the power structure to negotiate and/or by recruiting like-minded individuals to the terrorist's cause (Whittaker 89). V's revolutionary terrorism embraces the latter of these objectives, not insofar as he desires to create more terrorists, but insofar as he hopes to win public sympathy, creating a powerful grassroots movement that will sweep the Norsefire regime out of power. His failure to target innocent civilians sets him apart from the typical terrorist profile. His violence is directed against symbolic structures, villains, and law enforcement personnel. V's "violent theater" is a morality play, a struggle for the allegiance of the British people, torn between allegiances good and bad. However, the dichotomy between good and evil is initially inverted; the virtue seems wicked and the wicked virtuous. V's political theater must expose the villainous apparatus of the ostensibly righteous power structure. Ironically, within this same morality dynamic, the fanatically religious Chancellor Sutler and his fascist party are vicious, violent, maniacal, and inhumane, while the humanist aesthete, V, possesses the virtues of compassion, courage, and rationality, even as he pursues violent revenge against his former persecutors.

Targ argues that a terrorist's targets are selected for their "symbolic value" in the effort to "galvanize a population through fear or respect" (128). V too opts for marks that are emblematic. The destruction of the Old Bailey and the Parliament comments on Sutler's disregard for justice and participatory government, respectively. In addition, his multiple assassinations constitute attacks on the various institutions that were complicit in the Norsefire party's lunge for power. The murder of Prothero constitutes a simultaneous attack upon Sutler's propaganda apparatus, his military, and his national industries. Prothero is the spokesman for the Sutler regime, the voice of London, and he was a former military commander and a major stockholder in the company that created the cure for the St. Mary's virus. As a commander, he retained oversight of the "detainment facility" (or concentration camp), Larkhill, where the virus was developed on human subjects. The attack on Bishop Lilliman constitutes an assault upon the church for its collusion in the Larkhill experiments. Lilliman was paid a large salary and eventually received the title of Bishop for silently acquiescing in the crimes against humanity that brought Norsefire to power. The murder of Dr. Delia Surridge (formerly Diana Stanton) punishes the medical establishment for participating in the conspiracy to develop a biological weapon at the Larkhill facility. She was the primary physician in residence. Finally, the murders of Creedy and Sutler exemplify the responsibility of the executive branch of government, those who decided to release the virus on their own population, thus radicalizing the electorate and winning support for their unrivaled political domination. Creedy, described as "a man without a conscience," directs the government's covert apparatus, and Sutler acts as a despotic autocrat.

V explains the symbolism of terrorist violence in his effort to prevail over Evey's skepticism. When she asks if he actually thinks that he can transform England by "blowing up Parliament," he responds,

> The building is a symbol as is the act of destroying it. Symbols are given power by people. Alone a symbol is meaningless, but with enough people, blowing up a building can change the world.

Terrorism is meaningless without an audience, its purpose to direct the populace toward radical action or fundamental change, whether it be the suspension of civil liberties in the interests of national security, thus transforming the state from a liberal democracy to a fascist regime (as occurred fourteen years earlier in the post-apocalyptic England), or the consolidation of popular respect and support for the revolutionary cause represented by the terrorist act, the event that will occur after the Parliament has been destroyed. The Old Bailey stands in for the Parliament, a prelude to events that will transpire on November 5th of the following year. The British have one year to examine their consciences and mobilize their courage in support of V's heroic stand against tyranny.

The desired effect upon V's audience is realized in the final scenes of the film when thousands of citizens troop into the street to witness the demolition of that structure that signifies both Britain's history of participatory government and the proud English tradition of rebellion against despotism. For example, the monuments standing outside Westminster Hall, the Parliament building, are tributes to Queen Boudica, the indigenous

Briton who led a rebellion against Roman occupiers in the first century A.D., uniting the Iceni people and, for a brief period, putting the Romans to rout, and to Oliver Cromwell, the 17th century Parliamentarian who, in the interests of the Commons and of "freedom of conscience," deposed and executed the bungling monarch Charles I and ruled in his place for a decade. From the perspective of the people, the Parliamentary blast in *V/V* is merely a symbol, not an actual coup since as far as the people know the Sutler government will still be intact once the structure has been razed. The regime will have only lost credibility, not power, and it can continue its domination through brute force. The audience also signify their complicity by donning Guy Fawkes costumes, implying that they have endured enough abuse from their national leaders and are ready for drastic and risky measures. V's audience is personalized in the figures of Evey and Finch, who must decide to send the explosive laden train down the tube to Westminster. Evey remarks that the devastation of the building will give people "hope," and Finch concedes by refusing to stop her. The explosion only signals a new beginning, it does not create it; the problem of ousting Norsefire and creating a new government remains to be resolved.

State Terrorism

Brigitte Nacos observes that "the Western establishment has defined terrorism so as to exclude governments" (240). Nevertheless, there is a thoroughly explored category of terrorist violence related to the operations of the state in the effort to gain and maintain power. The differences between the actions of the revolutionary or ideological terrorist and the policies and practices of the state apparatus are often merely semantic. Annamarie Oliverio argues that terrorism is a discursive practice that is "historically and contextually produced" (48), a struggle for control of symbols, definitions, and ideas. Thus the determination of terrorist activities is dependent upon the perspective of the viewer. The state has the power to create official meanings, and these are calculated to guarantee the state's ascendancy, to consolidate power and generate legitimacy. If one accepts the myth that the purpose of terrorism is simply to create chaos (Stohl 15–17), a perspective adopted in government propaganda to demonize the political opposition, then the coercive activities of the state might reasonably be excluded from the appellation "terrorism" as the state's objective is to impose order. However, most definitions of terrorism cite fear as the defining element, and particularly fear as a means of coercion and intimidation. In this case, governments are among the very worst terrorist organizations. Stohl allows that "government terrorism kills far more than individual terror (2).

The Sutler regime is virtually a blueprint for state terrorism; thus it contests the idea that all terrorism is perpetrated by lone wolf or extra-/anti-governmental collectives. Norsefire conforms to William D. Perdue's definition of a police state which

> dominates through fear by surveillance, disruption of group meetings, control of news media, beatings, torture, false and mass arrests, false charges and rumors, show trial killings, summary executions, and capital punishment [42].

V's manifesto articulates the charges of state terrorism against Sutler's government; he cites the "cruelty and injustice, intolerance and oppression," and he reviles the censors and systems of surveillance coercing ... conformity and ... submission."

As with the traditional terrorists, the Sutler regime is dedicated to the exploitation and manipulation of the media, so much so that it retains complete control of the words and images that are broadcast to the populace. Prothero, the regime's *de facto* propaganda minister, keeps the population seething with hatred and suspicion of non–conformists to remind the audience of the chaos from which England was delivered during the reclamation and of the tumult that continues to engulf Europe and America. He is a nationalistic bombast whose principal aim is reminding the populace of their debt to Sutler (who delivered them from anarchy) and of their sworn allegiance to his authority. Because the media is state controlled, V literally has to hijack it in order to offer an alternative vision of England's past, present, and future. His occupation of Jordan Tower can be understood as a metaphor for the revolutionary or "expressive" terrorist's ("expressive terrorism" denotes those who merely desire to express outrage against the power structure; see Nacos 212) need to hijack the mainstream media in liberal democracies in order to be heard. *V for Vendetta* may be suggesting that all media to some extent is state controlled insofar as it articulates the historically and culturally constituted values of the society to which it speaks and within which it operates.

Words and ideas are value laden, and that value is determined by the context in which the words are uttered and understood. The individual's apprehension of words is intersected by a collective understanding, a culturally manufactured world view, and while these are by no means monolithic or trans-historical, they can generate a good deal of leverage in any given moment or epoch. The state sanctioned world view insinuates itself into the multidimensional apprehension of discourse and to a great extent dictates the audience's responses to sounds and images. Thus the terrorist, here V, must commandeer ongoing articulation of the official perspectives to turn the audience's heads in an alternative direction. Thus the takeover of the BTN can be understood as an expression of the often articulated idea the terrorist controls the media with his or her intermittent bids for attention; for a brief time, it annexes and rehabilitates the public discourse.

The Sutler government's policy regarding the media broadcasts is to keep the audience in a heightened state of apprehension, one might even say that it is a "national emergency state," one in which the boundary between order and chaos is always already crossed, not in terms of popular unrest, but in terms of the institutional response to the same. The permanent state of heightened awareness operates upon the certainty that given ample opportunity, the populace would revolt against domination. Without constant monitoring and extraordinary measures, the chaos, always bubbling beneath the surface, would issue forth, and it is the role of the media to keep the people mindful of the institutions of state that are simultaneously vulnerable and impregnable. The repeated allusions to the civil war being waged in the U.S. serves as a constant reminder of the potential for the same in Britain. Prothero argues that England was only saved from a similar chaos by divine grace and correct living. The government engages in a process of disinformation calculated to keep the populace too frightened to side with V or rebel against their authority.

However, the fear-mongering is not limited to tales of foreign wars or to drought and pestilence. The Sutler government makes it clear that the population has even more reason to fear the government than they do external threats. Paradoxically, the English must patiently submit to the tyrannies, cruelties, and persecutions of their own government in order to avert the seemingly greater threats of foreign terrorism and civil unrest. In the "national emergency state," the people have forged their own chains, opting for the familiar apparatus of authoritarian government rather than the erratic and random threats of political and/or religious malcontents. Creedy's secret service, the Fingermen, are the state machinery calculated to make the populace fear the government. The Fingermen are responsible for arrests and abductions, for tortures, murders, and disappearances. Here the narrative appropriates a form of state terrorism traditionally associated with Latin American dictatorships. The death in December 2006 of Pinochet, the former dictator of Chile (who was placed in power by the U.S. in order to undermine the communist government of President Allende), brought thousands of Chileans into the street to celebrate the demise of a man who tortured, persecuted, and murdered his political opposition, burying thousands of citizens in a soccer field. His practices gave rise to a new expression — "the disappeared" — which identifies those who had been abducted from their homes and never seen again (Duvall and Stohl 245), whose families, at their own peril, constantly petitioned the government for information about loved ones' whereabouts and/or for the return of their bodies. In *V for Vendetta*, Creedy's Fingermen are responsible for similar activities, and even the other agencies of government are critical of this practice. Finch complains repeatedly of the disruptive potential of Creedy's kidnappings. The inspector cannot "conduct his investigation" into the activities of the terrorist V if his witnesses "disappear ... into ... Creedy's black bags." The "bags" allude to the international outcry against the U.S. practice of hooding detainees at the Guantanamo Bay military base in Cuba, hooding having been identified as torture in international treaty.

As with "the disappeared," the fate of Creedy's abductees is mysterious, probably because few or none are ever released. The only direct information of these covert governmental activities that the film audience receives is represented in V's simulation of the same for the growth and edification of Evey, his effort to liberate her from fear through despair and suffering. Kept in a barren cell, she is daily interrogated, tortured, and threatened with summary execution, the inhumane treatment intended to solicit the location of her presumed co-conspirator. She, however, elects the firing squad over betrayal. The audience shares Evey's ignorance of her predicament, assuming that she has actually been captured by Creedy's agency, and by the time the viewers discover V's subterfuge, they have become resolutely committed to the revolutionary cause (if they were not already). Although the torture and incarceration are not an actual glimpse into the clandestine activities of Creedy's agency, they are based upon the accounts of two people who endured the same: Valerie, the film star who did not escape, and V, who lived to tell both tales.

The prevalence of injustice in Sutler's England is another dimension of the state terrorist apparatus. The repression of the populace cannot be entirely coherent or the population would not be sufficiently fearful of the government's potential for violence. If the populace can be certain they are free from arrest and prosecution by avoiding particular behaviors or if they can retain confidence that reason and argument can prevail against false accusations or unjust prosecution, they may not harbor sufficient respect for authority, sufficient submissiveness. When Evey is confronted by the Fingermen at the beginning of the narrative, her unjust treatment is intended to emphasize the irrationality and incoherence of law enforcement. She must submit to rape and potentially her own murder in order to avoid being arrested for curfew violations and even sedition. Her efforts to save herself serve only to legitimize her mistreatment. The continued condemnation of Evey Hammond over the course of the narrative proceeds largely outside of her control. It is true that V bears a significant amount of responsibility for her worsening predicament, but the legal apparatus assumes her guilt upon mere suspicion, and there is not any inquiry into the extent or nature of her guilt; merely gaining the attention of Creedy's Fingermen seems to be equivalent to a conviction since their powers are not restricted by reason or law and any interrogation into the matter is likely to prove fatal for the detainee. Finch expresses his desire to find Evey before Creedy does so that she can be questioned before she disappears. In the anxious days leading up to the 5th of November, Sutler becomes increasingly angry and desperate that the terrorist V has not been apprehended. Creedy defends himself and his organization from the accusation of ineffectuality, reporting that "arrests are as high as they have been since the Reclamation." This statement suggests that there is no necessary connection between the number of arrests and the crime rate. The numbers can go up at anytime depending upon the will or whim of the state's clandestine apparatus. Moreover, the branches of the Norsefire government distinguish between law enforcement or investigation, represented by Mr. Finch, and extra-legal activities practiced by Mr. Creedy's organization. If Finch enforces the law, then Creedy's role must be to prosecute the political opposition; thus the large number of arrests are simply the persecution of resistance, and since all organized opposition to the Norsefire regime was neutralized during the Reclamation, Creedy's increased arrests must be directed at individuals, who are merely considered a potential threat to the state, or perhaps the seizures are entirely random, inspiring apprehension among the populace that subsequently effects a docility intended to thwart suspicion. The random sweeps of the population inspire fear, conformity, and even gratitude in those still at large.

The clandestine monitoring of the population is reminiscent of the theory of "panopticism" articulated in Foucault's *Discipline and Punish*. Derived from Bentham's 18th century prison schemata, Foucault's panopticism attempts to theorize the application of power through surveillance, the panopticon a centralized prison architecture that facilitates the scrutinizing of inmates and prison employees twenty-four hours a day. The guard in a centralized tower is able to see directly into each cell as well as the surrounding work areas. However, the inmates and prison employees cannot see the monitors in the tower. Since they can never be certain they are being watched at any given moment, they have to behave as though they are constantly the objects of inquiry. Thus they become self-disciplining, fearful of the consequences of acting out (195–228). Panopticism is useful in understanding the representation of state terrorism in McTeigue's *V for Vendetta*. Moore and Lloyd's graphic novel was partially inspired by protests over CCTV, a video surveillance system installed in public areas throughout Britain in the 1980s, forming the most extensive network of popular surveillance in the world, and while the crime rate has decreased as a result of this scrutiny, many believe that it constitutes an infringement on the population's right to privacy. The positive effect that the apparatus has had on crime can be explained via panopticism. Since the potential criminals cannot know when they are being monitored, they are deterred from illicit activities at least in those locations where they know a camera to be present. We are to assume that those locations would include areas with a high degree of pedestrian traffic.

The monitoring of the London population in *VfV* includes both the audio and visual. The surveillance apparatus includes roving vans that take the temperature of the population. Based upon the information gathered, the official in charge of this operation is able to quantify the frequency with which a given subject is discussed on the various communication networks, providing the administration with an unofficial public poll. In one cabinet meeting, the official responsible for audio surveillance is able to cite a percentage of the population that believes V is still alive in spite of official reports to the contrary. Roving vans randomly pick up conversation in private residences, and some party members appear to be singled out for audio surveillance, either because their prominence warrants extra security precautions or because their influence makes them the subjects of suspicion. Bishop Lilliman's residence in Westminster Abbey is surveilled by a security van that is obviously not randomly placed nor new to the operation. When the Bishop entertains Evey, who is masquerading as a child prostitute in order to facilitate V's access to the residence, the eavesdroppers are not initially alarmed by what they hear. One listener salaciously remarks that it is "kiddie night at the Abbey," implying that the sexual exploitation of children is commonplace event in the Bishop's residence and that they have not and will not do anything to interfere with the pedophilic activities. Only after the transmissions reveal the Bishop's cries of alarm are the monitors compelled to intervene. The inversion of values is stunning in this scene: the legal apparatus does nothing to interdict child abuse, but is prompted to action by dangers to the molester. Other public figures are subject to audio scrutiny. Creedy is being surveilled by Finch's people and is certainly monitoring Finch's operations since the latter is repeatedly in trouble for investigating past matters, namely the St. Mary's and Larkhill incidents. Clearly the prevalence of spying is indicative of the inherent paranoia within the Sutler regime. The government is beginning to consume itself, the panopticon monitoring both the incarcerated and the incarcerators. Creedy also spies on Sutler, keeping men loyal only to himself close to the Chancellor, so that when Sutler, in frustration turns upon him, he can seize the leader and save himself.

The video surveillance is particularly prominent in the narrative line involving Evey Hammond. The attempted arrest and mishandling of the female protagonist by the Fingermen is captured on the CCTV. However, despite the obvious exculpatory imagery, she is condemned in absentia merely for being present at V's first public action. It is clear that she was not complicit in V's actions; she was even afraid that he might harm her, threatening to spray him with mace. Later, following the transmission from Jordan Tower, Finch observes that V is hesitant to take Evey with him after she is knocked unconscious, another indication that she is not in actuality his co-conspirator. Yet neither of the exculpating videos has any effect upon the presumption of Evey's guilt. The misinterpretation of the video surveillance demonstrates that the monitors still need to learn Othello's lesson that "ocular proof" can be deceiving. One must supplement the visual image with reason in order to attain the truth. The willful misreading of the visual media exposes the irrationality at the heart of the Sutler regime. The visual and audio surveillance are not practiced to attain truth or interdict crime but to gather information on people to be used in the construction of a pretense for arrest. The visual and audio tools actually serve the purposes of untruth.

A prominent feature of terroristic regimes is the employment of torture and death squads seemingly independent of the official governmental apparatus. These groups wage a campaign of intimidation and persecution — abducting, torturing, and killing members of the political opposition or anyone deemed dangerous to the state. While such groups frequently have no official connection to the government, they are, nevertheless, "linked with the ruling elite" (Perdue 19). Unlike many of the death squads typical of the Latin American strongman dictatorships, the Fingermen constitute an official form of clandestine surveillance intended to inspire obedience and discipline through fear. They are plain clothes officers who retain no hint of their official charges. The individuals who waylay Evey at the beginning of the film are downright sleezy in both appearance and action. The identification of their official role is obviously sufficient to strike terror into the average person. Evey initially tries to defend herself against her attackers until she sees their badges, at which time all her resistance melts away in spite of their lascivious and violent designs upon her. The reputation for cruelty and injustice is part of the mythology of Fingermen, the same that produces docility within a populace that can never be certain they are free of these watchful government spies. The irrationality associated with these men makes them frightening; their activities are ostensibly unrelated to the maintenance or enforcement of the law; thus no one can be certain that she or he is free of the Fingermen's violence, and innocence is not a defense, indeed as Evey's predicament reveals, innocence may actually be a defect. The Fingermen have *carte blanche* in their effort to interdict and summarily prosecute opposition or nonconformity. The infinitive "to finger" can mean to identify a malefactor, to ascribe blame. Thus the term fingermen may suggest that the role they play in the government is to manufacture dissent in order to sustain the ongoing state of emergency, the same that justifies the government's extraordinary measures in the suppression of its own population.

An identifiable strategy within the terrorist regime's arsenal of manipulative gestures is the willful creation and elimination of a threat to order and security (Stohl 6). This tactic permits the power structure to create a pageant of its own invulnerability. The legitimacy of power lies partially in its ability to guarantee order or to wage war in defense of its population. In the event that no insidious threats exist, the state may manufacture its opposition in order to define is itself via that which it opposes and create a spectacle of its supremacy by crushing and subduing that which it has demonized and radically excluded. Sutler's regime has ostracized and scapegoated religious, gendered, and ethnic minorities, fingering them as the threat to order and stability. If V had been manageable, he might have been a godsend to the Sutler government, who could have crushed him for the purposes of propaganda. While they do try to do just that, their long term goals are obviously thwarted by his success. The scapegoating of its antagonists is a part of the genesis of the Norsefire regime and the political clout of Adam Sutler. In order to create an atmosphere of panic, one in which he can offer his services and win the people's absolute obedience, Sutler condones the release of the newly created St. Mary's virus on his own population. The ensuing terror generates a national emergency, and Sutler steps into the ensuing panic, offering his services as the savior of the nation. Since the antidote was created in advance of the virus' release, the country's newly elected savior is able to produce a cure within weeks of his installation in power. Thus he owes his dominion over the nation to political theatrics in which he casts himself as protagonist.

The terrorist state frequently relies upon the "show trial" to consolidate power (Perdue 42). These highly publicized events serve a variety of purposes, including, but not limited to, demonstration that resistance to the regime's dominion is futile, that the standing government is the sole arbiter in the construction of truth and falsity, right and wrong, even in those circumstances where they are too much to blame, and that the regime at least maintains a pretense to an objective legal process. Having produced, unleashed, and subsequently cured the St. Mary's virus, the Sutler regime must ascribe blame to someone other than its own clandestine personnel, so it constructs a terrorist threat, fingering three innocent men — so-called religious fanatics — and creating a demonized opposition desperate for English blood and sufficiently frightening to inspire gratitude for and obedience to the watchful government. The trio were eventually found guilty and executed, a final theatrical gesture calculated to demonstrate the newly installed regime's counterfeit commitment to security and feigned respect for justice. Thus the subterfuge brought a fascist regime to power through popular vote, and all in the name of national security, demonstrating, once again, the slippery slope that liberal democracies tread when sacrificing civil liberties for safety.

Perhaps the most damning qualities of the Sutler regime include its visual and conceptual association with the most notorious terrorist government in recent memory — Germany's National Socialist Party. Through these associations, the film can turn the audience unequivocally against the Norsefire party and toward V in spite of his lone wolf terrorist activities. In such a scenario, resistance to power through revolutionary terrorism is not only desirable, but also morally defensible, and the allusions to Nazism are not subtle. Sutler's name is a synthesis of Susan (the name of the high Chancellor in Moore and Lloyd's graphic novel) and Hitler. Like the German *Fuhrer*, Sutler came to power riding a wave of nationalism in a time of crisis. The title "Chancellor" is one shared by both men, and both progressively exceed the power to which they were elected until they rule with absolute authority, sweeping away all opponents via a ruthless faction of secret police. While Sutler does not share Hilter's territorial ambitions, he does, as cited previously, coerce and manipulate the citizenry by scapegoating minorities. His concentration camps are composed of undesirables whom he exploits in fiendish medical experiments and then tortures and secretly kills. The tactics of his secret police, the Fingermen, are the same that were made notorious by Hitler's Gestapo: bursting into people's homes in the middle of the night to abduct, interrogate, and kill political resistance or merely undesirables, the stigmatized populations. The colors, emblems, and pageantry of the Norsefire party are also reminiscent of Nazi spectacles. One recurring image reveals the ranks of black clad soldiers marching triumphantly past Sutler, who is elevated on a grandstand that is draped in red and black flags, creating an analogue to the imagery of Hitler reviewing his troops in the lead-up to war. Even the name "Norsefire" alludes to the Wagnerian motifs or the Nordic sagas so fundamental to the Nazi mythologies. Sutler himself shares with Hitler his narcissistic borderline personality with a penchant for fiery speeches intended to arouse a defeated and demoralized population to action.

The dystopic image of England in *V for Vendetta* shares much with a previous film, one more contemporary with the graphic novel — Terry Gilliam's postmodern classic *Brazil.* The Kafkaesque absurdity and humor of Gilliam's film are not retained in McTeigue's, only the darkness and horror of a state gone mad in its pathological effort to combat terrorism and its rage for order and efficiency. The protagonist of *Brazil* is Sam Lowry, a befuddled bureaucrat with delusions of grandeur, who is led inadvertently into an ill-conceived rescue attempt of an idealized woman whom he believes is a terrorist. Like Evey, he is initially condemned by association, but progressively comes to identify with the anti-establishment agenda. While Evey escapes the long arm of the Sutler regime, the protagonist of *Brazil* only manages to escape into madness where he can no longer be reached by government torture. Perhaps the most striking visual parallel with *Brazil* in *V for Vendetta* relates to the activities of the secret police. The repeated images of the heavily armed forces bursting into private residences, training multiple laser scopes on the suspected dissidents, and bagging them in front of their loved ones is plucked right out of the precedent film. The captives' intense horror at the sight of the hood in each film constitutes a particularly striking parallel. The bags obviously symbolize the incarceration and torture apparatus of the secret police. The enigmatic title of Gilliam's film is indicative of the previously cited association between Latin American dictatorships and political abductions.

McTeigue's *V for Vendetta* seeks to conceptualize terrorism as a discursive practice, revealing that popularized notions of the term are overly simplistic and frequently manipulated to demonize political opposition. The debate within the film addresses several common questions about this international scourge: Is all revolutionary activity terrorism? If not, where is the line drawn between violent dissent and terrorism? Is terrorism restricted to unofficial violence perpetrated by non-governmental groups or individuals, or can it be a legitimate practice of social control? These questions resurrect the perpetual debate over the precise definition of the vexed term, a dispute not likely to be settled any time soon, since the nature of one's definition is often indicative of one's place within a socio-political structure. Although few may be tolerant of the random murder of unoffending and uninvolved citizens, some may find that violence perpetrated against innocents is a symbolic reprisal for the similar atrocities waged against non-combatants by those in power. The debate over terrorism is then a semantic struggle for the repulsion or appropriation of particular semantics. "Terrorism" is a socio-political negotiation between legitimacy and criminality, a struggle for the hearts and minds of the populace through a highly value laden discourse. McTeigue's film problematizes the overly simplistic refusal of dissent in the hasty ascription of meaning to the term. It specifically alludes to events from the history of Britain and America's struggle for independence and/or civil rights — the Boston Tea Party and the Gunpowder Plot — in which violence may have seemed reasonable in pursuit of a just resolution.

The progressive revelations of both Evey and Finch create an analogue for the movie audience, who are led to similar conclusions regarding the problematic nature of politically motivated violence. Both characters are radically opposed to V's activities at the beginning of the film, and they approach the issue from antithetical positions. Evey signifies the average law-abiding citizen and Finch the state law enforcement apparatus. Evey is powerless, Finch powerful. Nevertheless, they both eventually adopt V's point of view that the problems with Britain are so profound they require radical and fundamental action. Evey arrives at this conclusion emotionally and Finch, the inspector, through ratiocination. Both emotion and reason can comprehend the value of just violence against the wicked and powerful, but only because the crimes of the power structure are so great that they outweigh the comparatively tame malefactions of the traditional terrorist. While Evey and Finch are drawn by their realization, they also drag the movie audience along with them toward the recognition that the overly simplistic view of terrorism is dangerous to freedom, particularly when people consent to abridgements of civil rights in the interests of a false sense of wellbeing. In the 1980s and early 90s, scholars would have admired the extent to which *V for Vendetta* intercedes in contemporary cultural, social, and political practices by manipulating public discourse on the subject. The reversal or complication of the mimetic theory of art with the added dimension that art does not merely reflect reality but creates it, intervening in social processes removed from the realm of aesthetics, would have been a predictable line of inquiry (Montrose 15). Seldom do films make as heavy-handed an effort to intervene in complicated social processes that have the capacity to impact the disposition, direction, and duration of a political policy as does *V for Vendetta*, which warns its audience that a population should never trust its government to restore freedoms once they have been undermined in the interests of national security or shortly thereafter they will need to be secured from their own defenders. The international debate over terrorism is much more complicated than Western governments or the media choose to admit, and the most fearful kind of terrorism is not that practiced randomly by individuals or political factions, but that imposed systematically by a bloated power structure, claiming to save the people from themselves.

Three

---⟋⟍⟋⟍---

"Half Sick of Shadows"

Tennyson, Waterhouse, and "The Lady of Shalott"

In his subterranean residence constructed from an abandoned tube station, V collects a multiplicity of cultural artifacts rescued from the "vaults of the ministry of objectionable materials." Among these "monuments of unaging intellect" are some of those works formerly (within the context of the film) on display in London's various public museums: The National Gallery, The Tate, The National Portrait Gallery, and The British Museum. V immediately identifies himself as an aesthete at the beginning of the film by quoting Shakespeare, invoking the national memory of a long dead counter-cultural hero, and directing the *1812 Overture*, all while destroying the Old Bailey courthouse. The cultural heritage of contemporary London is constructed as a pivotal representative structure within the narrative. V acts as guardian of an interdicted culture that has been suppressed in the present of the film because it reminds the Sutler government of a decadent and chaotic past. He reconnects the afflicted population with the cultural artifacts that define them as Englishmen and thus liberates them from fear and hatred by restoring their national pride and simultaneously igniting a revolt against obligatory conformity and silent obedience.

Prominently featured in V's home is Waterhouse's 1888 painting *The Lady of Shalott*, which depicts the subject, already liberated from her tower, sailing down the river to Camelot. This is the only painting of the Lady after she has left the mirror and the web and begun her fatal journey. Waterhouse's canvas isolates a pivotal moment in the narrative of Tennyson's

60

poem and operates as a chorus or a "metatext," creating and interpreting a narrative structure within the film. Thusly the film foregrounds its own antecedent text, drawing the audience away from the restrictive confine of the movie reel and forcing an engagement with a broader culture, with what traditional aesthetic judgments might deem a "higher culture." The canvas allows the film to appropriate the prestige of high culture, signaling the audience to look beneath the surface of the cliché action or heroic narrative for traces of refinement, for advanced intellectual engagement that self-consciously places on display its indebtedness to other types of narrative, to the visual arts. The Lady's journey of discovery, her journey outside the restrictive texts that she views from her tower window and weaves into her tapestry, is shared by the film audience, who are pushed outside of the confined, the closed reading of the cinematic text. Mikhail Iampolski argues that the intertext is invoked whenever the internal features and details of the text become irreconcilable, forcing the viewer to grope for extra-textual supplements to meaning (30). In this fashion Waterhouse's painting, as well as many others in V's "Shadow Gallery," operate as a window on alternative dimensions of the text.

"The Lady of Shalott" — one of many poems in which Tennyson contemplates the ambivalent relationship between subject and object, between the personal artistic and the public spheres — depicts a young Lady who resides in a tower on an island in the midst of a river. Along the banks of this stream, a road runs down to "many-towered Camelot." In her tower, the Lady "weaves" a "web" or tapestry in which she captures the subjects passing by her window. However, if the Lady looks directly out the casement, a curse will fall upon her, and her quiet and methodical life will be destroyed. She observes and records the images of life as they are reflected in the mirror near her loom. Thus she experiences only a mediated or distorted image of the world outside of her insular environment, but she, "half sick of shadows," has grown tired of the repetitive activity. The Lady is lonely and unfulfilled, observing the external world without the opportunity to interact, and it is particularly the image of lovers on the road that evokes her melancholy. When she sees Lancelot, gleaming in his armor, ride past her window, she can no longer resist the temptation to look directly at the world, and she suffers the expected result:

> She left the web, she left the loom,
> She made three paces through the room,
> She saw the water-lily bloom,
> She saw the helmet and the plume,
>   She looked down to Camelot.
> Out flew the web and floated wide;
> The mirror crack'd from side to side;
> "The curse is come upon me," cried
>   The Lady of Shalott.

Apparently, the curse precludes the Lady from ever returning to her mirror and her loom, and her turning toward the window constitutes a direct involvement in the external world. She leaves her tower, writes her name upon the prow of a small boat, and drifts down to Camelot, singing a mournful but holy song and slowly dying. The spectacle of the boat arriving at dock distracts the celebrants in Camelot who muse over the identity of the stricken and deceased Lady. Lancelot remarks that she has a "lovely face" and invokes the heavens to "lend her grace," while remaining completely unaware of the role he played in her destruction.

Critics of Tennyson's poetry have produced no small pile of documents speculating on the meaning of the Lady's experience. While many may — for the sake of scholarship — quibble over the details of the Lady's symbolic predicament, most concur that her cloister is a metaphor for the requisite seclusion of the artist from the exterior or public world. For Buckley, the Lady's demise suggests "the maladjustment of the aesthetic spirit to ordinary living," for D. Culler, the "inescapable condition of the poet's art," and for Shaw, "the price the artist may have to pay for trying to make his world human" (qtd. in Chadwick 85). Smith argues that the Lady's condition creates a tension between the poet/artist's desire for creative seclusion and his or her conscience, which compels her to address and/or intervene in contemporary social problems (27–28), and Martin concurs, recognizing that the Lady's dilemma involves the contrast of privacy and social involvement (Chadwick 86). Shannon defines the Lady's journey as spiritual awakening, one that leads her from "sight to insight," from reality to "mystical revelation" (208). Other perspectives relate the Lady's condition to specific social ills, Chadwick recognizing in the Lady's isolation and her craft (weaving) the compulsory domesticity of women (88); for Armstrong the reapers in the poem suggest the exploitation of peasant workers in the 19th century (Joseph 28); and for Psomiades, "The Lady of Shalott" is the appropriate lens through which to view the critical reception of Victorian poetry in the twentieth century.

Waterhouse's painting, featured so prominently in V's Shadow Gallery, depicts the lady after she has left the mirror and the web, capturing the moment in which she lets go of the golden chain anchoring her boat and begins to drift toward to Camelot. She sits upon the tapestry that she wove in her tower, and she contemplates a crucifix fastened to the prow as well as a collection of three votive candles, while she sings her mournful song. The Lady's death need not be taken literally. Rather, her setting forth suggests awakening or revelation, the first tentative steps toward a better life. As the Death card in the Tarot deck does not signify death but great change or transformation, the Lady's death can be understood as a new beginning, one in which she embraces her mortality and opts for a brief but vigorous existence over a secure but isolated life of shadows. Alaya sees the Lady's death as an "initiation into a new creative life" (283), and this is the perspective from which the painting and the poem operate in the *VfV* film, a narrative that concentrates on its protagonist's efforts to awaken the slumbering population of England to the tyranny of the Sutler regime and to urge them to opt for a more dangerous but ultimately freer and more just society. The Lady's journey to Camelot can then be understood as a passage to a greater justice, a point of view reinforced by the traditional construction of the Arthurian court as an idealized society.

The Lady of Shalott's progress from the distorted images of the mirror and the industrious preoccupations of weaving, from the dread and fear of an undefined curse to the exhilaration of release and the freedom of movement is embodied and reiterated throughout McTeague's cinematic narrative. The mirrors abound within the film, one scene after another, some suggesting vanity and/or self-care, others self-analysis or crisis. The opening scenes of the narrative link V and Evey through a series of parallel edits, both primping in front of the mirror as they listen to Lewis Prothero's nightly tirade on the television. The result is a not so subtle equation between Evey's cosmetics and V's mask, a parallel that would make the early modern satirist proud. Both of the principal characters dwell behind a façade, Evey's suggesting conformity, an effort to pretend that there is nothing wrong with her life or the society in which she lives, and V's divulging the discontentment with Sutler government that compels him toward revenge. Thus from the very beginning, the mirror signifies misrepresentation as both characters employ it to manufacture an imprecise image of themselves for the world.

The mirror may signify lies and self-delusion. Lewis Prothero primps and showers in front of the mirror, his luxurious bathroom walled in reflective glass. As he washes, he listens to a tape of his vituperative television address and proudly recites the content of his speech. The image of the man naked and almost facetiously reveling in the harsh rhetoric of his monologue creates a contrast between the imperious and self-assured bully of television and the fleshy middle-aged creature in the mirror. The disparity becomes even more marked when V startles him by appearing at that moment when the television broadcasts Prothero's defiant challenge, one in which he boasts that a man who hides behind a mask and threatens innocent civilians is a "goddamned coward" and that given a chance he would deal with the terrorist himself. Prothero's subsequent denials of his former life as a military commander and his simpering effort to save himself reinforce the fraudulence of his television persona. However, the end of his broadcast signifies in a fashion that he could never have expected — "Good guys win, bad guys lose, and, as always, England prevails." He inadvertently acknowledges the discrepancy between appearances and reality. Prothero loses in a profound way when V kills him and leaves his signature rose lying on the corpse.

In yet another scene, Evey cleans an antique mirror in V's bedroom/library. Initially, the glass is so smudged with age that it offers no reflection at all, but as she progresses with her cleaning, a Latin inscription is revealed, which V identifies as a quotation from *Faust*: "By the power of Truth, I, while living, have conquered the universe." The cleaning of the obscured mirror suggests the first step in the progressive revelation of Evey's courage, the inscription signaling the passage to the country's liberation. Evey and her countrymen must overcome fear and uncover the truth of their recent past in order to secure a more just and tolerant future. Here the mirror seems to signify contrary to the same in Tennyson's poem. The Lady of Shalott's glass draws her in and transfixes her, creating a false sense of security. Evey's engraved glass repels, driving the subject into the public realm, not flying from loneliness and bondage (although at the time Evey is indeed being held against her will), but pursuing a revitalizing and restorative impulse. Immediately following her episode with the Faustian glass, Evey agrees for the first time to participate in one of V's murderous intrigues, and while her resolution waivers, the instance does signify the tentative first step of a future revolutionary.

The embedded story of Valerie, the lesbian who shared a cell next to V's when he was interred in the Larkhill detention facility, a story which Evey learns while she is being tortured by V, also features a mirror. The story of Valerie is a "coming out" narrative in which she confronts her parents by introducing them to her girlfriend Christina. The father, while staring into a mirror above the mantel in their living room, banishes his daughter from their home, instructing her never to return. The father's inability to look away from the mirror while he addresses his daughter, whom, in all probability, he sees reflected in the image, suggests that he is unwilling to look beyond his own preconceived ideas of his daughter's sexual orientation, ideas partially generated by his vanity and self-absorption. Valerie defends her actions, complaining that she only sought to tell her parents the "truth," adding that "[o]ur integrity sells for so little, but it is all we really have." The young woman is subsequently forced out of the insular and secure space of her family home, where she is eventually swept up in Norsefire's genocidal purge of the gay and lesbian population. Following a few years of blissful cohabitation with Ruth, Valerie and her partner are arrested, tortured, and killed. As with the Lady of Shalott, Valerie, banished from the mirror, experiences a brief period of liberation, followed by a premature death. However, in both cases the women consider mortality an acceptable price to pay for their freedom and happiness, for a brief period of truth.

Perhaps the most dramatic use of the mirror image and the one most pertinent to the examination of the Lady of Shalott occurs in the Shadow Gallery following Evey's departure. When she discovers that she has been tortured by V rather than Mr. Creedy's Fingermen, she initially feels betrayed and resentful; however, once she accepts that V's actions were intended to liberate her from fear of the outside world and, specifically, of Sutler's government, she experiences a revelation. The internment, torture, and death sentence were perpetrated to liberate her of vanity and worldliness, to make her "half sick of shadows" and lies so that she will develop a new appreciation for the brief period that she spends enfolded in this mortal coil and can embrace a newfound courage, one born out of the assurance that living a dignified and principled but potentially brief life is of more value than living long cowering in fear. Her revelation is followed by a desire to be "outside." Declaring that "God is in the rain," she emerges in a downpour on the roof of a tall building, looks out at the shining city below, and raises her arms in exultation. This imagery of becoming is juxtaposed to reiterated shots of the scorched and faceless V emerging from the flaming ruins of Larkhill. The rain and fire suggest creation and destruction respectively, antithetical principles inherent in revolution. The baptisms of fire and water also determine divergent prospects for the respective protagonists. V's immolation necessitates his subsequent donning of a mask to hide his deformities both physical and psychological, while Evey's inundation signals liberation from masks. She no longer needs to primp and pretty herself for the world; her head shaved and her face untouched by cosmetics, she leaves the security of V's hidden chambers. V, by contrast, returns to the mirror in his dressing room and smashes it with his mask, unable to experience the rejuvenation that she enjoys, unable to abandon his self-destructive vendetta and pursue his newfound love, and because of his disfigurements, both emotional and physical, unable to live among the rest of humanity.

Thus the paradigm created by the Tennyson and Waterhouse metatexts is fully enacted albeit with two rather than a single participant. Evey figuratively turns from the mirror and walks out of hiding to embrace the city, simultaneously dangerous and exhilarating, fraught with potential and peril. Her curse includes the need to embrace responsibility for herself and for the long suffering country in which she lives, and her new awareness coincides with a pattern of social reawakenings throughout London. V's destruction of the mirror suggests a separate curse, one specifically for himself. It is an acknowledgment that V is trapped rather than liberated, not just by the revenge to which he has sworn, but to the limitations of his physical appearance. Destroying the glass with his Guy Fawkes mask suggests an identity crisis, one initiated during his liberation from internment. He cannot show his disfigured face to the world and thus remains isolated, trapped in a tower. The destruction of the mirror certainly suggests that V too is "sick of shadows," but unlike the Lady of Shalott, who has "a lovely face," his cannot be countenanced, and the romantic desire that he has harbored for his companion cannot be fulfilled.

The mirrors in the film have an analogue in the televisions and/or computer screens appearing in many scenes of the narrative, and these alternative glasses also undermine certitude and veracity. Several times the imagery of the film reveals televisions reflected in mirrors, specifically at moments when there is a clear discrepancy between appearances and reality, as in the scenes where Evey and V sit at their respective vanities preparing their faces and Prothero mimes his own vituperative broadcast in his bathroom mirrors, divulging a cowardice that invalidates the bravado of his pontifications. Like the mirror, the television screens/broadcasts generate a distorted reflection of reality; however, while the mirror reveals the individual conscience, the television operates on a collective or social level.

The plethora of television and computer screens in the film display the increasing influence of media in directing the lives and perceptions of the populace. However, in the Sutler regime, the media are not the watchdogs, but the instruments of government. The counter-cultural power of the media has been usurped by and appropriated into the operations of a regime bent upon total "hegemonic" domination. Thus media broadcasts are either escapist or vehicles of governmental propaganda, and that which is permitted to be broadcast to the public is tightly controlled by censors. The light and escapist nature of much television entertainment keeps the populace distracted from the unpleasant realities of the world outside. On the day that Evey arrives for work at Jordan Tower, she passes a security guard watching a program similar to *Xena: Warrior Princess*. She remarks, "I can't believe you watch that shit." The guard responds with an affirmation of the program's entertainment value: "What? Laser Lass is banging." The man who should be vigilant, scrutinizing those who enter the presumably secured space, is distracted by fantasy and particularly the erotic fantasy embodied in the implied Amazonian voluptuousness of the protagonist. The guard's indifference can be understood in a specifically pro-institutional fashion, revealing that his lack of vigilance may have allowed a terrorist access to an important governmental apparatus, but it can also suggest that a dearth of caution exercised by the populace allowed the Sutler regime to make repeated intrusions into their civil liberties until the citizens were virtual prisoners in their own homes, a foolish indifference and credulity that V interrogates in his usurping broadcast shortly thereafter.

The domination of media in collective environments is reflected throughout the film, creating a narrative movement parallel to Evey's liberation from fear and shadows. Indeed the storyline is punctuated by a series of collective television viewings that register the populace's movement from naive patriotism and xenophobia to a general mistrust of government. The Norsefire regime's news broadcasts and editorials are measured against the faces of attentive viewers throughout London. The camera moves through a series of brief shots depicting multiple collective viewing environments. There are two separate families who are repeatedly shown watching and intently listening to the scaremongering broadcasts of the news media and of Lewis Prothero. The same transmissions are the center of attention in the many London pubs, in the recreation rooms of a rest home and veterans association, and on the big screens of Westminster's Piccadilly Circus, perhaps the busiest place in London. In the course of the film, the selection of television viewers becomes progressively more skeptical of the information that they receive from the media, and they are given impetus in their cynicism by V's hijacking of the BTN, in which he urges them to acknowledge the problems with their country and rise up against tyranny on Guy Fawkes Day (November 5th) one year later.

The image of the populace watching from enclosed spaces as the shadows of the nightly broadcast play across the television screen and believing in the reality of that which they perceive reenacts the seclusion of the Lady of Shalott in her cursed tower. The news reports are calculated to remind viewers of the dangers of venturing outside, both because of the potential for terrorist violence and chaos and because of Creedy's sleazy Fingermen. The scaremongering seems to be successful. The imagery of the film is highly claustrophobic; rarely are there exterior shots and even more rarely are there people milling around outside. Most of the exterior images before the film's denouement reveal deserted streets.

The conservatism of the population is revealed in the television viewing scenes. The families practice an abundance of caution, fearing for the safety of children and rarely leaving their domestic environments in the evening. The images of the rest homes suggest the inherent conservatism of the aged, who commonly harbor a fundamental belief in the superiority of the past. In the rest homes, there are Norsefire symbols placed prominently within the décor, suggesting that many of the elderly are veterans of past conflicts, perhaps the same that brought Norsefire to power, and thus are unlikely to invalidate their sacrifices by questioning the sagacity of their former operations. The retirement home occupants might also suggest that portion of the populace who are too tired and defeated to long for renewal and change. The pub imagery is perhaps the most damning of the population's varied lethargies, the occupants of the clubs anesthetized by alcohol, more interested in escaping reality than in effecting fundamental social change.

The effort to jar the population out of its quiet desperation begins with V's takeover of Jordan Tower and the subsequent illicit television broadcast in which he apologizes for the intrusion into the nightly routine of the audience and assures them that he too enjoys "the security of the familiar" and "the tranquility of repetition," but that social circumstances force a reexamination of living conditions and inspire a nostalgia for those rights or freedoms — of expression, movement, and privacy — sacrificed in the effort to attain national security. He explains that it was fear of "war, terror, [and] disease" that "conspired to corrupt" the people's judgment, making them complicit in their own subordination. Paradoxically, they consented to their bondage in the interests of safety. When he points a finger at those guilty of facilitating the present government, V tells his audience to examine themselves: "if you are looking for the guilty, you need only look in the mirror." Here the glass suggests compunction or self-examination, but it also continues the analogy between the looking glass and the television screen. The directive to look at oneself in the mirror is not literal, but is a charge to examine one's interiority, one's conscience. Just as the mirror generates a double who teaches the viewing subject to approve or amend a portion of his or her life, V's challenge sends the viewing subjects into a similarly charged dilemma. Here, he exemplifies the revolutionary potential of the English population, his image calculated to inspire a comparative self-examination. His charge includes a social dimension. The resulting inspection of the self involves a consideration of the collective past and the national identity, sentiments that inspire a pre–Norsefire patriotism, a national tradition of resistance to tyranny. The television audience becomes "sick of shadows" and begins to doubt the wisdom and necessity of the lives they lead under the current regime.

V's revelation that he destroyed the Old Bailey contradicts the official story offered by the government controlled media, vexing the audience's efforts to suspend disbelief, forcing them to confront the open secret that the Sutler regime lies to them in order to maintain control. However, the government's misdirections exceed mere lying. The politicians manufacture the truth, making England's government appear simultaneously vulnerable and unassailable. According to the state controlled media, the threats against order and safety are constant, but the interdiction efforts of the state law enforcement agencies are so successful that unrest rarely succeeds in disturbing the status quo. However, even when V succeeds in destroying the Old Bailey, Sutler's propaganda machine denies that the explosion was the work of terrorists, offering the explanation that the building was destroyed in an unpublicized demolition. The paradoxical idea that the state is susceptible and invulnerable operates effectively in the practice of population control. The belief that the country may be imminently subject to assault from terrorists and insurgents keeps the population docile; they silently consent to the repressive measures that exploit national security as a pretext for the annulment of civil liberties: however, the power structure must also present itself as monolithic and invincible in order to deter actual dissent either by insurgents or critics. Dascomb, the official in charge of the media, reveals his institution's complicity in the recurring distortions of reality, but places blame for the practice on the Norsefire government. When asked by a colleague whether he believes that the public will accept the official explanation for the Old Bailey's destruction, Dascomb responds, "Why not? This is BTN. Our job is to report the news, not fabricate it. That's the government's job." The equivocal element of the Dascomb's response lies in the play on the term "news," which does not necessarily mean reality or truth. The government defines those events that constitute the news, and the media reports them. Thus the television producer claims no responsibility for the content of the broadcast or the accurate representation of current events.

Television lies are distortions of the mirror rather than a window on reality, and virtually every television broadcast includes misrepresentations of the external world, which are intended either to alarm the audience by reminding them of the imminent potential for disaster or to reassure the populace with demonstrations of the effectiveness of security institutions. The news agencies falsely report that V killed unarmed civilians during, but that he was himself killed in a shootout subsequent to his takeover of the BTN. The images that the media use to reinforce this falsehood are equivocal, depicting a figure (actually a station employee), wearing a Guy Fawkes mask and cape, being killed by a S.W.A.T. team even as he pleads for his life. The image sends all of the wrong signals, suggesting the competence of the emergency response team and the cowardice of V. In order to conceal the terrorist's continued activities, the media, when Prothero is killed, reports the incident as a simple heart attack. Evey's association with V is consistently misunderstood and misrepresented by the country's surveillance operatives. They believe she willfully assists him in his revolutionary activities, even though in their first encounter she is as frightened of him as the Fingermen from whom she is rescued, and all of this is captured on the government's surveillance cameras — the Fingermen's assault, V's rescue, and Evey's terror of both. These instances emphasize the unreliable nature of visual surveillance even when it is not disfigured by unprincipled and equivocal editorializing. The government must learn Othello's lesson that "ocular proof" is not necessarily reliable.

The film also comments on the media's preoccupation with bad news, which tends to increase the state of alarm, subjugating the masses through fear. In the final act of the film, the narrative fixes on a media broadcast that runs through the "American war," the "avian flu," "water shortages," and "new airborne pathogens." The concluding item suggests that V may have been responsible for the viral attack on children at St. Mary's elementary school, the same that initiated Sutler's rise to power fourteen years earlier. The preponderance of bad news may be a satire of American and British media and culture, through which the population are conditioned to fear all of the wrong things. This practice detracts from the real threats and problems in their lives whose solutions could prove inconvenient or unprofitable to political or financial establishments (Glassner xviii). As long as the news remains frightening, the populace will support the repressive measures deemed necessary to avert chaos or disaster, and they will disregard the more imminent threats in favor of those whose chaotic potential is exaggerated.

As inspector Finch investigates the circumstances that brought the Norsefire Party into power, he finds that many of the momentous events were manufactured by the government and the media or misrepresented to the population and that a careful effort to cover up the subterfuge followed the installation of the Sutler regime. Records surrounding the Larkhill Detention Facility — the locus for the manufacture of the insidious pathogen that killed 100,000 citizens — have been erased, even tax records were partially deleted, and he discovers that the most horrifying terrorist attack in British history was in actuality a convincing piece of British theater, enacted by ambitious politicians and businessmen. The image of the Lady of Shalott's mirror is duplicated yet again in Finch's search through records online; he spends much time watching the play of lies on his computer screen, but the accumulation of falsehood paradoxically leads to the revelation of truth. The newspaper headlines of fourteen years earlier scroll rapidly across his computer screen, and the enormity of the crime and the betrayal weighs upon him. The men who were held responsible for the terrorist outrage and were eventually executed were coerced into confessing to cover up the true culpability in the crimes. Ironically, the play of fabrications on the computer evokes Finch's crisis of "shadows," causing him to turn away in disgust, but with a growing resolution to expose the true malefactors.

The inspector's query to his colleague, Dominic, captures a dilemma similar to that at the center of Tennyson's poem: "What if it was someone else who killed all those people, someone who works for our government? Would you really want to know?"

Is it better to keep one's head buried in the sand than to face a reality that will alter one's priorities and beliefs irrevocably? Accepting the truth will create a much more dangerous world, and accepting the responsibility to alter the state of affairs accordingly will bring grave personal peril. Finch implicitly concludes that a more dangerous and potentially brief life of fidelity to truth and reality is superior to a longer life of fraud, delusion, and misdirection. The result of his resolution is the redirected social action in which he permits Evey to destroy the Parliament. He ventures down a perilous path, but one with integrity, one that accurately places responsibility for crimes against humanity.

A similar exchange of theories on the relative merits of truth and lies occurs between V and Evey earlier in the narrative. Following V's takeover of the BTN, Evey shares a portion of her tragic life story — the death of her brother and her parents — and quotes her father's comparative analysis of art and politics: "Artists use lies to tell the truth while politician use them to cover up the truth." Her decision to share her father's observation follows the viewing of the 1934 film *The Count of Monte Cristo*. She seems to recognize that the film narrative parallels V's incarceration, his escape, and his calculated revenge. Thus reality is mediated and interpreted by art. In a broader sense the comment defines the fashion in which many of the objects which are on display in V's Shadow Gallery signify within the context of the film. The various pieces of art have been selected to reflect a portion of V's story, not least of which is Waterhouse's *Lady of*

Shalott and by extension Tennyson's poem of the same name. This particular piece of art tells the fictional story of an artist who records the distorted representations of the mirror in her tapestry but grows weary of her craft. As stated above, her revelation, her turning away from her art and her mirror, is the subject matter of Waterhouse's canvas, and this moment of discovery and resolution constitutes a lesson in the repressive nature of fear, encouraging others to embrace uncertainty and danger. The paternal aphorism also emphasizes the social responsibility of art, the need for art to intervene in the communal by addressing contemporary social problems in a fictionalized setting, the same topic at play in Tennyson's poem, according to a preponderance of the scholarship addressing the work.

Evey, however, cannot anticipate the horrifying application of her father's words. V abducts and subjects her to interrogation and torture, makes her believe that she is in the merciless hands of Mr. Creedy and his Fingermen, that she has little or no expectation but to be killed whether or not she reveals the location of V's hideout. While incarcerated, she reads the secret diaries of Valerie who is presumably occupying the adjoining cell. The diaries tell of the writer's coming out and coming of age, her brief period of happiness with her lovers, and the terrifying brutality of Sutler's crackdown on sexual diversity. When Evey's jailer realizes that he cannot break her will, she is released only to find that V has been the perpetrator; he has made her believe that she is in imminent peril in order to transform her into a socially active subject, in order to encourage her, in a manner of speaking, to turn away from the mirror and the preoccupation with her own image and safety and embrace the perilous flux of the world. When she upbraids V for his cruelty, he reminds her of her father's words: "Your own father said that artists use lies to tell the truth. Yes, I created a lie, but because you believed it, you found something true about yourself." Thus artists veil social commentary in metaphor to reveal the absurdity, horror, or intolerable nature of contemporary events in a context where their irrationality is underscored.

The contrary practice of politics in which lies are used to conceal the truth is documented at length above; however, it may be productive to examine the dialectical construction of the politician and artist in the father's aphorism, which treats the two groups as antithetical processes operating within a single social arena. The artist's output comments upon human interests and preoccupations, pointing toward the resolution of conflict both physical and psychological, exposing and offering solutions to the causes of human suffering. As discussed above, Tennyson's poetry, including the "Lady of Shalott," debates the contrary compulsions of the artist: the tendency to withdraw into isolation, into the "palace of art" where creativity is easy and the subject matter light and entertaining and the contrasting impulse to use art as a instrument in the mitigation of human suffering, injustice, and tragedy (Smith 23–55). The contrast between artist and politician may be represented in the contrasting environments — Shalott and Camelot — of Tennyson's poem, Shalott associated with meditation, withdrawal, and/or introversion and the latter with debate, merging, and involvement. While the social is an inevitable element of the creation of art which requires an audience for its sustenance, the inclusion of overt social and political commentary within the subject matter may be merely an unconscious result of the intertext, language and images playing off of each other in unpredictable ways. While the politics of art was for Tennyson a choice, in our contemporary age, all art is considered to have a political dimension regardless of the creator's intentions — Fredric Jameson's "political unconscious" (Dowling 114–142) — and for Evey's father, the artist is a force for liberation and revolutionary change, manipulating fiction and reality to counter the lies and misdirections of politicians whose objective is to amass power for personal advancement. Politicians labor to obstruct truth while artists endeavor to expose it; they operate on the opposite sides of a single cultural axis.

The father's aphorism also suggests that truth will be liberating for the masses and that the revelation of the same will motivate the people to enact fundamental change. Gordon Deitrich's televised satire of Sutler's paranoia, his desperate effort to suppress the terrorist V, fictionalizes a truth, exposing the open secrets none will publicly express, specifically the knowledge that the Chancellor's government is misleading its citizenry. The faux Sutler tells the talk show host that the terrorist V has been neutralized at the same time that a faux V is tying the Chancellor's shoestrings together under his chair. The resulting farcical pursuit of the masked man emphasizes the absurdity of continuing to believe the government's lies. The program ignites a widespread chorus of dissent, signaling the populace's frustration, and as a result, the population begin to turn away from the mirror in which they have been transfixed, their priorities misdirected by the Norsefire propaganda. As in the tale of the Emperor's new clothes, a single prominent, derisive voice can break the spell, after which the collective is no longer willing to maintain the open secret.

Throughout the film, the populace is depicted primarily in interior environments where they are mesmerized by the images on the television screen. However, after V's broadcast at the BTN and Deitrich's satire of Chancellor Sutler, the television audience increasingly voices its skepticism over the images on the screen. Following a lengthy series of alarming news headlines, a pub denizen voices his aggravation and disbelief at the unrelenting bad news, the same intended to keep the people frightened and docile. The citizens of London and more broadly Great Britain are not unlike the denizens of Plato's cave who have lived their whole lives constrained, watching the play of shadows across the interior wall, shadows which they believe to be reality. Behind the bound troglodytes, who are unable to turn their heads, a fire burns and people carry artifacts above their heads which cast shadows on the walls. The captives believe that the reflections are reality because the captives have never turned to see the actual figures casting shadows. Plato suggests that his image of the cave is an allegory of human perception, one which captures his theory of ideal forms, of the paradigms that exist within the metaphysical world, the foundational structures for the disfigured representation of objects and ideas that humanity experiences in this world. The Greek philosopher then imagines the reaction of a cave dweller who was released and allowed to experience reality directly. She or he would at first experience pain at the glare of natural light but eventually become acclimated and refuse to return to the counterfeit reality of the cave, preferring even a painful truth to the play of shadows on the wall. Plato imagines that the newly enlightened cave dweller would find it difficult to convince any of his companions of the exterior realities, of the falsity of that which they have always believed. The influence of Plato's allegory on Tennyson's "The Lady of Shalott" has formerly been noted (Culler 230; Chadwick 93) in the Lady's revolt from the shadows of her tower and her subsequent journey through the exterior world.

Plato's escapee is an artist or philosopher, an enlightened mind that glimpses an alternative life and attempts to share his revelation with a reluctant audience. Likewise, the insights of V and Deitrich cause the populace to look away from the shadows on the screen and wander out of the cave, confronting the world directly. Having grown "half sick of shadows," the populace emerges from hiding and clusters in the streets of Westminster to witness the promised destruction of the Parliament on November 5th. The camera rapidly runs through the now familiar television viewing locations — pub, living room, rest home, and so on — to reveal that they are all empty while the Chancellor offers his final address, one that urges the population to be mindful of the threats to national security and promises to prosecute all of those who leave their homes to participate in or witness the terrorist attack. Just as the "Lady" in Waterhouse's painting has already left the security of her tower, tapestry, and mirror and embarked on her fatal journey to Camelot, the populace of London have initiated their own perilous course, confronting the overwhelming military power aligned in front of the capitol with nothing more than civil disobedience. The activated populace prefers death to the false realities manufactured by the Sutler regime and the complicit media institutions.

The social and political activation of the long dormant masses depicted in the final scenes creates an analogue for the real politics of *V for Vendetta*. The film, as a cultural artifact, operates in a fashion similar to that of Waterhouse's painting and V's television broadcast, urging the audiences to recognize the necessity of social activism and political change. When V delivers his speech at the BTN, he is not only speaking to the fictional audiences of the film, but also to the movie audiences in Britain and America, who sat idle while their scare-mongering governments have attempted to abridge their civil liberties, and all in the name of national security. V accuses his film audience of having betrayed their principles and their national heritage by quietly acquiescing while a particularly cynical and dishonest administration robbed them of their freedom from governmental intrusions, of their rights to counsel and to due process, and of their right to participate in and oppose the policies of their government, and all in the name of preserving the very same freedoms that the respective administrations have violated. In the resulting meta-cinematic and self-reflective trope, the movie screen recreates the Lady's mirror in which the audience must see their own indolence and quiet desperation portrayed, not in documentary form but in those lies that tell truths. The shadows on the movie screen are not historically accurate, are not a faithful depiction of contemporary reality, but are a representation of contemporary political practices taken to their logical extreme and resulting in a police state. Thus the film offers a valuable commentary on contemporary politics, but a commentary embedded in a fictional context. *V for Vendetta* urges the audience to turn away from the lies on the movie, television, and computer screens and engage in social action that can obstruct the passage to radical nationalism and dictatorship. In the final image of the film, the population breaches the military lines in front of the Parliament, creating a metaphor for the newly activated movie audience, who are invited to take back their governments from dishonest and power hungry politicians. The refusal of the legion of Fawkesian rebels to engage the military suggests that the resumption of power need not be inaugurated through violence, but through the civil disobedience of the masses. Thus the resolution is not for a government such as the Sutler regime, but for a society that has yet to capitulate its right to bring change through demonstration and ballot.

The film also illustrates that endless interplay of the intertext, leading the audience through many layers of complex signification, a movement that destabilizes the narrative integrity and closure of all the relevant texts. McTeigue's *V for Vendetta*, based on the graphic novel, invokes Waterhouse's *Lady of Shalott*, based upon Tennyson's poem of the same name, which is a reconstitution of Plato's *Allegory of the Cave*, and these are merely the significations evoked by the presence of a painting in a few frames of the film. The social and political intertexts also animate the commentary, providing the fictional story line access to contemporary events and narratives.

Four

V and *The Count of Monte Cristo*

When Evey awakes from her first night in V's hidden residence, she finds herself room crowded with books stacked to the ceiling, and while none of the titles are visible in the film, the aged hardcover books suggest the time-tested volumes of canonical literature and classical erudition. If one can extrapolate from the remarks V makes regarding the content of his art gallery, then one can assume that the books within his chamber also constitute knowledge interdicted within the Sutler regime. Just as the art has been stolen from the "Ministry of Objectionable Materials," the books have in all probability been censored, removed and subsequently resurrected by V. Without any titles, it is difficult to make connections between the content of V's library and the events of McTeigue's film; however, one can assume that among those books is Alexandre Dumas' *The Count of Monte Cristo* because so many of V's personal aspirations, labors, and tribulations are shared with the protagonist of that 19th century French novel. The Dumas novel is a shadow text buried somewhere amid the innumerable books of V's bedroom library, its text exerting an enormous gravitational pull on the cinematic narrative.

As she emerges from the bedroom library, Evey hears the sound of sword play and assumes that V is fighting with an unknown assailant, but when she follows the sound into the Shadow Gallery, she discovers V fencing with an empty and immobile coat of arms in the center of the room. His curious behavior is immediately explained by the film playing on his television screen — the 1934 production of *The Count of Monte Cristo*, starring Robert Donat and Elissa Landi — which V emulates in his mock combat, particularly the climactic duel between Edmond Dantes, the Count,

78

and his rival, Mondego. In response to Evey's inquiry, V names the movie and invites her to watch. Later she views the film a second time, and in each instance cries over the happy ending where Dantes is reunited with Mercedes. Recognizing the parallels between the cinematic adaptation of Dumas' novel and the circumstances of V's captivity, release, and revenge, Evey specifically christens the unnamed V "Edmond Dantes" at the conclusion of the film.

For the few unfamiliar with *The Count of Monte Cristo*, the naming of V might be highly enigmatic, particularly since the declaration of V's new name is offered so portentously that the viewer is initially inclined to believe she or he has missed some important detail explaining the protagonist's newly ascribed identity. The curiosity raised by this designation creates an incision in the cinematic text, inviting a closer examination of the contents of its belly, and even the most cursory account of Dumas' narrative reveals much continuity between the two texts. Indeed, the parallel between the French novel and *V for Vendetta* are so extensive that they are akin to postmodern "quotation" or "appropriation," the retelling of the antecedent tale in a radically altered context (Orr 133–134).

Both protagonists are unjustly incarcerated to facilitate the advancement of unscrupulous and ambitious politicians. Dantes' apprehension results from his inadvertent involvement in an effort to restore Napoleon to power from his exile on Elba. He is asked by the dying captain of his ship, the *Pharaon*, to receive a letter on the Isle of Elba and to deliver it to a Mr. Noirtier, a Bonapartist. Dantes is not aware of the content of the letter, but his ambitious shipmate Danglars overhears the captain's request, and hoping to replace Dantes as the new captain of the *Pharaon*, he reports these activities to an ambitious lawyer, de Villefort, who is also the son of the letter's recipient. In Dumas' novel, de Villefort is convinced that Dantes had no knowledge of the letter and did not willfully participate in any activities treasonable to King Louis XVIII; nevertheless, he incarcerates Dantes in the Chateau d'If, a notorious island prison off the coast of France, because he fears that his father's involvement will be exposed and his, de Villefort's, professional ambitions ruined. Because Dantes knows the name of the letter's recipient, he must be silenced. De Villefort himself uses the letter to ingratiate himself with the King, and because of this subterfuge, becomes the Crown's Attorney, a rich and powerful man. The third involved in the scheme to remove the lowly Dantes is Mondego, who betrays him for the love of Mercedes, the former's fiancée. The three conspirators suggest the three principal motivations for betrayal — love, money, and power.

The incarceration of V is similarly motivated although the three (love, money, and power) are not necessarily embodied in single individuals, and at least one of them is represented in a radically altered form. The narrative is unclear regarding the specific circumstances that brought V to the Larkhill internment facility since, like the Count of Monte Cristo, V's former identity has been obliterated by his suffering and subsequent liberation, and he does not talk about his past. But those who are detained at Larkhill must be the same social and political undesirables reviled elsewhere in the narrative — Muslims, foreigners, and homosexuals. Add to this group political opposition to Norsefire's ascendancy and the population of Larkhill may be complete. While several frames within Moore and Lloyd's graphic novel suggest that V may be gay, the film is even more vague about this facet of characterization, unless, of course, one assumes that stereotypical qualities such as refinement, gentility, and aesthetic proclivities imply the same, nor is there any implication that he is either Muslim or foreign, which leaves only political dissident, a quality associated (albeit unfairly) with Edmond Dantes as well. Even if V was chosen randomly to participate in fiendish medical experiments conducted at Larkhill, his fate is nevertheless dictated by politics, since the viral experiments are conducted by the covert elements of government in order to invent a new means of waging war, and the eventual release of the virus against the population of Britain is intended to bring Sutler absolute power and to make millions for the stock holders in the pharmaceutical industry who withhold the cure until Sutler is conveniently installed in office. The element of love in the motivation for incarceration is not embodied in a romantic rivalry but in a paranoid and homophobic government that seeks to interdict desire between members of the same sex. In effect, the marriage of Valerie and her partner is called off and replaced with a dungeon, all to serve the malice and ambition of unprincipled individuals, and as in *Monte Cristo*, the antagonists represent various social and political institutions — the media, the medical establishment, the pharmaceutical industry, the church, and the executive branch of government.

The conditions of the incarceration in the respective texts share a significant number of analogous features as well. The protagonists are not so much imprisoned as buried. They have been convicted of no crimes and received no sentences, so their incarcerations can have no explicit duration since terms of imprisonment are presumably based upon the severity of the crime and the extent of favor and/or mitigation in the case. The extralegal internment of the individual can have no conclusion because the revelation of the released prisoner's unjust treatment could be a political or financial liability to those responsible. If V were released when it became apparent that he would survive the St. Mary's virus, he could have informed the world of his maltreatment, of the horrific inhuman medical experiments being conducted in the interests of military buildup and so-called national security. Dantes can never be released because he could hold to account (either publicly or privately) those who conspired to remove him, thus undermining Mercedes commitment to Mandego, Dangler's credibility as a financier, and de Villefort's integrity as the embodiment of justice. Thus both Dantes and V must be removed permanently without hope of release and without communication with the outside world. The men are essentially kept in their respective dungeons where they are to await their slow deaths.

The prison environments of the two narratives share additional features. Dantes is placed in one of the lowest lying cells in the Chateau d'If structure so that he can have no contact with others, save the prison guards, and so that he cannot escape. His cell has stone block walls and is completely unadorned except for a cot along one wall. The environment is dark and dank and the prisoner drawn increasingly closer to madness. While the audience is denied specific imagery of V's cell, one can assume that the incarceration of Evey is indicative of the condition of her captor's parallel imprisonment; after all, he does long to teach her the same lessons about life that he learned while incarcerated, so in all probability, he made the environments parallel. However, whether or not his dungeons resemble the conditions of his actual incarceration, they are visually equivalent to the imprisonment scenes of the 1934 version of *The Count of Monte Cristo*. Evey curls up on the floor of her cell because she has no furniture, not even a cot. The room is dark save for a small amount of light emanating from the single portal, her food dropped through a small opening in the door, imagery that constitutes a specific quotation of the 1934 film. One significant departure is the interrogation and torture of the prisoner Evey. There is no torture or prolonged contact of the guards with the prisoner Dantes unless one considers being kept in solitary confinement a form of torture. Unlike Evey, Dantes has no information that the staff requires; their orders are merely to disallow any contact between the prisoner and his fellow inmates.

Nevertheless, the prisoners in both narratives manage to make contact with another through a hole in the wall. Edmond Dantes hears the tunneling efforts of the detainee in the adjacent cell. The two men have resided alongside each other for many years and have not even been aware of the other's existence until they first communicated by tapping on the wall. Eventually, they manage to remove the final stone between Dantes' cell and Abbe Faria's tunnel. The subsequent friendship between the two includes continued labor on the tunnel, companionship, commiseration, and edification. Despite his undeserved reputation for madness, Faria is a highly literate (speaking multiple languages and completing a treatise on the Monarchy in Italy) and educated man, and he struggles to teach Dantes all that he knows. The older man's underground cell has been covered with diagrams and images — calendars, equations, figures of human anatomy, maps, scales of justice, and religious iconography — that to Faria represent the "sum total of man's knowledge." Upon his deathbed, Faria leaves his treasure map and all of his knowledge, remarking that he does not have to worry about dying because he has replicated the contents of his mind in Dantes'. Faria acts as both a priest and a teacher, guiding the younger man morally and intellectually, and he implores Dantes to use their common knowledge "as an instrument of justice," to act as "an avenging angel doing the work of God" rather than as a madman who seeks only personal retribution. The death of Faria creates an opportunity for a rebirth of the younger man. Hiding himself in Faria's burial shroud, Dantes is cast into the sea, an apt metaphor of death and rebirth, both physically and spiritually, and after his escape from Chateau d'If, he is no longer Edmond Dantes, remaining unrecognizable to everyone save Mercedes.

The circumstances of Evey's imprisonment by V are quite similar to those of Dantes. She too makes contact with another prisoner through the wall of her cell. She finds a narrative written on toilet paper stuffed into a mouse hole. The document is the autobiography of Valerie, a lesbian film star incarcerated for her deviation from obligatory heterosexuality. She expresses her fear that she will die in prison without ever relating her personal history — her love affair with Ruth and her apprehension by Creedy's secret police. The opening lines of her narrative are strikingly similar to the words of greeting offered by Faria to Dantes. Faria remarks, "I thought you might be a jailor trying to deceive me," while Valerie acknowledges that she has no way to reassure her reader that the note is not a deception of his incarcerators. Ironically, in *VfV*, Valerie's autobiography actually is a trick of the jailor; however, the jailor is not Creedy but V. The edifying qualities of Valerie's notes are not intended to school Evey in "the sum total of man's knowledge," but to teach her the courage and resolution necessary to defy her perceived tormentors within the Sutler regime. When she elects to die rather than reveal the identity and whereabouts of V, she is liberated both physically and spiritually. Like Dantes, who is thrown into the sea, she is reborn through water in that ecstatic moment when she realizes that "God is in the rain." However, even with release from incarceration, her education is not complete as she has not yet become an instrument for divine justice. She has courage, but not yet hope. In a manner of speaking, she has made it no further than an adjoining cell.

The interaction between *V for Vendetta* and *The Count of Monte Cristo* seems at times to be more like allegory than intertextuality. In complex allegories, such as those produced by Edmund Spenser, there is often no consistent one to one correspondence between object or persona and the idea that the figures embody. The characters may reveal a given idea in only a single scene, or the attributes of a single reference may be spread across several embodiments. In *V for Vendetta*, both V and Evey, at particular times, replicate the experiences of the Count. For example, while Evey names V Dantes at the end of the film, in the captivity scenes, she experiences the tribulations indicative of Dumas' hero. Indeed, the relationship between V and Evey may be thought of as a master apprentice affiliation such as that shared by Dantes and Faria. After all, the person communicating the story of Valerie's life is not Valerie, but V, the other Edmond Dantes. His object is to bring Evey to the same emotional and rational conclusions as he achieved; thus he plays the role of priest to her Dantes and his home becomes a place of education and training for the younger and less experienced malcontent.

When Evey is released from her cell, she emerges into a space analogous to Faria's illustrated cell, namely V's shadow gallery, which might also be described as containing the "sum total of man's [culture]." The paintings, statuary, historical artifacts, cinema, books, and music are indicative of a lost world preserved for eventual reintroduction when the political order is itself annihilated. While Evey is no philistine before she meets V, the contents of V's home signify the necessity of a counter-reclamation, a restoration of the beauty that was lost when Norsefire came to power. When, upon his death, V leaves the contents of his home, as well as his revolutionary prerogative, to Evey, an inheritance parallel to Faria's legacy, she replaces V as the guardian of the interdicted culture and the instigator of reform. He leaves in her now capable hands the restoration of the British cultural traditions. The shadow gallery also stands in for the treasure of Monte Cristo, a dazzling cache that provides her the means and the impetus to vindicate her suffering countrymen.

The charge with which Faria leaves Dantes is to be "an avenging angel doing the work of God," rather than a madman pursuing a reckless and bloody path to retribution and self-destruction. Dantes must learn patience to carry out his revenge in a coherent, methodical, and, perhaps most importantly, symbolic fashion, making his torturers suffer in a fashion appropriate to the crimes that they have committed against him, the strategy most likely to meet with success. Thus Dantes must become a sophisticate who can match wits as well as swords with his persecutors. His predicament is partially due to his naïve belief in the honesty and integrity of humanity and the law, but his liberation introduces to the world a sophisticated man who is a consummate intriguer and dissembler. Evey's growth as a character parallels this same edifying process. She naïvely believed in the integrity of her government and the wickedness of its enemies until she met V and adopted a more discriminating and skeptical view of society. The woman who masquerades as a young school girl to entertain the Bishop and then naïvely believes that she can sway him to her cause by saving him from V's vengeance, emerges at the end of the film fully masculinized, her head shaved and her resolution for destruction and violence fixed. Like Faria, V leaves to Evey the responsibility for completing his work, for fulfilling his promise to the British people. She then must make a rational, rather than an emotional decision to blow up the Parliament building. It is the arrival of Finch just in time to stop her from engaging the train that guarantees the rational consideration of her actions. She has the perfect excuse not to follow through since Finch is threatening her with a gun, but she has also learned in V's torture chambers not to fear death when principle is at stake. She pauses briefly to rationalize her decision and then follows through, putting the welfare of the country before her own peril.

While Evey plays the role of Edmond Dantes, V, having already lost his former self, adopts the demeanor of the Count, and the two personages of Dumas' novel are, in many ways, treated as separate entities. When Dantes is thrown into the sea, his former self dies, and he becomes the Count of Monte Cristo, subsequently avenging himself in the third person, a dissociative experience that allows for patience in the pursuit of his long awaited vendetta. The Count's discovery of his death certificate, the same that he presents at his trial, is one of many signifiers of his passage from one identity to the next. Evey undergoes a similar shift following her incarceration and enlightenment. Part of her maltreatment included V's shaving of her head to liberate her from frivolous preoccupations with appearances and vanity. Both the experience and the shearing render her unrecognizable even to those who know her well. The woman who was fixing her hair in front of the vanity at the beginning of the film takes on the appearance of a concentration camp detainee; her unadorned face has become a mask.

Dante and Machiavelli

V for Vendetta's French shadow is shadowed in its turn by precedent texts. Dantes' namesake from Italian literature figures into the content of the novelistic hero's character and objectives. The damned in Dante's *Inferno* are punished in a fashion that illustrates the nature of their sins. In addition, the *Divine Comedy* is concerned with humanity's passage through perdition and purgatory toward ecstasy, and the same paradigm can be understood as a thematic pattern within both the *Monte Cristo* and *V for Vendetta* narratives. The protagonists endure the suffering of the damned for, in this case, unspecified sins. The liberation from their unique agonies initiates a period of labor in which the characters must purge themselves of the residual emotions of their former lives, not only the rage and vindictive resolutions, but also, in the case of Dantes and V, desire for lost loves — Mercedes and Valerie, respectively. Evey must be purged of fear and trepidation. Ironically, the cleansing of their souls involves murder, death, and ruin. The attainment of bliss in 1934 film version of *Monte Cristo* is a deviation from the original text; Dantes and Mercedes are reunited to live in harmony with Mandego's son and the son's wife, de Villeforte's daughter. In the final image of the film, sampled twice in *V for Vendetta*, the blissful couple, Dantes and Mercedes, seek solitude in a tree, refusing to allow Albert and his wife to join them, probably a ridiculous reference to "love birds." This happy ending repudiates the purgatorial guilt that Dantes experiences at the end of Dumas' novel, in which the revenger compares himself to Satan, usurping God's judicial prerogative. Prior to the first viewing, Evey asks if the film has a happy ending, and V affirms, "like only celluloid can deliver." The idea that film is the exclusive province of happy endings is contradicted by the conclusion of *V for Vendetta* in which one protagonist dies and the second is set upon a course of potential self-annihilation in her own vendetta against the Sutler regime. However, each is free of his or her respective weakness — Evey of dread and V of hatred.

In the conclusion of Dumas' novel, Monte Cristo sends a letter to Maximillian explaining the life lessons that he has attained in his pursuit of revenge:

> there is neither happiness nor unhappiness in this world; there is only the comparison of one state with another. Only a man who has felt ultimate despair is capable of feeling ultimate bliss. It is necessary to have wished for death, Maximilian, in order to know how good life is [531].

The same pattern that Dantes describes applies as well for his Italian namesake. *The Divine Comedy* reveals that antithetical construction of the Christian cosmos, an endless contest between good and evil, bliss and agony, freedom and restraint, and so on, and the protagonists of *V for Vendetta* learn similar lessons. Evey's mishandling by V is calculated to teach her that living in fear is not living at all. The pattern also explains V's lifestyle. He lives in a room filled with beauty, the aesthetic treasures of many generations surrounding him. It is a "palace of art," suggesting that he embraces life fully, living without regret or trepidation, enjoying life because he knows how fragile pleasure and beauty can be. The upshot of Valerie's narrative is the same. She remembers the few rapturous months cohabitating with her girlfriend before the bubble of her delight was burst by the intrusion of the state. Nevertheless, she finds it easier to face her death because she was allowed those brief months of happiness, which she captures in her references to the roses that she and her partner grew on their window sill. V uses this same metaphor when he eliminates the targets of his revenge, placing a rose, a Scarlet Carson, on the corpse of the dead, a symbol of the love that was shared and lost between Valerie and her mate and a traditional reminder of the brevity and fragility of "this mortal coil."

Dante's imaginary journey through hell or *The Inferno* concludes with the horrifying image of Satan, his torso frozen in a sheet of ice and his head, a blasphemy of the holy trinity in that it includes three faces, protrudes from the frozen waste. In the mouth of each face is lodged one of the great traitors of Western history — Judas, Brutus, and Cassius — chewed for eternity, signifying the perpetual punishment of those who ruminated over their respective conspiracies. The tripartite villainy represented in the punishment is analogous to the three conspirators in Edmond Dante's ruin, and they will all receive special attention from the revenger and perhaps, by extension, from the father of dissimulation in Hell. While V's revenge is more ambitious than Monte Cristo's, encompassing at least five people, there certainly is a preponderance of infernal imagery in the contemporary film, not least of which is V's fire baptism at the Larkhill facility and his remorseless and even gleeful punishment of transgressors. The subterranean action of the film and the fiery destruction of the Parliament also reinforce the "Dantesque" analogues.

Upon his liberation from the Chateau d'If and the acquisition of his treasure from Monte Cristo, the Count dedicates himself to the pursuit of revenge against those who tried to destroy him. His efforts begin in Italy despite the fact that all of the perpetrators are residing in France. In a circuitous and subtle effort to reintroduce himself into the lives of both his rival and his former love, the count ingratiates himself to Mandego's son Albert during the Italian carnival. However, the scenes in Italy invoke another tradition, and one particularly related to revenge and dissimulation. In Dumas' novel, Abbe Faria mentions Machiavelli's plan to unify the many contending kingdoms of Italy, to create a single powerful empire (50), and he has been composing a manuscript entitled *A Treatise on the Possibility of a General Monarchy in Italy*. The writings of Machiavelli, to the consternation to the 16th century, sought to describe what is efficacious in politics as opposed to what is honorable (Ruffo-Fiore 37). Thus he jettisoned the moral and the ethical in favor of the practical and was declaimed (particularly on the English stage) for condoning villainy and intrigue (Ruffo-Fiore 141). The present age has become accustomed to the often unprincipled behavior of politicians, assuming that underhanded, manipulative, and destructive activities are requisite to success among power brokers and that most of those kinds of transgressions can be winked at in the service of greater political ends. However, Machiavelli's contemporaries, who expected obedience to established authority because power and rank were divinely ordained, and wished to pursue enhanced influence, upset the divine, social, and natural orders. Machiavelli's *The Prince* offers strategies that advocate intrigue and subterfuge in the pursuit of lofty goals and often in the interests of "common welfare" (Ruffo-Fiore 46), and it is easy to see the direct application to Monte Cristo's predicament, even as a justification for activities that might otherwise undermine the reader's sympathy for the protagonist.

Like Machiavelli's Prince, the Count must learn to dissimulate, to use subterfuge in the pursuit of his revenge. Machiavelli conceptualizes life as a struggle between *virtù* and *fortuna*, between the individual's personal virtues and abilities and the vicissitudes of fate. The Prince must engage the former in the mitigation of the latter (Plamenatz 159–160). In like fashion, Dumas' Count begins with the planned abduction of Albert, which as stated above, serves as a calculated introduction to Mandego's family. The Count's subsequent activities are a careful and patient effort to ruin his antagonists in a fashion that is indicative of the crime perpetrated against him. He ruins Danglers financially by convincing him to make a poor investment, but only after he has won the former ship accountant's trust with many successful ventures. He destroys de Villefort's credibility as an attorney by exposing his mistreatment and his misrepresentations of Edmond Dantes, and he ruins Mondego by revealing his treachery to Ali Pasha and his family, whom the rival betrayed and sold into slavery. Like the Machiavellian villain of the English stage, Monte Cristo demonstrates patience, aptitude, and remorselessness in the execution of his vendetta, however, unlike Iago, Richard III, Bosola, Vindice, Ithimore, Aaaron, Barabas, and DeFlores, the count is motivated by real personal injury rather than vaulting ambition. Indeed the count is prepared to resign his place of immanence in Paris once his accounts have been settled, and the gracious and munificent treatment of Valentine de Villefort, the daughter of his enemy, demonstrates the rational limitations of his revenge. It is a flaw in the character of the stage Machiavelli to place another's interests before his or her own, to value anyone or anything more than success and personal security. But Monte Cristo is solicitous of the success and happiness of several others even to the extent of enriching them at his own expense.

V too is Machiavellian in his unswerving commitment to revenge and to the memory of Valerie Page. Edmond Dantes is warned by Abbe Faria to exercise his revenge in a careful and methodical fashion, and the Count is faithful to this advice. He waits ten years to initiate his actions, in the meantime building his wealth and his network of accomplices, all of whom are indebted to him and committed to the execution of his will. V shares Monte Cristo's patience, taking more than a decade to build his revenge and revolution, skulking in the dark rooms beneath the city and studying the subtle points of the Norsefire bureaucracy in order to use that information to the regime's destruction. Moreover, he attempts to remain unfettered by bonds to individuals, conflicting loyalties that could compromise the success of his destructive endeavors, but like Machiavelli's Prince, he is motivated, at least partially, by a sense of civic responsibility. Nevertheless, V is surprised by love; although he tries to remain immune to Evey's allure, he eventually succumbs and his revolutionary zeal momentarily wavers. While he does follow through with the plan to kill Sutler and Creedy, receiving a mortal wound in the process, his decision to leave the destruction of Parliament up to Evey's discretion is a gamble and a potential failure of his planning. He spent ten years laying the track that will carry the explosive-laden train to the Parliament, yet he decides at the last minute to allow Evey the choice of destroying the symbol of Britain's representative government, and while he has little reason to believe she will follow through with the demolition, she is eventually respectful of his wishes. The death of V constitutes an affirmation of human relations; he dies in Evey's arms — in the posture of Michelangelo's *Pieta*— both lamenting the unrealized potential of their love.

The shared narrative strings of *V/V* and *The Count of Monte Cristo* create a compelling glance into the network of interrelations that is the intertextuality. The pursuit of textual precedents and paradigms in this one instance stretches back over six hundred years, invoking a variety of textual analogues, nor does the string end there. The precedent texts for *The Divine Comedy* can be trace back to classical literature and to Scriptures. The boundaries of the intersecting texts are porous, facilitating the interpenetration of various narratives. The wormholes in the text do not lead in a single direction, but move backward and forward, as the thoughts of the reader wander in the unconfined spaces of the multiverse and the intertext.

Five

1984 and the Dystopian Genre

In his notes on the casting of *V for Vendetta*, James McTeigue remarks that he selected John Hurt for the role of Adam Sutler partially because of his former role as Winston Smith, the dissident romantic, in Michael Radford's version of the Orwellian classic *1984*, auspiciously released in 1984. Similarly, Moore and Lloyd cite Orwell and Huxley as early influences on the genesis of the *V for Vendetta* project (270). Perhaps to as great an extent as *The Count of Monte Cristo* (1934 film version), Orwell's novel and the Radford film version, as well as several other cinematic dystopias, shadow and structure the *VfV* text. One might say that after Orwell's *1984*, there was little else to do in the genre of dystopia than to create variations on and footnotes to the extraordinary creative insight of the author, who in 1949 managed to anticipate many of the technological developments of the next sixty years, and whose efforts were so successful that his narrative became a paradigm for visions of future societies in which government hegemony has become absolute, the state gone mad with surveillance, committed to the task of obliterating creative and abstract thought, thus producing a culture in which language is so impoverished that it is no longer sufficient to conceptualize or express rebellion or sedition. While institutional control in V's England has not reached the monolithic intrusiveness of *1984*, in which individuals are carefully monitored for minute indications of dissident thought or emotion, the Norsefire government has, nevertheless, adopted many of the surveillance and disciplinary techniques common within Orwell's Oceania. The *1984* references within McTeigue's film are not derived exclusively from the Orwellian text, but also from texts (cinematic and literary) that followed the influential novel, and McTeigue's film in its turn appears to have impacted the more recent film *Children of Men*, or at least one cannot help but view the latter in the context of the former.

The societies of both *1984* and *V for Vendetta* evolved in the wake of an atomic apocalypse, a significant concern in the year that Orwell was writing, as the possibility of an all-out atomic exchange had become credible if not likely. America had only a few years earlier exploded atomic bombs over Japan, and the Soviet Union had countered the threat in 1949 by detonating its first nuclear weapon, a blast that signaled the forty year arms race and cold war. Writing at the beginning of this process, Orwell predicts the exchange of nuclear weapons between the great military powers of the age within ten years of Russia's atomic genesis; however, he also imagines that the shock of the limited nuclear conflict compels governments to abandon this devastating weapon, concerned that they will otherwise destroy human civilization along with the very powers they crave (194). The result is ceaseless internecine warfare between the three superstates — Oceania, Eastasia, and Eurasia, a conflict that involves no risk of conquest or annihilation, its purpose only to distract the population, to act as a legitimation for greater governmental control, to justify increasingly greater demands for individual sacrifice on behalf of the power structure. In *V for Vendetta,* the constant threat of war or terrorism and chaos ensures that the population will not question the judgment and the demands of the seemingly besieged government, for to do so would undermine the war effort and thus national security. Orwellian critic John David Frodsham has identified this "need for a mass mobilization effort" as commonplace within communist and totalitarian states (153). In *V for Vendetta,* Europe has been devastated by a nuclear conflict, and America has collapsed into chaos and civil war. England, which appears to have escaped much of the former devastation, save for some areas outside the city referred to as the quarantine zone, has become wary of international influences or intrusions that may interfere with the country's safety and renewed prosperity. The shock of the faux terrorist attack involving the St. Mary's virus has led to popular support for the repressive gestapo tactics of the Norsefire Fingermen. The people are conditioned to believe (via constant television broadcasts and misinformation campaigns) that they need the strict controls of a totalitarian state in order to avoid further attacks upon their national sovereignty. Both Terry Gilliam's *Brazil* and Alex Cox's 2002 cinematic version of Cyril Tourneur's *The Revengers Tragedy* also share this post-apocalyptic dystopian landscape. While *Brazil* does not specifically mention nuclear war, all imagery of the countryside reveals utter devastation of the environment, the landscape laid to waste by war or rapacious and destructive industry. The images of Sam Lowry's, the fumbling and benighted bureaucrat's, fantasy pastoral landscape are a sharp contrast to the devastated countryside, and they form a specific allusion to Winston's dreams of escape from the urban nightmare that is London to a safe bucolic setting that includes forbidden romance, as depicted in Radford's *1984*. Cox's futuristic version of Tourneur's 17th century tragedy begins with a satellite image of northern France and southern England in which a vast hole has replaced the landscape making Liverpool one of England's southern most cities. In the wake of the nuclear devastation, Britain's class hierarchy has not collapsed but has intensified. Having escaped destruction, the aristocracy became even more exploitative and predatory than they were previously.

The dystopian societies of these films recognize the virtues of producing misinformation in the interests of social control. Frodsham sees this as customary within the totalitarian system as well — the government controls "all mass communications and all organizations (153). *VfV*'s BTN is a government sanctioned and manipulated media that rehabilitates or rewrites the news so that it reinforces ruling party interests and priorities. The director of the BTN, Mr. Dascomb, sits on the Chancellor's cabinet. Several times he is commanded by Sutler to spin the news in order to make the government seem unassailable. In the nightly news report, V's destruction of the Old Bailey becomes a planned demolition and includes a lecture on the dangers of clinging to the old structures, "symbols of a decadent past." V's murder of Prothero is reported as a massive heart attack, and V's invasion of the BTN studio, according to that organization, ends in his death at the hands of heroic public servants. Dascomb remarks that it is the government's task to alter the news and the BTN's merely to report.

Orwell's Winston Smith is actually employed in the editing and rewriting of historical reports and official records. Because the Party constructs itself as infallible, a complete rewriting of history must be undertaken whenever the administration shifts its policies. When international hostilities and alliances shift from Eurasia to Eastasia or visa versa, all databases must be altered to make it appear as though the alliances have remained the same. Big Brother's party slogan states, "who controls the past, controls the future, who controls the present controls the past" (35), and Winston Smith is employed in the rehabilitation of the past to safeguard party control of the future, yet he has become increasingly dissatisfied with his work. The country has been at war with Eastasia and allied with Eurasia, and when alliances abruptly shift, he cannot bring himself to forget the past (as is required in the practice of "doublethink") even though it is his occupation to alter it. He becomes increasing disillusioned by the lies to which he is privy. His odyssey of discovery is analogous to Finch's in *VfV*; the inspector doggedly follows the trail of deleted and forgotten information about the Norsefire rise to power, only to discover the lies upon which the power apparatus was constructed. At this time, he actually begins to participate in its destruction. Gilliam's *Brazil* is a culture that has gone mad in the collection and control of information, and vast institutions have been created to process and safeguard this practice. Moreover, there is an assumption on the part of the state that the institutions are infallible because they are mechanized. No one will take responsibility for the fact that Buttle was arrested in place of Tuttle and that Buttle's bank account was debited for the arrest rather than Tuttle's.

The telescreen that is ubiquitous in the lives of the Orwellian party members is echoed in *V for Vendetta* as well as *Brazil*. The latter film includes a conceptualization of technology that produces a strong visual overlap between the two films. In each, the advanced technology seems to be based upon a 1940s or '50s aesthetic. In *1984*, the advanced offices and telescreens appear to be futuristic versions of a 1940s work station. In the Gilliam film, the screens themselves constitute a visual quotation. The tiny black and white screens are reminiscent of early television rather than the video and computer technology of today. Moreover, the long rows of cubicles within the work environment of Radford's *1984* are reiterated in the industries of Gilliam's dystopia. The denizens of both attempt to escape the drudgery, squalor, and collectivism of their workaday lives through fantasy, in *Brazil* by altering the channel of the computer screen and in *1984* by escaping the omniscient eye of the telescreen. The Orwellian screen operates both as a receiver and a transmitter, monitoring the party members in their most private moments, but also serving as a source for patriotic news, music, and oratory as well as other programming that advances state interests, such as the interactive exercise program in which Winston is chided by his instructor for failing to make an adequate effort. The role of the telescreen in population control suggests Jeremy Bentham's "panopticon," an idea popularized among literary critics by Foucault's *Discipline and Punish* (200–217). The panopticon generates self-disciplined bodies by hiding its mechanisms in plain sight. The guard tower in Betham's penitentiary architecture offers visual access to all areas of the localized prison structure, but those under observation are only able to see the tower, not those who may or may not occupy the same. Thus the structure functions by evoking self-consciousness in the detainees, who do not know whether they are being observed at any particular time; thus they must assume that and subsequently behave as though they are always under scrutiny. Similarly, Winston is never certain whether he is being watched by the government apparatus, thus he must assume he is. After all, the principal evidence in the prosecution of "thought crimes" is derived from the telescreen's capture of somnolent speech. Winston must, therefore, hide his thoughts, even in his sleep.

While the television in *VfV* can be interactive, such as that used in Chancellor Sutler's cabinet meetings, the screens operate almost exclusively in the circulation of propaganda. Non-governmental programming, such as Gordon Deitrich's show, is censored. Most of the broadcasting seems to consist of government propaganda in its many forms, such as the misleading news reports, nightly editorials by Lewis Prothero, and occasional fiery speeches by Chancellor Sutler. Population surveillance is more conventional in McTeigue's fascist London than in Orwell's dystopia. Much monitoring is conducted by roving vans with high-powered antennas mounted on the roof; thus little or no effort is made at concealment, but the nocturnal activities and long distance detection of this spy apparatus makes it somewhat less conspicuous. In addition, more traditional surveillance is conducted by plainclothes Fingermen, who cannot be identified until they flash their badges. In Terry Gilliam's *Brazil*, a Kafkaesque dystopia in which public works, mechanization, and information collection have proliferated to the point of absurdity and madness, surveillance is achieved through ID tracking and through CCTV cameras mounted throughout the bloated social institutions.

Frodsham recognizes the need to purge historical artifacts as indicative of totalitarian rule, "Anything old and for that matter anything beautiful, was always suspect" (145). The authoritarian regimes of both *1984* and *VfV* consolidate power by purging cultural artifacts, the same that would verify and validate an alternative past, one contrary to that constructed by the ruling party. As cited above, the Orwellian dystopia engages in a full-scale revision of history whenever an alteration occurs that would tend to discredit official constructions of historical and contemporary events, including the deletion of all written references to people who have been eliminated by the state. There is also a systematic effort to eradicate material reminders of an alternative past, reminders such as antiques which testify to a bygone culture that revered novelty and individuality. The production of entertainments, such as reading materials, have been relegated to a government institution that mass produces narratives considered harmless to the interests of the state, and the purpose of these entertainments is escapism. The absolutist control of the population does not extend to the Proles, who are considered beneath consideration and contempt; they are merely distracted from political engagement through pornography and cheap liquor. One particularly callous party slogan states that "animals and Proles are free." From one of the few remaining antique shops in the Proles' sector of the city, Winston Smith purchases an innocuous glass ornament that encases a chunk of coral; its simplicity and impracticality fascinate him, and he feels compelled to conceal it from the telescreen because it might constitute evidence of thought crime, evidence that his ruminations have strayed beyond the simple consideration of duty to the state. Radford's version of the Proletarian antique shop is a dusty and desolate room filled with junk, the mostly mechanical leftovers of a culture completely devastated.

The institutional control of cultural artifacts in *VfV* has been touched upon previously in this discussion. V's home is virtually a museum in which he safeguards the interdicted relics of past ages. Director McTeigue told his design and art department that he wanted the Shadow Gallery to contain "little pieces of civilization that aren't available anymore" (Lamm and Bray 196). His home becomes a repository for the portions of a fragmented and fragmenting civilization. While there seems to be no concerted effort to control people's thoughts or eliminate individuality as Frodsham observes in *1984* (151), there are efforts to abolish all materials that would seem to challenge governmental hegemony. For example, after V broadcasts Tchaikovsky's *1812 Overture* and blows up the Old Bailey, Sutler, demonstrating his philistinism as he is unable to identify the familiar music, quickly has it added to the list of "objectionable materials" that are to be publicly banned because they challenge his power. As in *1984*, public displays of art in *VfV* are replaced with government propaganda posters, particularly those tending to promote a fear culture founded upon the threat of terrorism from foreign powers and interests. London of *1984* is plastered with posters depicting Big Brother, hostile foreign soldiers, and party slogans. The same is true in other cinematic dystopias: the walls of Gilliam's *Brazil* are plastered with parodies of propaganda, including many nonsensical and absurdist placards; Cox's *Revengers Tragedy* is decorated with banners and billboards advocating the cult of personality that has grown up around the Duke and his decadent family. Similarly, Sutler's London includes images of the Chancellor and the party mantra "Strength through Unity: Unity through Faith."

The respective dystopian societies of *1984* and *VfV* are cultivated by hatemongering. The blighted outer party members of Orwellian London are obliged to engage in a virtual ecstasy of hatred on a daily basis, a practice known as the "Two Minutes of Hate," in which the image of "Emmanuel Goldstein, the Enemy of the People" appears on the telescreens along with the broadcast of his fiery seditious rhetoric that denounces the goals of Big Brother's regime and demands peace as well as a restoration of civil liberties. The population are required to repudiate the message of the subversive and his clandestine organization — "The Brotherhood." Of course, the text suggests that both Goldstein and the Brotherhood are mythic, created to channel the hostilities and tensions of the population into a harmless carnivalesque display of powerful emotions. The potentially seditious pressures associated with everyday coping in a totalitarian regime are burned up in an innocuous display of loathing for an over-determined face and dogma. Big Brother is then constructed as the savior of the state, standing between the people and the chaos of Goldstein's destructive agenda. Ironically, Big Brother himself is in all probability a fabrication generated by the party to give a face to its agenda and to create a simplistic duality between good and evil in the socio-political spectrum, one in which the choice of the present regime is made easy. The book which contains Goldstein's anti-totalitarian manifesto was actually written by O'Brien, the inner party member who betrays and then interrogates Winston.

The power of the Sutler government in *VfV* is similarly based upon hate-mongering and divisive rhetoric. The Norsefire party came to power, as we know, by scapegoating a group of Muslims who were blamed for the worst bio-terrorist attack in the history of the nation, one actually perpetrated by ambitious politicians. However, the hate-mongering in Britain obviously pre-dated Norsefire and was merely exploited not created by Sutler and his cronies. The medical experimentation on Muslims, homosexuals, and foreigners antedated the Norsefire power play. For much of the narrative the government propaganda is effective. The bourgeoisie, even Evey, are compelled to believe that V is a terrorist and a threat to the safety and prosperity of the nation; however, the repressive tactics of the increasingly nervous government eventually turn the people's sympathy toward the revolution or restoration that V embodies.

The internment camps in *1984* and *VfV* are identically named "reclamation camps" (Orwell 163), and V's association with the indestructibility of revolutionary ideals — "Beneath this mask there is more than flash.... Beneath this mask there is an idea, Mr. Creedy.... And ideas are bullet-proof" — is echoed in O'Brien's recruitment speech to Winston — "The Brotherhood cannot be wiped out because it is not an organization in the ordinary sense. Nothing holds it together except an idea which is indestructible" (Orwell 176). Of course, O'Brien's statements are equivocal. The Brotherhood is literally only an idea and one that is created, perpetuated, and contained by its nemesis. It cannot be destroyed because it is too useful in creating the antithesis against which power defines and maintains itself. The idea that V embodies is inevitable wherever inordinate power exists; he is the oppositional principle that periodically reasserts itself when governments become overly arrogant and intrusive. In *1984*, subversion has been eradicated via the perpetuation of war with Eurasia or Eastasia. Making danger omnipresent eliminates the threat that it will ever make any head against total government hegemony. It has been appropriated into the government's own mechanisms and is spectral, merely an illusion always already eliminated at the moment of its inception.

In *VfV*, the antithetical political philosophies of liberty and oppression are cyclical, suggesting a periodic reevaluation and re-evolution. Orwell's government is systematically eliminating the very words that describe sedition, a process which Henry Giroux identifies as "the language of 'eternal fascism,' which produces an 'impoverished vocabulary,' and an 'elementary syntax' whose purpose is to 'to limit the instruments for complex and critical reasoning'" (18). Conversely, Sutler's power structure may be more authoritarian than totalitarian, not so much seeking to control every facet of the people's lives — including their language — as attempting to manage political expression, and thus it may be more vulnerable to the vicissitudes of the public will than is Big Brother. The people can think about changing their government whenever they are sufficiently scandalized or enraged, but they dare not express the will until there are sufficient numbers to mobilize a mass effort. Indeed the mass demonstration of the populace at the end of *VfV* may be a specific negation of the hegemony O'Brien sees in Oceania, where the Proles or masses will never rise to put down the Party.

Rebellion against tyranny, which is so commonplace a theme within the dystopia genre, frequently takes the form of interdicted romance. The totalitarian regimes of these narratives attempt to control the population by controlling the alliances that people form with each other, the individual loyalties must be reserved exclusively for the state. O'Brien explains,

> We have cut the links between child and parent, and between man and man, and between man and woman. No one dares trust a wife, a child or a friend any longer. But in the future there will be no wives and no friends. Children will be taken from their mothers at birth, as one takes eggs from a hen. The sex instinct will be eradicated. Procreation will be an annual formality like the renewal of a ration card. We shall abolish orgasm.... There will be no loyalty, except loyalty toward the Party. There will be no love except the love of Big Brother [Orwell 267].

Winston's increasing dissatisfaction with Big Brother eventually takes the form of a traditional romance that is based upon attraction and desire as well as a mutual contempt for the repressive environment in which the protagonist and his forbidden love, Julia, are forced to live. Their romance is a luxurious reprieve from the emotional wasteland of their lives in which they are compelled to marry according the wishes of the state, and any sign of mutual attraction guarantees that the couple will not be permitted a marriage license. Winston despised his wife, particularly her belief that sex was a duty to the state conducted exclusively for the purposes of procreation, for the purposes of creating citizens for Oceania and Big Brother. Both Winston and Julie are certain that their romance will eventually lead to their capture, interrogation, torture, and execution, but their desire is fed by the sense of danger and freedom. They defy the state by loving each other, and they swear they will continue to love each other in spite of Big Brother's tortures and the inevitable mutual betrayals. They know that they will confess and will implicate each other, but they will resist the compulsion to stop loving each other.

Gilliam's *Brazil* involves a similar thematic. The bureaucrat Sam Lowry, a combination of Walter Mitty and Kafka's Joseph K, falls in love with a woman, Jill Layton, whom he first sees in his dreams, but who later turns out to be a real person fighting the establishment to win the release of her neighbor Mr. Buttle, who has been mistaken for the renegade repairman Tuttle. When Lowry sees the incarnation of his fantasy woman, he pursues her across the wasteland of futuristic London, an environment in which bureaucracy and the pursuit of information have taken a pathological turn, the entire city wired for surveillance and flowing with missives shuttled through vacuum tubes. Although his fantasy woman is actually a truck driver, he assumes that she is a terrorist, and in his efforts to rescue her from herself and from Information Retrieval's fascist thugs, he inadvertently implicates them both in the very activities from which he mistakenly sought to extricate Jill. Just when Sam believes he has successfully deleted her from the institutional records and saved her from Information Retrieval, the storm troopers or Black Maria Guards burst in upon the couple's private interlude and drag them off for interrogation. As in *1984*, the protagonist's desire for his love interest appears to be partially motivated by the excitement of pursuing a forbidden romance; here Sam's fantasy life intrudes upon reality creating an antagonism between Jill and the law. In the process of living out his fantasy of rebellion against the increasingly inhumane establishment, he creates a forbidden romantic interest from a simple truck driver and subsequently destroys both of them.

Huxley's *Brave New World* envisions a futuristic society in which emotional attachments between individuals have been obliterated. Child birth is no longer conducted via the womb, but is instead industrialized, restricted to the test tube, guaranteeing that bonds will not be created between mother and child. Social and genetic engineering, however, does not mean that the denizens of the new society are deprived of happiness and sex. They are instead encouraged to engage in recreational drug use and promiscuity. It is the emotional attachments (either romantic or familial) between individuals that have been eliminated via indoctrination and social pressures. A single individual, John the Savage, who grew up on a reservation outside of the World State, challenges the social norms by falling in love with Lenina, but he is first confounded and later infuriated by her continued promiscuity until he murders her and commits suicide. Here powerful sentiments for others have been systematically obliterated, and the check upon romantic attachment has been internalized through socialization and indoctrination, and those who experience powerful sentiments of love are banished to outlying regions.

VfV includes several manifestations of the same thematic discussed in the above narratives. The potential romance between V and Evey is doomed from the start for several reasons. First V's physical condition does not permit him to be sexually intimate with another person, his body ravaged by the fires at Larkhill. His refusal to remove his mask to allow Evey to see his face is not merely a reticence born of disfigurement and self-loathing, but also a metaphor for another obstacle, V's commitment to revenge. As we already know, his mask is the face of Guy Fawkes, Catholic revenger and revolutionary from the early 17th century. His disguise signifies his commitment to the process of social change and specifically the elimination of fascism and its subsequent persecutions and discriminations. He can tolerate nothing that would dissuade him from his obligation to revenge. Evey constitutes a distraction, a temptation to opt for happiness rather than social justice. However, the thematic of interdicted love in the dystopian state is most clearly represented in the motivation for V's vendetta — the persecution and death of Valerie Page. The dystopian obsession with interdicting inappropriate sexual relations is revealed in the same sex romances of the film and graphic novel. Valerie risks everything, even her life, for a few years of happiness with Ruth, and continues to live openly even as it becomes clear that the state is systematically rounding up homosexuals for shipment to internment camps. The reinvention of the dystopian forbidden love premise seems calculated to demonstrate that our increased contemporary prohibitions against same-sex bonds constitute a step toward fascism, that prohibiting and criminalizing desire constitute an infringement upon personal liberties that should not be tolerated.

The fascist tactics of the Sutler regime within the romance thematic are particularly reminiscent of Gilliam's *Brazil*, including the hooding of detainees and the intrusion of black clad storm troopers into the domestic space, multiple guns trained on unoffending and basically harmless individuals. Indeed this later aspect is so similar that it may even be a visual quotation of the antecedent text. Both *1984* and *Brazil* focus on the thematic of "the walking dead." In both narratives, a man's life has become so blighted by governmental control that he considers an antiestablishment and inevitably self-destructive union with a likeminded woman preferable to a continuation of a tedious single-minded pursuit of safety and longevity. The same is true of Valerie Page. In all three, the sadistic power structure intercedes to punish the seditious romantics.

Most of the antecedent texts also share with *VfV* the subject of terrorism, as an impetus for restrictive social control. The periodic rocket attacks upon Oceania may or may not be originating from Eurasia or Eastasia, but they have the effect of mobilizing public support for war and for the government of Big Brother that heroically battles to ensure public safety. Random violence tends to legitimize the restrictive practices of the totalitarian regime, which cites external threats as justification for repressive tactics at home. The population must fall in line to battle the threat from outside. However, in Oceania, since the power of Big Brother has become hegemonic and monolithic and the threat of war has become perpetual, the violence of rocket attacks operates largely as a tool to stir the rage of the population and consolidate the requisite support and self-sacrifice for war. *Brazil* also develops terrorism as central to the power of the state. But terrorism has been more broadly defined, expanding to include activities that merely disrupt the meticulous functioning of their morbidly obese institutional bureaucracy. Tuttle is a dangerous subversive and fugitive because he makes repairs to structures without appropriate permission from the public works institutions. Moreover, the routine tortures at the Bureau of Information Retrieval are legitimized on the grounds of necessity; they serve to interdict terrorist and subversive activities. Sam and Jill disagree on the relative merits of the state's abductions for the purposes of information gathering. Jill complains of the mistaken arrest of her neighbor Buttle, and Sam quips, "I suppose you would rather have terrorism." In *VfV*, Sutler's government literally consolidated its power by manipulating terrorism as in the St. Mary's viral attack. But the news media and the government censors also invoke terrorism to turn public sentiment against the activities of V, activities which are actually designed to discredit the establishment and restore a representative political process. Thus the people's hysterical fear of terrorism is manipulated to their own detriment, encouraging them to oppose their own liberation. And it must be said that V's explosions are not designed to kill innocent people but to draw attention to the repressive tactics employed by the fascist regime bent on social control and to ignite a popular rebellion.

The institutional scare-mongering in the dystopia genre creates an interpretive context in which the *VfV* audience can read the totalitarian potential in contemporary events such as the post–9/11 Bush administration's penchant for spying, torturing, detaining suspects without representation or due process, price gouging, violating the right to privacy, and demonizing of the political opposition. The allusions to *1984* in *VfV* invoke the most well-known governmental nightmare of literature and cinema; however, the latter film alters the political orientation from left to right. Orwell's dystopian novel has long been acknowledged and often condemned as an unfair attack on the communism of the Soviet Union (Frodsham 143). *VfV* effectively reminds the audience that repressive and controlling government can emerge from either the left or the right and in the present time, most likely from the right, which has already begun the process of depriving the population of civil liberties with the justification of national emergency and national security. By implication, if the trend continues, the people will need security from their own national security apparatus. In his article, "Representations of the Unreal: Bush's Orwellian Newspeak," Henry Giroux recognizes in the George W. Bush administration's reductive, divisive, and impoverished rhetoric the language that Oceania's bureaucracy shapes and manipulates for the purposes of deception. Big Brother misnames its social and political institutions in order to create positive connotations and engage the practice of double-think — the place of torture and interrogation named the "Ministry of Love" or the source of propaganda dubbed the "Ministry of Truth." The Bush administration created the Healthy Forest Initiative and the Clear Skies Initiative, both of which permit the exploitation and degradation of the respective resources they should ostensibly protect, and the misleading rhetoric in the case for war against Iraq is now notorious.

The dystopian genre also observes and interrogates the anti-intellectual bias of a large portion of the population who merely accept the government propaganda without intellectual engagement. The masses want to remain uncritical, an idea richly satirized in the film *Idiocracy,* in which a future society has succumbed to this trend, and all of humanity has devolved into idiots. The same can be seen in the image of Orwell's Proles, who would rather be distracted by cheap booze and pornography than evaluate the world around them and particularly their living conditions. *VfV* includes a periodic summary of the reactions of the population to V's activities. The imagery focuses on people drinking in pubs or clustering in front of the living room TV screen or resting in the old folks' homes. In his BTN address, V reviles the population for its critical indolence, the same which facilitated the Sutler regime's rise to power and subsequent exploitation, persecution, and genocide. He urges them to abandon their indifference and struggle for the rehabilitation of their society along democratic lines. *VfV*'s anti-neoconservative, anti–Bush subtext simultaneous rebukes the film audience or rather the indifference of Britains and Americans to the disastrous foreign and domestic policies of their respective governments, policies that include constant and increasingly brazen encroachments upon civil liberties. The film suggests that the population is partially to blame for the failures of government because they did not impeach government propaganda in the lead up to the Iraq war. Thus the subject matter urges the population to confront government intelligence reports with skepticism.

The irony of *VfV*'s invocation and condemnation of surveillance and propaganda through cinematic quotations of *1984* is that the former film, as a cultural artifact, operates in a similar fashion to the Orwellian surveillance apparatus. Cinema in Orwell's novel and in Radford's screen adaptation largely serves the purposes of "political propaganda" (Varricchio 98). The political commentary that is explicit and implicit within McTeigue's film serves as a type of propaganda just as in the Orwellian nightmare, and while the actual film appears to advocate a politics of liberation, one that reveals the potential for positive social change, it nevertheless functions as a type of scaremongering, urging its audience to fear the dystopian potential of contemporary events, a process that could just as easily promote rightwing policies, as is the case in the more recent film *300*, or initiate a leftwing totalitarian backlash. *VfV* is, like Big Brother's broadcasts, an example of the manipulation of the public via the mass media, making its audience mindful of potential misery that follows a fascist power play. Moreover, the obvious terrorist predisposition of *VfV* constitutes a reversal of much popular cinema, but the film irregardless attempts to steel the audience against the suffering and sacrifice that will be requisite to liberation from repression. Thus the potential power structure legitimizes itself by identifying and combating its antithesis and expecting the population to accept extraordinary circumstances, to adopt a siege mentality bracing for the eventual attainment of the socio-political goal that has been attained. However, there is no guarantee that the object will ever be attained, or that if it is, the power structure will loosen its grip appropriately. Like the war on drugs, the war on terrorism, the same that inspired our current national security entrenchment and subsequent repressive policy decisions, will never end, particularly not so long as we continue those policies that attempt to interdict it, policies that exacerbate hostility toward Western governments rather than diminish it. The television/telescreen/movie screen analogues remind us of the reality of the misuse of media while paradoxically embracing the same as an instrument of liberation.

Six

$\rightleftharpoons$❦❦❦$\rightleftharpoons$

Knight, Death, and Devil

The antecedent voices penetrating the porous boundaries of the *V for Vendetta* text, shaping and informing its narrative devices, its characterizations, its imagery and dialogue, its ideology, its foundational thematics, even its musical soundtrack, are legion, including several examples of nineteenth and twentieth century medievalism. V crosses swords with a coat of arms while watching the 1934 film version of *The Count of Monte Cristo*, eventually defeating the inanimate antagonist by knocking off its helmet in a single stroke. The sparring suggests the revenger's delight in the trappings of medieval romance. And the symbolic offering of the helmet to Evey, which rolls to her feet, may be homage to courtly love in which the knight vowed loyalty to a lady and performed his valorous actions in her name. The knight was a crusader, both at home and abroad, rectifying the injustices of a fallen and corrupt world, particularly aiding in the defense of helpless women. These additional intertextual pressures on both McTeigue's film and Moore and Lloyd's graphic novel include Goethe's *Faust*, Scott's *Ivanhoe*, and Bergman's *The Seventh Seal*.

Faust

In Book I of the graphic novel, Moore and Lloyd offer a list of canonical texts that shaped the consciousness of their revenger. V points to a bookcase where the titles of his reading materials are legible (I.18). Among the collection is Goethe's *Faust*, the story of an early modern scholar who offered his soul to the devil in exchange for power, pleasure, and knowledge. Goethe's *Faust* is unique insofar as it does not mention the traditional 24 year time period in which the conjurer is permitted to live in all luxury before Mephisto closes their bargain and drags him off to hell (Gillies 48). Indeed, Goethe's Faust is a nineteenth century *ubermann* whose epic appetites and ambitions define the spirit of the nineteenth century, which embraced unchecked advancement in human understanding and technology (Peacock 168). Faust will never be damned until he has become fully contented, bereft of all desire and longing. Thus Faust and Mephisto embark upon a world tour of delight and debauchery as the devil tries to bring him to complete satisfaction (Gillies 75). The most poignant and pertinent facet of Goethe's epic drama is the destruction of Gretchen, a young woman who is seduced and abandoned by the self-centered and unwitting Faust. Gretchen, pregnant from her encounter with the conjurer, kills her baby and sinks into madness. Subsequently, she is apprehended, tried, convicted, and executed. The consequences of her affair also include the deaths of her mother and her brother; she is left entirely alone. When Faust learns of her imminent execution, he struggles to liberate her, but she perceives the opportunity as a temptation to capitulate to the devil's agenda, a participation in the Faustian bargain (Gillies 217). Gusta Barfield Nance describes her choice of death over degradation:

> And by the hard way, by experience, Gretchen learns the power of choice and chooses death and the salvation of her soul rather than physical freedom with a lover bound to the spirit of evil. She is a tragic character not only because of an error in judgment, but tragic also in that she, with her tender sensitiveness to life, has to discover how brutal life can be [78].

The principal trace of *Faust* in the cinematic version of *V for Vendetta* is much less subtle than the book case reference in Moore and Lloyd's graphic novel, and indeed the verbal references to the play are accompanied by the adaptation of a pivotal scene within which Faust sees a vision of a "heavenly image in the magic glass.... The loveliest image of any woman" (84–85). The mirror image accompanies the Faustian reference in *V for Vendetta*. Evey, while cleaning a mirror in V's library, discovers a Latin inscription adorning the glass: "Vi Veri Veniversum Vivus Vici" ("By the power of truth, I, while living, have conquered the universe"). The iteration of V's in the etching is consistent with revenger's self-celebrating wordplay. The inscription itself defines V's hubris as he strives — single-handedly — to topple the Norsefire system. However, the mirror scene is derived from Goethe's tale of epic ambitions. Just as Faust sees in the reflection the most beautiful of women, the mirror in the V's home reflects both V and Evey, predicting the birth of their mutual desires. This is the point at which Evey first offers her assistance in V's seditious campaign. While she does use the opportunity afforded by V's assassination of Lilliman to escape, it is clear that the revenger and his captive have already formed an emotional bond. When V rescues her from the Fingermen at Gordon Deitrich's home, he subjects her to a painful incarceration and interrogation, an action which seems cruel and ill-considered for a potential lover, but in his nightmarish world, the experience is merciful as it permits her to develop a more courageous demeanor toward the regime's potential violence; it teaches her of the mercy and understanding that she can expect from Creedy's covert agents, who would never believe in her innocence, and even if they did, they would kill her anyway in order to remove even the potential for sedition. Moreover, if he cared nothing for her, he might have left her to her own devices and her inevitable death since she, in all probability, could not have identified him to the authorities as he is a man in a mask, living in an underground bunker. V's declaration of love at the conclusion of the film is shared by Evey, who begs him not to follow through with his vendetta for the sake of his own safety and their mutual affection.

However, the mirror in V's library does more than prophesy their future adoration. The placement of the mirror in the library is appropriate because it literalizes the mimetic theory of art, that attempts to account for the relationship between the cultural artifact and the world, as Hamlet so eloquently defines in his coaching of the players before their performance:

> the purpose of playing, whose end both at the first and now, was and is, to hold, as 't were, the mirror up to nature, to show virtue her feature, scorn her own image, and the very age and body of the time his form and pressure [III. ii. 20–24].

The mimetic theory holds that art reflects life, offering behavioral and verbal paradigms for navigating life's pleasures and aggravations. V constructs his own identity from the various fragments of culture with which he has surrounded himself, particularly his books, as they are a principal means of transferring knowledge from one generation to the next; moreover, books are a particularly potent metaphor for sin, for the understanding acquired via the tree of interdicted knowledge, and, by extension, for the Faustian bargain. Both Marlowe's Dr. Faustus and Goethe's Faust have been reading forbidden books when they decide to conjure the devil. Dr. Faustus even vows to burn his books in order to appease the angry God that damns him at the conclusion of the play. The mirror in V's chamber vaunts of worldly dominion, the same that might be represented by the knowledge contained in his books, the knowledge that includes a glorious history of revolution and sedition, egging him on in his vendetta against the state. However, the mirror is also for Evey and the cinematic audience. The former must decide if she will continue to live, evading the radar of the state and hoping for the persecution to pass, or whether she too will "take up arms against a sea of troubles." Paradoxically, in that moment before the mirror, she chooses both. The mirror also invites the members of the cinematic audience to consider whether they are willing to look the other way as overly aggressive administrations in both England and America, fueled by hysteria over terrorism, make steady encroachments upon civil liberties, a process which could culminate in a fascist national security state. Evey's dilemma is the audience's — to become involved or to quietly hope that terror passes.

As they both gaze into the Faustian mirror, V informs Evey that he needs the assistance of someone with some acting skills and enlists her in his nefarious designs against the Bishop. The moment is pivotal for Evey, because even though she intends to use the opportunity to escape her captor, she will nevertheless be inextricably and inexcusably implicated in V's terrorist agenda. Her choice is the same that many in the film must make, a choice between damnation and redemption, between fear and principle, and, figuratively speaking, between earth and heaven. V elects long before the film opens to put the pursuit of principle before earthly or physical needs, and although he enjoys the luxuries in this life, he, nevertheless, will toss them all away to settle his long-term grudge. He is in the world, but is no longer of the world, as his liminal physical status would attest. Evey's complaint about Monte Cristo, that he loved revenge more than he loved Mercedes, is a commentary on the same process. While V is faced with a Faustian dilemma and while it may seem that he has chosen the path to perdition, he has actually chosen redemption; he has made Gretchen's choice to die rather than practice appeasement, to place mind before matter and principle before a long and sumptuous life. While he would appear to be in league with the devil, he is in fact a dark avenging angel who rescues humanity first through his miraculous curative blood and later through his self-destructive determination to overthrow tyranny in England. Evey's redemption in V's dungeons is a reenactment of Gretchen's choice. She is offered a chance to save herself by embracing the devilish enterprises of the fascist state, but she chooses death rather than betrayal, death rather than a capitulation to bullies and worldlings. The rejection of the state to which she had all her life acquiesced actually saves V, at least within the artificial world of his simulation. Similarly, *Faust* scholars have suggested that Gretchen's rejection of the rescue attempt facilitates Faust's own redemption, as her capitulation would have bound both her and Faust to the devil forever (Gillies 217). Evey and Gretchen both choose death over capitulation and a life of guilt, fear, and shame.

Bishop Lilliman is an example of the contrary, a man who has abandoned his principles in favor of worldly pleasures. He is the true Faustian figure in the film, sullying rather than preserving innocence, using his power to procure sexual favors from young girls; indeed this is the lure that V uses to gain access to his chambers — dressing up Evey like a preteen and sending her in the place of the priest's usual victims. In his bed chamber, he is surrounded by reminders of his pastoral vows and obligations, however, these do not serve to elevate him, but operate as foils to his debauchery, illustrating how far he has fallen from his righteousness. When Evey appeals to him for assistance in escaping V, he mocks her, assuming that she is engaged in a sexual charade to heighten his pleasure. He burlesques his own priestly ministrations by calling their conversation the "confession game" and becomes verbally and physically abusive when she resists his aggression. Fifteenth century German painter Matthias Grunewald's *The Crucifixion* (a.k.a. *The Isenheim Altarpiece)* sits on an easel in the Bishop's chambers. The painting is a ghastly image of the dying Christ, one that emphasizes his suffering — particularly the spectacle of his ruined hands and feet — and the grief of those surrounding the cross. In *V for Vendetta: From Script to Film*, McTeigue describes his intentions for the Bishop's room, indicating that he had placed the Grundwald painting above the bed and flanked it with two Balthus paintings of young women with their legs lifted in sensual and inviting poses. McTeigue laments that all of the images did not make it into the final cut as he had to edit the Bishop scenes to shorten the film, and that the unseen Balthus paintings were intended to emphasize the Bishop's lechery (Lamm and

Bray 205). Perhaps the most damning aspect of the clerical chamber is the Bible that contains a hidden gun. The book that ostensibly serves as hope and salvation harbors an instrument of death, which Lilliman attempts to use against the intruding assassin. This holy book is a metaphor for the Bishop's exploitation of religion in pursuit of wealth, pleasure, and power, Faust's own ambitions. His exploitation of Evey and other young girls is reminiscent of Faust's insensitive seduction, impregnation, and abandonment of Gretchen, the unwitting victim of his marauding appetite.

The same pattern can be extended to the Norsefire regime and particularly to the life and ambitions of Adam Sutler, "a deeply religious man," who allowed the desire for power to corrupt his better parts. In the name of religion and order, he lied, tortured, persecuted, and killed to pacify a restless and fearful nation and to gain absolute power. Of course, Sutler's Faustian bargain is shared by much of the nation who elected to live in fear and bondage to the state rather than brook the threat of terrorism. The instrument of Sutler's rise to power, the St. Mary's virus, constitutes another link between V and Faust. The triumph that inspired Faust's *hubris* was his success in curing the plague. Just as it operated in the middle ages, the plague is the impetus for living life fully and quickly, for the *memento mori,* the reminder that life is fragile and should be fully enjoyed each and every day, a sentiment that drives Faust's commitment to experience all potential pleasures.

Ivanhoe

Another example of 19th century medievalism that informs the *V for Vendetta* text is Walter Scott's *Ivanhoe.* The same bookshelf that holds the copy of *Faust* in the graphic novel features the aforementioned Scott text more prominently, and there are both cursory and extended connections with the film and with the other circulating texts. These include analogous socio-political milieus, parallel characterizations, and similar plot devices. More broadly, *Ivanhoe,* as a shadow text, illustrates the long British tradition of resistance to tyranny. The events of the narrative are set at the end of the 12th century. Moreover, the inclusion of Robin Hood in the narrative invokes a national mythology that lionizes terrorism and theft in the pursuit of social justice.

King Richard I has long been treated as a subject of national pride, particularly through his efforts at conquest abroad. While his endeavors to liberate the holy land may seem ill-considered in the present, in his own age and long after, he was a national hero, canonized for his militant virtue. His cruel and usurping brother made the people long for Richard's return; thus his virtue was exaggerated to counterbalance the weight of villainy and tyranny borne by the future King John. *Ivanhoe* depicts a country still divided between Saxons and Normans four generations after William the Conqueror, and Prince John's regency has intensified the divisions since the Norman nobility have been given a free hand in the exploitation of the Saxon population. Cedric the Saxon and Prince John occupy opposite ends of this political and ethnic divide. King Richard is the personality who can bridge the gap between the polarized ethnic factions. Ivanhoe, himself a Saxon, has elected to follow Richard to the holy land, a sign of Richard's capacity for reconcilement; moreover, he succeeds in reuniting Ivanhoe with his nationalistic Saxon father, Cedric. If Richard can be viewed abstractly as the embodiment of English pride and national unity, then the political environment of 12th century England can be understood as analogous to the dystopia of *V for Vendetta*'s post-apocalyptic England. Just as Walter Scott's England awaits liberation from the oppression of the usurping tyrant, England of McTeigue's film groans under the oppression of the Norsefire regime. Sutler has suspended the people's hereditary rights, allowing his inner circle — Norsefire Party members — to abuse and coerce the population at will. Just as the kingdom under John's regency has become factional, the power within Sutler's party has also been compartmentalized with various branches competing for power. The application of the Ivanhoe political paradigm to *V for Vendetta* reveals a nation awaiting the return of a hero who will liberate it from bondage to tyranny. The return of the true King in the novel can be understood as the restoration of the participatory government or of rule by acclamation. In this process, V is not King Richard, but Ivanhoe fighting for the reclamation of the British people's civil rights. Thus Richard, abstractly, is good government in England; he signifies the restoration of justice and human rights.

Ivanhoe offers an analogue to *V for Vendetta*'s justifiable resistance to tyranny. If the film is attempting to demonstrate that there are circumstances under which terrorism may be justifiable, then the Scott novel offers an additional exemplar in the characters of Robin Hood and his band of well-meaning outlaws. Just as *V for Vendetta* invites its audience to support a terrorist/assassin/villain, the legends of Robin of Locksley create a folk hero who, through subversive and disreputable activities, sought to restore justice for the poor and downtrodden, maintaining an organized resistance to the usurping regent and his abusive, parsimonious, and exploitative nobility. The longing for a restoration of King Richard is the longing for coherence, justice, and order. In Scott's novel, Robin Hood and his cohorts assault the castle Front-de-Boeuf to liberate the abducted Saxon lady Rowena — specifically Ivanhoe's true love — from the ardent and lustful De Bracy. The assault upon the castle is ostensibly an assault upon the legitimate power structure, but what redeems the act (beyond the moral imperative) is the fact that King Richard or justice fights on the side of the assailants. In a similar fashion, the destructive and chaotic activities of V are justified against a power structure that persecutes its own people; he is vindicated by justice, ethics, and morality, his efforts calculated to create a tolerable living environment for the long suffering Englishmen, whether or not they have the courage or the right to expect the same. Like both Ivanhoe and King Richard, V perpetrates his violence and destruction in disguise and defends those who are victimized by the Norsefire regime, laboring to bring about a period of greater compassion, openness, and coherence in government.

The allusion to the crusades in Scott's novel creates a yet unexplored dimension to the *V for Vendetta* intertext. One of the ostensible origins for the contemporary hostilities between the West and the Middle East is the distant memory of the violence and destruction of the Crusades. Indeed the Arabic term *jihad* for holy war was coined in the wake of the aggressive religious conflicts waged by Europe against Palestine in the Middle Ages, and the memory of those onslaughts still impacts the relations between Christianity and Islam today. The meddling of Western powers in Middle Eastern affairs is regarded as a new crusade to control and exploit the region and its vital natural resource. While the wisdom of these efforts is not thoroughly interrogated in Scott's novel, the consequences of Western meddling in the East are vital to the politics of McTeigue's film. In Sutler's England, Islam has been so completely abrogated that Gordon Deitrich is summarily executed for possessing a copy of *The Holy Koran*, even though it is an antique, which he appreciates only for its poetry and imagery. Moreover, the presumed terrorists scapegoated in the wake of the St. Mary's catastrophe are described as Muslim extremists, a group systematically persecuted in the effort to create an antidote for the virus, the same process that created V. Moreover, the exhausting futility of the Crusades that killed so many soldiers or brought them home demoralized is implicit in what the film defines as the "war they [America] started," that followed them home, resulting in the subsequent internecine conflict or civil war. Meddling in the Middle East created the atmosphere of paranoia that made Sutler's political ruse and rise to absolute power possible. It was the population's belief in the probability of Islamic terrorism that made the St. Mary's conspiracy believable and made Norsefire seem like the appropriate solution to that fear.

The anti–Semitism that operates as the film's a shadow text, a ghostly paradigm never explicitly named, but prevalent within the structure and imagery, is shared with Scott's novel as well. Isaac, the Jew, and his daughter, Rebecca, are central to the conflict in *Ivanhoe*. While the Saxons and the Normans may hate each other, they are united in their contempt for the Jews, and Isaac is repeatedly subject to dangers from those who would have his wealth or would simply act out unmotivated aggression. In the opening pages of the novel, Isaac must escape from Cedric's manor in the middle of the night in order to avoid being killed by the Templar Bois-Guilbert. The same man will later abduct the Jewess Rebecca, fall under the condemnation of the Templar Grand Master, Lucas-de-Beaumanoir, and defend the charge of witchcraft against the unoffending Lady in order to save himself in the eyes of his brethren. In addition, extravagant taxation or extortion of the Jews is repeatedly practiced even by Prince John who keeps them under his protection because he wants their money. The anti–Semitism of *V for Vendetta* operates at the level of imagery and innuendo. Jews are not openly reviled within the film, but the familiar shadow of the holocaust looms over the action of the novel, implicitly equating the persecution of the "Muslims, foreigners, [and] homosexuals" to the victims of Nazi genocide. The Norsefire regime is obviously based upon the Nazi party (including the Nordic nationalistic implications of the name), Sutler upon Hitler, and the Larkhill Internment Facility on the Nazi death camps. This subtext constitutes a warning that a recurrence of fascism within Europe will lead to persecution, to racial and ethnic cleansing similar to that practiced in Germany of the 1930s and 40s. The surrender to fear and extreme nationalism is a slippery slope.

The Jews are not the only oppressed minority (or majority) in the England of Scott's novel. The Saxons are downtrodden as well, perhaps suggesting that those abused by power must not square off against each other, but retain a mutually beneficial and helpful posture toward fellow sufferers. Cedric is more civil to the Jews than are most of the Normans, but only begrudgingly so, allowing Isaac food and shelter in his home out of principle, not out of respect or good will. The same parallel seems to be at work in *VfV*, which invites the citizens of Sutler's England as well as the cinematic audience to consider the consequences of silently consenting to the abuse of the politically powerless. The population of the film did nothing while minorities were rounded up, subjected to fiendish experimentation, and eventually killed, and subsequently those same people who looked the other way are prisoners now in their own homes, contained by the repressive policies to which they quietly acquiesced when hostilities were directed only against marginalized groups.

In both narratives, a disguised hero returns to restore justice and decency, but can only do so by attaining popular acclamation. The knight Ivanhoe and King Richard I return to England without revealing their true identities, and both act to correct social and economic injustices that have arisen in their absence. Ivanhoe's marriage to Rowena constitutes a reunion of both the biological and the ethnic Saxon families. Ivanhoe's reconciliation with his father suggests a reunification of the defeated and fractious Saxons, a fractiousness that had arisen from Ivanhoe's much reviled cooperation with the Norman invader, King Richard. Moreover, Ivanhoe's rescue of Rebecca draws more closely the parallel between the Jews and the Saxons, both of whom are ill-treated by the Normans. King Richard's liberation of Rowena begins to rehabilitate the vexed affiliation between Normans and Saxons, suggesting the utopian potential of both ethnicities working together for the common good rather than for the interests of a small group. Similarly, in *V for Vendetta,* a masked avenger reemerges after long absence to punish transgressors and to restore integrity and participatory government to the English system, and, just as in the case of Richard and the Saxons, his success requires that he win over hearts and minds of the oppressed majority. As the revelation of Richard's identity is sufficient to drive his usurping brother from power, the exposure of Norsefire crimes and abuses is sufficient to mobilize widespread support for V's revolutionary agenda. The restoration of the formerly supplanted government is achieved by popular acclaim.

In the peril of Rebecca at the hands of the knights templar, *Ivanhoe* dovetails nicely with both *Faust* and *VfV.* The love stricken knight Bois-Guilbert pleads with Rebecca to escape burning by running away with him, but she would rather embrace her own mortality than be indebted to the man who placed her in that danger, a man too craven to defy the Grand Master's threats against his honor and freedom, and a man who embodies the imperialism of the occupying Normans. The imperiled lady's defiance is echoed in both of the precedent texts — *Faust* and *Vf V*—where an innocent Lady is corrupted and imperiled by a prideful and self-centered male who considers only his own safety: Faust abandons Gretchen when he flees from the law in the wake of her brother's death; V abducts and imprisons Evey partially for her own good and partially for his safety, as Creedy would force her to reveal the terrorist's hideout if and when she fell into the spymaster's hands; and Bois-Guilbert, as discussed above, abducts Rebecca for his lust, but betrays her to save himself from shame and disenfranchisement (he stands to lose his place as a Templar). In each case, the lady is given a choice between a shameful safety and an honorable death, and in each case the lady opts for death; however, in only one case — *Faust* — is she actually killed. Each of the men is tormented by guilt at having compromised the lady's safety, but, once again, only in the case of *Faust* does the man survive his own disgrace.

The surfacing of *Ivanhoe* as precedent or shadow text to *V for Vendetta* invokes the longstanding English tradition of resistance to tyranny, both in the Saxon unrest and in the allusions to the future King John, whose historical antecedent will be forced to sign the *Magna Carta,* guaranteeing the rights of his peers. If one looks at King Richard as a liberating hero parallel to Ivanhoe, the militant King shares another similarity with V. Richard has been held captive for years by the Duke of Austria, a captivity facilitated by Richard's brother who seeks to rule in his place. When Richard escapes, he returns to England in disguise while he musters support to supplant his usurping brother. This context resembles the imprisonment, abuse, and escape of V who is held at the internment facility only to escape and, incognito, plot the overthrow of those who tortured him and oppressed an entire nation.

The Seventh Seal

A more contemporary example of medievalism that appears to be operating within the cinematic version of *VfV* is Ingmar Bergman's film

The Seventh Seal (1957). Like Ivanhoe, Antonius Block is returning from the Crusades to rediscover a suffering homeland, this time plague-ravaged Sweden. The pestilence has begun to devastate his homeland before Block and Jons, his Squire, have reached its familiar shores. Greeted by Death on the shore, the knight is only permitted to venture further because he challenges the specter to a game of chess, agreeing Death can take him if he (Block) loses. The succeeding narrative is a literalization of a medieval personification of death — the *Danse Macabre* or the "Dance of Death" — a tradition from the visual and literary arts in which death — usually a skeleton — leads a chain of doomed souls toward the grave, a group that forms a microcosm of society, constructing Death as the social leveler and making all equal in mortality. The camera follows Antonius as he struggles to understand and to outwit the phantom; thus the film is also an illustration of the *psychomachia*, the internal moral or ethical struggle. The knight would know what comes after death before he answers its inevitable call.

The storyline follows the knight through a serious of metaphorical locations and encounters. Like Death, Antonius collects an entourage, the same group who will follow Death into oblivion at the conclusion of the film. In addition to this Squire, Block collects his own wife, a blacksmith and his adulterous lady, an actor, a maiden, and a lapsed and despicable holy man. Only the family of actors — Joseph, Mary, and the infant Michael — escape the reaper's scythe to witness the ensuing *Danse of Death*:

> I see them! Over there against the dark, stormy sky. They are all there. The smith and Lisa and the knight and Raval and Jons and Skat. And Death, the severe master, invites them to dance. He tells them to hold each other's hands and then they must tread the dance in a long row. And first goes the master with his scythe and hourglass, but Skat dangles at the end with his lyre. They dance away from the dawn and it's a solemn dance toward the dark lands, while the rain washes their faces and cleans the salt of the tears from their cheeks [Bergman 163].

The family — Joseph, Mary, and child — watch the grim procession from a safe distance having escaped pestilence for the present. The dawn suggests the passing of the specter of plague, but, like all of humanity, the family are, nevertheless, postponing their expected mortality, an idea emphasized in an earlier scene when the knight, the squire, and the family enjoy strawberries and fresh milk (metaphors of life's transitory sensory pleasures) on a blanket near the shore, while above them on a post hangs the *memento mori*, a mask of the death's head, a reminder of his universality.

Like so many of the previously cited referents of McTeigue's film, *The Seventh Seal* invokes the specter of plague, thus shadowing the St. Mary's virus portion of the *VfV* text. Moreover, Prothero's malicious attribution of the plague to "Godlessness" (a masterpiece of hypocrisy since he knows very well the terrestrial and malicious origins of the virus at the hands of unprincipled, high-level, Norsefire party members, including himself) is echoed in the speeches of Bergman's Dominican Monk who leads a train of mourners and flagellants, hoping that through their humility and self-mortification, they can diminish God's wrath and save themselves as well as others from the Black Death. The lead Monk is merciless in his scorn for humanity and his emphasis on the inevitability of death:

> God has sentenced us to punishment. We shall all perish in the black death. You standing there like gaping cattle, you who sit there in your glutted complacency, do you know that this may be your last hour. Death stands right behind you. I can see how his crown gleams in the sun. His scythe flashes as he raises it above your heads. Which one of you shall he strike first? You there, who stands staring like a goat, will your mouth be twisted into the last unfinished gasp before nightfall? And you, woman, who blooms with life and self-satisfaction, will you pale and become extinguished before the morning dawns? You back there with your swollen nose and stupid grin, do you have another year left to dirty the earth with your refuse? Do you know, you insensible fools, that you shall die today or tomorrow or the next day, because all of you have been sentenced [Bergman 124].

If one can, for a moment, entertain Pollitzer's theory that black rats, which carried the plague, were imported to Europe on ships returning from the Crusades (Bray 45), then the same pattern of "bloody instruction ... return[ing] to plague the inventor" can be found in both *VfV* and the antecedent film. The high level members of the Norsefire Party responsible for the St. Mary's outrage are systematically assassinated by V, who, in most cases, uses a poison, which may be derived from the same virus they unleashed on a hapless population, a conspiracy inspired by a misguided religious motive to purge the nations of undesirables and immorality. Similarly, in this context, blame for the Black Death can be laid at the feet of the Church officials who encouraged the medieval warlords in their attempts to liberate the Holy Land, an equally misguided venture that created untold suffering on an intercontinental scale. The storyline involving Raval illustrates the guilt of Churchmen in the misadventures of the returning Crusaders. Jons corners the former professor from "the theological college at Roskilde," addressing him with the title "*Dr. Mirabilis, Coelestis et Diabilis*" and reviling him for encouraging Antonius Block to undertake "a better class crusade to the Holy Land" (Bergman 117). The Squire mocks the idea that suffering is a manifestation of God's wrath:

> Our life was too good and we were too satisfied with ourselves. The Lord wanted to punish us for our complacency. That is why He sent you to spew out your holy venom and poison the knight [Bergman 117].

It is difficult to imagine that the Squire is sincere about the divine inspiration for the Crusades when he refers to the idea as "holy venom and poison." While Jons cannot bring himself to kill the professor/churchman turned rapist and thief, he promises to brand him the next time they meet.

Historically, many clergymen abandoned their vows and obligations in order to flee in advance of the marauding pestilence, and in other instances, the official apparatus erected to care for the sick was itself decimated leaving no one to care for the dying. Religious officials made blanket proclamations, absolving all plague victims of their sins when no priest could be found (Kelly 159, 193, 200). According to his vows as a man of God, Raval should spend his time comforting and ministering to the grieved, sick, and dying, but instead he steals from the deceased and abuses the living. Raval's demise constitutes poetic justice. He contracts the plague and is denied the very comfort that he too withheld. He begs the Knight's train to offer him a drink of water to slake his parched throat, but none will go near him; thus he dies anguished and unaided. His pleas for the pity that he never showed are echoed in the pleas of V's antagonists who sued for mercy after having perpetrated an unprecedented outrage upon the masses. Sutler, who counted himself a deeply religious man, and who killed over one hundred thousand people for the advancement of his secular power and subsequently oppressed an entire nation for over a decade, could not, without great irony, appeal for mercy in the name of his God nor beg the grace and forgiveness of the revenger. Just as the medieval Church used the ventures in Palestine and the plague to consolidate power at home, the Norsefire Party manipulated chaos abroad, plague, international terrorism, and widespread hysteria to seize power in England.

Perhaps the most striking resemblance between *VfV* and *The Seventh Seal* is the image of V himself, who resembles Bergman's personification of Death with a stark white face against all black sartorial choices. Death's grand theatrical gestures, such as the iconic image of the specter, his draped right arm extended, inviting the mortified Block into his embrace, is echoed in numerous images of V posing with arms outstretched with a thespian flare such as when he directs the phantom orchestra through the *1812 Overture* that ends in an explosion at the Old Bailey. When V visits Delia Surridge, he stands quietly in the shadows near her bed calmly discussing her guilt in the Larkhill experiment and her impending death. In their screenplay for the film, the Wachowski brothers refer to V in this scene as "a dark angel" who "floats at the edge of her bed" (Lamm and Bray 90). The quiet conversation between the two is reminiscent of the encounter between Death and Antonius Black on Sweden's shore at the beginning of *The Seventh Seal*. In each case, the doomed mortal inquires after the identity of the intruder; Death reveals that he has been stalking the doomed for some time; the mortal attempts to bargain or reason with death; and "that fell sergeant," showing no outward malice, is, nevertheless, "strict in his arrest."

Bergman's initial scene is archetypal in its iconography:

> Behind him stands a man in black. His face is very pale and he keeps his hands hidden in the wide folds of his cloak.
>> Knight: Who are you?
>> Death: I am Death.
>> Knight: Have you come for me?
>> Death: I have been walking by your side for a long time.
>> Knight: That I know.
>> Death: Are you prepared?
>> Knight: My body is frightened, but I am not [100].

Compare the above with the exchange between V and Surridge:

> Delia wakes with a start. Something stirs along the dark edge of the room.
>> Surridge: It's you, isn't it? You've come to kill me.
> From the shadows, V answers.
>> V: Yes.
>> Surridge: Thank God
> V floats at the edge of her bed, a dark angel.
>> Surridge: After what happened, after what they did ... I thought about killing myself.... But I knew one day you would come for me....
>> Surridge: Are you going to kill me now?

He shows her an empty syringe:

> V: I killed you ten minutes ago while you slept.
> Surridge: Is there any pain?
> V: No.
> Surridge: Thank You [Lamm and Bray 90–91].

Block's sense of guilt and familiarity with death through the Crusades is analogous to Delia's recognition of her participation in the catastrophe of the St. Mary's virus. They both bargain with death, Antonius by proposing the chess match and Delia by claiming ignorance of the intended use of her experiments. While it might appear that Antonius is given temporary reprieve while Delia is summarily killed, Berman's film can be understood as a strictly subjective experience played out at the moment of death, a journey home.

The "dance of death" that structures Bergman's film can also be observed in McTeigue's. If V is an angel of death as described in the passages above, then his systematic campaign to murder the Norsefire Party members can be understood as his dance to the grave. His victims are a microcosm of power with a representative of military/media/industry (Prothero), the Church (Lilliman), the medical establishment (Surridge), and the government clandestine and public (Creedy and Sutler, respectively). The characters can even be understood as a parade of the seven deadly sins: Prothero is guilty of greed — he profiteered off of death, and he dies celebrating himself in the bathroom mirror; Lilliman — unmistakably lust, dying even as he tries to rape Evey; Sutler — wrath as evidenced in his emotional ruptures in cabinet meetings and in the media; Surridge's sloth can be seen in her failure to do anything but hide when she discovered the objectives of the unprincipled politicians; and Creedy — envy, yearning for Sutler's power. All of the Norsefire characters are guilty of pride having placed their personal ambitions before public service and safety. While there is no gluttony directly represented, one might say that all of the characters have intemperate appetites for power, wealth, and fame. As death and his merry chain dance away from the dawn in Bergman's film, they suggest that the scourge has been a blessing, bringing renewal via destruction, V's final catastrophic gesture can also be understood as a renewal. The images of the multitude of V's at the end of the film is also a portion of the Dance of Death as many of those who reveal themselves in the final unveiling are those who died earlier in the narrative, such as the little girl killed for spray painting a Norsefire prop-aganda poster. The image of Block and his companions greeting death at the entrance to their dining hall is reminiscent of the legion of V's star-ing apprehensively at the military barricades and the doomed Parliament building, awaiting an apotheosis of destruction that will liberate them from repression and political indolence.

Death's cunning is embodied in the respective gaming metaphors from the two films. Death's success at chess and his subterfuge in discov-ering Antonius' strategy suggest his inevitability. While Block thinks that he has a chance to out wit death, he is already named in the register of Time's conquests. The game was only a delaying tactic, part of Death's incontrovertible strategy. In like fashion, V plays with dominoes, creat-ing a vast structure displaying his terrorist logo, and when the first domino falls, the events leading to the destruction of the Sutler regime, events that he has planned for over a decade, begin to fall into place until there is only one left standing, which he extricates and places in the subway car that will carry his dead body and tons of explosives to the Parliament. Like death, he circumvents all subterfuge, calculating several moves ahead of his opponents.

Perhaps one of the most important analogues between the two films is the scapegoating of the powerless in the wake of pandemic. The St. Mary's virus, created through the suffering and death of persecuted minori-ties, was then blamed on those who were the principal victims. Similarly, the burning of the witch, fourteen year old Tyan, in Bergman's film reveals the desperation with which the plague ravaged population sought to under-stand the cause of their tribulations. The pestilence is attributed to the woman's presumed copulation with the devil, a charge that she is unable to refute, not only because it is so utterly irrational, but also because she is addled and broken by torture. She invites Block to look into her eyes if he desires to see the devil, but he sees only "an empty numb fear ... noth-ing else" (Bergman 146). The burning of the witch to hinder the pesti-lence plays into the AIDS motif of McTeigue's film, alluding to the continued irrationality of human populations facing epidemic. The vic-tims of the HIV virus were blamed for creating it in the laboratories of their sinful lives, a suggestion that on its surface is so absurd it confounds rebuttal. One who could believe that a virus is the wrath of God cannot be appealed to in the name of reason. She or he has discounted reason and science with the very accusation.

Conclusion

The instances of medievalism in the contemporary film can serve a number of effective purposes. As so many other of the film's references and quotations, the medievalism demonstrates the long history of particular belief systems and social practices and processes. The Middle Ages may be an appropriate referent for a narrative such as *VfV* since it was a time that paradoxically celebrated valor and virtue while simultaneously remaining firmly in the grip of superstition and irrationality. Perhaps it is the Manichean duality of pure good and pure evil that is so attractive to contemporary popular culture. At a time in which the most fundamental assumptions about faith and God are subject to constant scrutiny and repudiation, in which the membrane between right and wrong has become demonstrably porous (these antitheses even interdependent), then stories derived from a culture that perceived a clear separation between vice and virtue may serve to feed the emotional needs of the masses, the need to believe in coherent and stable categories of right and wrong. However, none of the above works were created in the Middle Ages, and they all comment on the dangers of scouring the past for a way to live and believe in the present. The narratives demonstrate that our contemporary biases are implicated in a long inglorious history of irrationality. In all of the above, a heroic yet sullied figure attempts to promote virtue to rescue innocence, and cheat death and/or the devil in human or infernal form, and each discovers that faith is not a sufficient force out of which to create a coherent universe. Good and evil are a mirage arising from hope and/or hysteria. The heroic figure may be a degraded sensualist such as Faust, a ruined aesthete such as V, or a misguided crusader such Antonius Block or Ivanhoe. Heroism can manifest itself in the desire or willingness to die rather than to live. Villainy can appear righteous and virtue malicious.

Seven

---❦---

"Odds and Ends Stolen Forth of Holy Writ"

Shakespeare and the Invention of V

Harold Bloom, in his voluminous study *Shakespeare and the Invention of the Human*, argues that this most celebrated writer in the English canon is responsible, as the title suggests, for nothing less than the creation of the modern consciousness, of introspection and self-analysis (2). Humanity has subsequently modeled life on the paradigms for behavior and self-construction that Shakespeare created through his art. From this perspective, the bard becomes a principal intertextual analogue in the representation of modern subjectivity. Representations of humanity are always already spoken — playing upon a "ghostly paradigm of things" — a Shakespearean Platonism in which the individual intentionally or inadvertently invokes the playwright's constructions of subjectivity. Even without our knowledge, we are living Shakespeare's lives, or rather those of his dramatis personae, analyzing, categorizing, evaluating, embracing, and repudiating with — in a manner of speaking — someone else's mind or language. This idea plays out on multiple levels in *V for Vendetta:* first in V's conscious construction of attitudes, objectives, and behaviors along Shakespearean lines, second in the writers' and director's invocation of the Shakespearean analogue for the construction of the villain hero, and third in the broader appropriation of artistic paradigms to capture the psychological predispositions of the cinematic characters.

The identity assumed by the terrorist V is constructed upon a Shakespearean or, more generally, a theatrical paradigm. V's vanity evokes the cliché image of an actor's dressing room, replete with lighted mirror and a seat for lengthy cosmetic preparations. Here he dons his Guy Fawkes and Rookwood masks; the latter for his meeting with Finch and Dominic at the St. Mary's Memorial. The dressing room entrance is draped in red, which also suggests a theatrical setting and calls attention to the idea that V has only those identities that he puts on in that room, his memory having been wiped away by the St. Mary's virus and his face by the subsequent fire in the Larkhill laboratories. Along one wall of the dressing room stands a bust of Shakespeare and directly across from it hangs a copy of John Everett Millais' *Ophelia,* a corner of it can be seen in the background of a brief shot, and particularly Ophelia's grey dress as it flares out in the brook where she drowns. Above the vanity is copy of Paul Delaroche's *The Execution of Lady Jane Grey,* completed in 1833 but depicting an event from the mid-sixteenth century, when the Protestant claimant to the English throne, following the death of Edward VI, was executed by the rising Catholic claimant Mary Tudor. Thus within this room, there are several ciphers to V's assumed identity. In his preparations, V is surrounded by melodramatic images of women in distress, revealing that his vendetta is inspired by the unjust treatment and untimely death of a woman — Valerie Page. V's self-construction is reminiscent of the late medieval and the early modern periods of which Shakespeare often wrote. He is the chivalrous gallant and/or courtly suitor, an affected pose, but one not out of place for a man who has no face and who lives exclusively behind a mask.

V assumes his courtly demeanor particularly in his own residence where he is revealed to be a man of sophisticated taste, filling his chambers with high art and artifacts from bygone eras. He practices fencing with a coat of arms, conducts himself with grace and gentility, speaks eloquently in elevated English with a self-effacing tone, and is patient and solicitous of Evey's needs, making her breakfast and quietly enduring her several tantrums. He adopts a didactic manner in his relations with her, attempting to bring her to an understanding of his motivations for revenge. Even the abduction and torture scenes are done to teach her to live without fear, and when he deems her capable of fending for herself, he permits her to leave in spite of his concerns for their safety.

Macbeth

But the Shakespearean references in the film are not limited to art works and courtly manners. V repeatedly quotes from Shakespeare's plays and often in such a way that it is clear he is shaping his behavior in conformity to literary paradigms. Following Bloom's argument, he models his post–Larkhill identity on Shakespeare's characters, filtering his experiences through a Shakespearean sieve. Indeed, the first words that V speaks in the film are drawn from *Macbeth*: "The multiplying villainies of nature do swarm upon him" (I.ii.13–14). With these words, Shakespeare's Captain describes Macdonwald's rebellion; the traitor has raised insurrection within the kingdom, which has subsequently been put down by the heroic Macbeth and Banquo. The passage evokes Macdonwald's accumulation of sin and vice in his person as well as the attractiveness of his cause to the kingdom's malcontents and base villainous persons. The traitor's ranks are swelled with an influx of discontented rabble who are swiftly put to the sword by the just and revenging Thanes. As V begins to extricate Evey from the perilous situation with the Fingermen, he quotes again from the same Shakespearean exposition: "Disdaining fortune with his brandished steel, which smoked with bloody execution" (I.ii.19–20). If the first passage was intended to characterize the behavior of the Fingermen and particularly their loyalty to and employment by a vicious dictator and unjust usurper of the English government, then the latter quotation captures V's claim to a just violence. He portrays his actions as heroic and, despite the state sanctioned authority of his victims, as a contribution to stability and order. He is executing, not murdering. Of course, the "brandished steel" alludes to V's exclusive use of daggers in combating his opponents.

The passages are employed in an ironic fashion, one contrary to their usage in the precedent drama, or rather contrary to the interests of power. In the first act of the play, Macbeth faces a dilemma. He goes from the defender of King Duncan to his murderer in a few brief scenes. The Captain's speech portrays Macbeth as a patriot, exhibiting loyalty by risking his life to uphold the power structure. The use of the passages in *V for Vendetta* creates an antithetical context. Here the "villainies of nature" are the power structure (albeit criminal), and the "bloody execution" is the first blow in an agenda to discredit and subsequently topple the country's leadership. However, V can still be understood as a patriot seeking to liberate his country from the grip of a despotic tyrant. In *Macbeth*, on the other hand, the relative vices and virtues of the characters are reversed. The King is so blameless that his Thane can think of no reason to depose him save for "vaulting ambition"; Sutler, by contrast, has created many good reasons for his destruction. Moreover, Duncan treats Macbeth with honor, gratitude, and respect, while Sutler and cronies consign V, along with many other Englishmen, to death in order to facilitate the Norsefire bid for power. Perhaps the Macbeth figure is then more indicative of Sutler, who embodies the tainted and degenerate Thane who cannot wipe the blood from his hands, who has become increasingly paranoid and dangerous, who has progressively alienated even his closest companions, and whose final destruction results from the ripple effects of the "unnatural" crimes that brought him to preeminence. To problematize the comparison still further, V seems to share Macbeth's "charmed life, which must not yield/To one of woman born" (V.vii.12–13). While V is not ultimately invulnerable, he does seem to be; his strength, dexterity, and invincibility make him virtually superhuman. He is the only subject to survive the viral experiments at Larkhill, and out of his blood is created the cure for that same pathogen. He emerges reborn from the laboratory fires, his eyes and features burned away, yet his faculties undiminished or perhaps even strengthened. He is able to combat and successfully kill large groups of heavily armed and highly trained men, usually without injury to himself. Only at the conclusion of the film do we learn that he has been wearing a bullet proof vest, yet it strains credibility that all of the gun play would not have found a chink in his armor until the final battle with Creedy's forces. In all probability, his resolution in the vendetta drove him to extraordinary feats of strength and endurance; he would not allow himself to die until he had revenged Valerie Page. Thus while his seeming invulnerability resemble Macbeth's, his objectives are more like those of Macduff, who seeks vengeance for his murdered family and is infused with a ferocity and determination that will not be suppressed. V is motivated by the injury to himself, but more so by the injury perpetrated against this fellow prisoner/medical subject.

The confusion of literary analogues continues with V's next quotation from the same play. On her first morning in his home, he cooks breakfast for Evey. She expresses her surprise that he has used real butter, since the staple has obviously been unavailable for many years. V explains that he stole the butter from a supply train bound for Chancellor Sutler, a revelation that inspires Evey to doubt his sanity. His reply, "I dare do all that would become a man," is derived from *Macbeth* (I.vii.47–48), in which the titular character balks at the idea of killing the King because the act would tarnish his reputation, adding "who dares do more is none" (I.vii.48) Macbeth's protestation indicates that he is committed to doing only those deeds which would tend to make a man look good or enhance his honor. Those who would exceed such limitations are not men but monsters, a pronouncement that foreshadows the future King's descent into sociopathic behaviors that have no "relish of salvation" in them. Macbeth becomes increasingly conscienceless, a trend reaching its nadir in his subornation of the murder of Macduff's family and his indifference to his wife's death. The scenes from which the screenwriters draw the Shakespearean text operates antithetically to the one in which the text is placed. Macbeth's refusal to sully his reputation with contrived murder is followed by Lady Macbeth's infamous seduction of the Thane in which she equates his resolution in the murder plot to his masculinity and his worthiness as a husband and lover. Paradoxically, Lady Macbeth urges him to murder for her love, thus initiating a thematic in the play, aligning love with violence.

The circumstances in which V offers this final quotation from Macbeth are ironically reversed in the context of their utterance. V identifies with Shakespeare's works as cultural artifacts and his language as expressive and constructive of subjectivity. He is not identifying himself as Macbeth exclusively, but is mining the Shakespearean lode for apt and eloquent gems. While the analogies to the Shakespearean texts are numerous, they are not consistent with or faithful to the original. In Act I, scene vii, Lady Macbeth encourages her husband in his villainy, and he capitulates but only with great trepidation. By contrast, Evey remains dissuasive of V's unlawful acts, reminding him of the dangers he plucks by rousing the Sutler government to action. Thus the traditional male/female roles which are reversed in *Macbeth* are rehabilitated for *V for Vendetta*. In the seduction and regicide scenes of Shakespeare's play, Macbeth behaves in a fashion that Lady Macbeth believes is inconsistent with the contemporary masculine ideals, particularly those of a soldier. Macbeth becomes timid, afraid, and overly emotional both before and after the murder of Duncan. Macbeth's feminization is contrasted with Lady Macbeth's masculinity at the beginning of the play. She takes charge of the assassination, suppressing her emotions and trying to hold her husband together. However, the roles of the tragic characters are reversed by the end of the drama where Macbeth has become a conscienceless killer and his wife has been driven to suicide by her paranoia, guilt, and grief. In the kitchen scenes of Mac-Tiegue's film, traditional gender roles are sustained. Evey displays timidity, admits to being "afraid all the time," and tries to deter V from his criminal enterprises, albeit not very enthusiastically. Like Macbeth at the outset of Shakespeare's play, V is a cultured man who has traits one might consider feminine in contrast to the most rigid and reductive standards of contemporary masculinity — "hegemonic masculinity," that which a social body has determined to be the standard behaviors indicative of uncompromised masculinity (Connell 111). V is a great lover of the arts, is cultivated and well-spoken, is not afraid to perform tasks that chauvinist might consider women's work, is gentle, considerate, and serviceable, and is obsessed with a female film star. In short, V may conform better to the British standard of genteel masculinity than the American rugged individualist. Despite his cultivation, V is capable of unleashing an extraordinary violence, one of the most definitive attributes of traditional manhood. Moreover, when V protests that he "dare do all that would become a man," he ironically defends his theft of government supplies, an activity that under most circumstances would be understood as more than "would become a man." He is determined to live his life on his own terms rather than be cowed by the dictates of a fascist government committed to his destruction.

Shakespeare's *Macbeth* includes a debate between two contrasting constructions of masculinity: one defined by the witches' imperative, "be boldly bold and resolute" (IV.i.79), which is the ideal of manhood to which Lady Macbeth would have her husband conform; the second construction of manhood, this one embodied in Duncan, King Edward of England, and Macduff, includes traditionally feminine virtues, such as "mercy, lowliness/Devotion, patience" (IV.iii.93–94). The idealized man within Shakespeare's tragedy must be more well rounded than the "bloody, bold and resolute" soldier who honors only his own will and ambition (Waith 265–268). V's conformity to a less reductive notion of masculinity, in contrast to the Norsefire party's hyper-gender-consciousness, makes him more likely to succeed. Norsefire is limited in its responses always opting for the most violent and obtrusive solutions to social unrest. V, on the other hand, has a vast repertoire of literary and artistic precedent from which to draw for his dissimulations; he uses these to the detriment of his more heavy-handed and less imaginative antagonists. Unlike Macbeth, V does not become increasingly masculine, but his more genteel side as well as the justice of his actions is progressively revealed. His changes are embodied in the revelation that he loves Evey romantically. In contrast to Lady Macbeth, Evey becomes increasingly masculine and invulnerable. Her head is shaved; she no longer tries to beautify herself either sartorially or cosmetically; she loses her fear of the Sutler regime and of death; and she drops her conformist objections to the V's campaign against Norsefire. In effect, she becomes a revolutionary.

The departure of this character development from the Shakespearean analogue illustrates a shift of values in our contemporary age, an alteration in the way that we understand gender. Shakespeare's tragedy includes an essentialist conception of gender. While Macbeth and his wife may briefly assume opposing gender roles, inevitably they will drift back to those that were deemed native to their respective sexes in the early 17th century, which saw gendered behaviors as natural extensions of sex rather than cultural constructs. V's conformity to traditional gender roles is problematized from the beginning of McTeigue's film. First manifest in his thespian flair, his gentility becomes increasingly more pronounced, while ironically and simultaneously more heterosexual. His genteel demeanor does not change, but his romantic attachment to Evey does. He becomes enamored, a fact which constitutes his greatest vulnerability as Evey makes him appreciate and value his own life. Unlike Macbeth who, by the end of the play, feels nothing, V grows increasingly passionate, embracing his emotional attachment to Evey and thus reinforcing the sense of loss, particularly lost love at the end of the film. In contrast, Evey is highly vulnerable when she first meets V. Her weakness and timidity are emphasized visually through the careful art direction of the film. In V's gallery, she is repeatedly shadowed by a painting of a cowering girl who is attempting to conceal her nudity from prying eyes, but perhaps the most literal manifestation of her naivety and trepidation is revealed visually in her "baby-doll" disguise, designed to entice the pedophilic Bishop Lilliman. While Lady Macbeth moves from hardened and violent to vulnerable, Evey becomes increasingly unemotional, resolute, and aggressive. She is transformed into a revolutionary of politics and gender. While Lady Macbeth is torn apart by her conscience, opting for suicide rather than a life of compunction, Evey loses her loyalty to and sympathy for those who have perpetrated crimes against the people of England and against humanity. The fluidity of gender within the narrative demonstrates the 'constuctedness' of such roles, inviting women to join the struggle against oppression and injustice.

The paradoxical union of love and murder that recurs in *Macbeth* is also present within the McTeigue and Wachowski film. Dissimulating, Macbeth tries to explain his motivation for killing King Duncan's guards, whose apparent culpability required interrogation. Macbeth defends himself:

> Who can be wise, amaz'd, temp'rate and furious,
> Loyal and neutral, in a moment? No man.
> Th' expedition of my violent love
> Outrun the pauser, reason [I.ii.9–12)

Macbeth explains that he became so overwrought with rage that he summarily executed the seemingly guilty grooms; he was unable to remain neutral long enough to uncover the truth. Similarly, Lady Macbeth had coerced him into pursuing his plot against the King by suggesting that he was unworthy of her love if he could not remain resolute. Macduff too kills for love, swearing vengeance for the murder of his family and risking the dangers of the battle field and of single-handed combat with a highly skilled and celebrated war hero.

Similarly, when V's motivations for pursuing his vendetta are finally revealed, the audience discovers that he has followed his violent course not to attain retribution for the monstrous way in which the Sutler government treated him, but to revenge the innocent and vulnerable Valerie Page, whom he came to love and revere in absentia. While he desires the liberation of England from tyranny, it is the attachment to an individual that ignites his rage. One may argue that Evey harbors a violent love. Her alliance with V against the Sutler government must be at least partially motivated by the untimely deaths of her entire family, particularly her younger brother who died in the St. Mary's viral attack. Her parents were killed in subsequent protests against the government. In addition, her love for V doubtlessly motivates her to complete his revolutionary agenda. Following his death, she sends the explosive laden train down the tracks toward Parliament.

The quotations from *Macbeth* may be included because it is in this play that Shakespeare commented on the recently exposed gunpowder plot, the same that is central to the *V for Vendetta* narrative. While it is highly unlikely Shakespeare felt any sympathy for the traitors or their efforts, he may have felt the need to distance himself publicly from the events as the rebels operated out of safe houses near Shakespeare's Stratford home (Asquith 216). Moreover, Shakespeare had close ties to Catholicism through work, friends, and family, and may have been Catholic himself if he had had any strong religious sentiments. Following the revelation of the gunpowder treason, many innocent Catholics loudly deplored the scheme, both because it was audacious and inhumane and because they did not want to appear sympathetic to the cause as they knew savage reprisals would follow. Macbeth includes a debate on the nature of Kingship as well as a lengthy lament over the suffering of the ailing country (in this case Scotland). One of the most dramatic comments on the narrowly averted catastrophe condemns the loss of innocent lives including children, namely those of the King who would be in attendance at the opening of Parliament on Nov. 5th:

> And pity, like a naked new-born babe,
> Striding the blast, or Heaven's cherubin, hors'd
> Upon the sightless couriers of the air,
> Shall blow the horrid deed in every eye,
> That tears shall drown the winds [I.vii.21–25].

The image is apocalyptic, decrying the universal suffering and loss of innocence that would have followed in the wake of the blast. Of course, within the context of *V for Vendetta*, the historical infamy of 1605 is rehabilitated, offered as a reasonable response to tyranny. Irregardless, the film does not suggest that the Parliament will be filled with legislators at the time of its destruction.

Hamlet

V also quotes from *Hamlet* while rescuing Evey from the overly aggressive and lascivious Fingermen:

> We are oft to blame in this —
> 'Tis too much proved — that with devotion's visage
> And pious action we do sugar o'er
> The devil himself [III.i.46–49].

This particular quotation is not included in the graphic novel, thus it is an extrapolation upon the Shakespearean paradigm invoked by Moore and Lloyd. It is an interpretation of the author's perceived project in the shadow or precedent text, a process which continues in subsequent scenes. Polonius' commentary on hypocrisy (the same that "lashes" the King's "conscience" in Shakespeare's tragedy) has an alternative meaning within McTeigue's film. Ostensibly, the quotation constitutes a direct response to Fingerman Willy's plea for "mercy" in the name of "Jesus Christ," suggesting a piety that he did not practice in life, one that he invokes only in self-preservation. V offers him no mercy. By extension, the same brief exchange becomes a broader commentary on the religious hypocrisy of the Sutler regime, the same that exploited religion to legitimize its brutal and discriminatory policies, actions resulting in the murder of thousands of innocents. Here V's quotation suggests that pious language and posturing only serve to obscure the devilish motives that informed the implementation of Sutler's genocidal designs — xenophobia, racism, and homophobia.

However, Polonius' remark actually constitutes a moment of self-analysis, and one that is unfavorable to the speaker. He suggests that his lofty objects — namely the discovery of the source of Hamlet's madness — may only be a smoke screen veiling a delight in intrigue and dissimulation. Thus Polonius acknowledges that the actions in which he is presently engaged are not entirely altruistic. He is preparing to compromise his daughter's honor and integrity in order to further the King's understanding of his unbalanced nephew, a action which Polonius himself earlier equates to turning an animal out for breeding ("I'll loose my daughter to him" II.ii.162). His pang of conscience reveals that he relishes the intrigue beyond the beneficial outcome for the King or for his own place within the King's court, confidence, and affections. He enjoys spying on other people, and particularly other people in erotically charged situations. The usage of the Shakespearean passage by V can be understood as self-reflection and even self-condemnation, V acknowledging a certain amount of fiendish glee in being able to finish off the brutal Fingermen. He acts not exclusively out of a desire for justice, but also out of a pleasure in violence.

V's usage of the Shakespearean passage shares much with Polonius' self-analysis. In *Hamlet*, hypocrisy such as Polonius' is frequently equated to wearing a mask, particularly a mask of cosmetics, one that creates a better face than one's own. Indeed, Claudius' reaction to his companion's comment includes a reference to women's "painting":

> How smart a lash that speech doth give my conscience!
> The harlot's cheek, beautied with the plast'ring art,
> Is not more ugly to the thing that helps it
> Than is my deed to my most painted word [III.i.51–54].

Both men acknowledge that their dissimulations undermine their integrity, requiring some enthusiastic maintenance to rehabilitate their self-righteousness. Everyone in the subsequent scene is wearing a mask: both Polonius and Claudius pretend to have Hamlet's best interests in mind while each actually pursues self-interests — Polonius courtly ambitions and Claudius freedom from a potentially dangerous rival — Ophelia feigns interest in Hamlet's amorous advances while actually serving the political aspirations of her father; and Hamlet is pretending to be mad in order to vent his repressed rage and to keep his rivals in confusion while he contrives his revenge. Similarly, V wears a Guy Fawkes mask to hide his identity or rather to hide the fact that he no longer has an identity or face, and Evey wears a cosmetic mask just like Claudius and Ophelia, one which she applies with great care during the opening scene of the film.

The situation in which V intervenes is a sexually charged one. In the graphic novel, Evey is actually trying to prostitute herself out of desperation, and the Fingerman in the film assume as much when they apprehend her after curfew. There are multiple implied references to prostitution in the Shakespearean analogues for this scene. V's citation from *Macbeth* delicately skips over a reference to "fortune," the "rebel's whore," a phrase that is included in Moore and Lloyd's parallel scene. Claudius' reaction to Polonius's conscience includes a reference to a harlot, and Hamlet himself accuses Ophelia of being a whore because she allows her father to exploit her for his own gain. His infamous imperative, "Get thee to a nunn'ry"(III.i.122) alludes to a brothel as well as a cloister. Even the source for *Hamlet*— Belforest's *Histio-Tragic*— reinforces the prostitution motif since the nunnery scene of Hamlet is modeled on an encounter in which the uncle, Feng, hires a prostitute to pierce Amleth's disguise of madness.

Despite multiple prostitution allusions, the cinematic Evey has merely violated curfew and is innocent of carnality and sedition, yet she is being sexually assaulted by sleazy and unbalanced Fingermen who believe her to be both a rebel and a whore. However, while Polonius stands idly by watching his daughter's distress, V intercedes liberating the distraught captive. Thus V's Shakespearean rejoinder to the Fingerman's plea can be understood as an acknowledgment that he actually enjoys harming and even killing such people. He intercedes out of a sense of fairness and civic duty, but that does not mean he does not enjoy the brutal reprisals that he executes on deserving thugs. The madness of Hamlet's behavior in the nunnery scene is not lost within the film context either. Unsettled by his violence and his excessive cordiality, Evey asks if he is "a crazy person," an assessment that she offers at multiple times during the film. However, V's "madness" is not a ruse as is Hamlet's. He has merely been liberated from the restraints of an excessively restrictive rule bound society, one that, for him, has lost all credibility and legitimacy (not unlike the madness of Ginsberg's "angel-headed hipsters"), and his freedom manifests itself in daring, indifference, and confidence.

The statement "sugar over the devil himself" proves to be a motif in *Hamlet*, describing multiple scenarios. Claudius, like Polonius, pretends to care about Hamlet's mental health more than his own safety when in reality he wants to determine the source of his nephew's distraction so that he can know if Hamlet is ambitious for the throne and should be neutralized. When he sends Hamlet to England, he does so ostensibly to protect the Prince from retribution for the murder of Polonius, but in reality he has sent a message to the English King to strike off Hamlet's head without even the opportunity for "shriving" or repentance. When Claudius kneels to pray for forgiveness of his sins and Hamlet contemplates killing him, both men are "sugaring over the devil," Claudius because he appears pious while unable to repent and Hamlet because he imagines that he is doing God's work by refusing to kill his uncle in the cleansing of his soul. Hamlet neglects his sworn duty to revenge because he wants to make certain his uncle goes to hell. Laertes sugars over the devil when he feigns reconciliation with Hamlet, speaks of honor, and carries a poisoned sword to murder the Prince.

The Shakespearean adage has a similarly broad application to *V for Vendetta*. While V makes no claims to religious piety, he does assume a very self-righteous demeanor in his self-declared war on the Norsefire establishment, and he maintains that the extraordinarily brutal history of the same warrants a violent and remorseless response. The act of terrorism is so completely abominated within Western culture that it is difficult for an audience to appreciate the circumstances or applaud the outcome of such an act no matter how righteous the cause may be. Thus the explosion at Old Bailey and Parliament, as well as the takeover of the BTN studio, may be understood as devilish activities cloaked in the garments of devotion and piety. The ongoing debate between Evey and V regarding the latter's activities captures the alternative views of his tactics. For a while, Evey perceives the terrorism and assassinations as wholly indefensible while V affects confidence in the justice of his cause. By the end of the film, the two have switched places, V no longer certain he should complete his promised destruction of Parliament and Evey confident that it is the best way to issue in the new society. "Sugaring over the Devil" has an even more pertinent application to the Sutler regime that assumes a facade of "pious action and devotion" even as it perpetrates ghastly crimes against humanity—abduction, torture, and mass murder. Finch, who is basically a descent fellow in the film, continues to believe in the legitimate rule of law and the integrity of the regime even after he has uncovered the inhumane subterfuge that brought Norsefire to power. It is only on the tube station platform in front of the explosive laden train that he finally concedes and abandons his commitment to his party, his profession, and his government.

When Hamlet prepares for his journey to England with his schoolmates, Rosencrantz and Guildenstern, he understands that they have been suborned to bring about his death, and he vows that he will circumvent the King's murderous designs by destroying his traveling companions before they can do the same to him:

> There's letters seal'd and my two schoolfellows,
> Whom I will trust as I will adders fang'd,
> They bear the mandate; they must sweep my way
> And marshal me to knavery. Let it work.
> For 'tis the sport to have the enginer
> Hoist with his own petar, and 't shall go hard
> But I will delve one yard below their mines,
> And blow them at the moon [III.iv.209–216].

Hamlet will see his opposites "hoist upon ... [their] own petar," or destroyed by their own machinations, blown up by the explosives (petar) they would use to annihilate another. This idea operates as a blueprint for action in the play: Polonius, who meddled in the King's business, is mistaken for the King and inadvertently killed; Laertes is poison by the very sword that he envenomed to kill Hamlet; and Claudius "commends th' ingredients of ... [his] poison'd chalice/To ... [his] own lips" (*Macbeth*, I.vii.11–12).

A similar pattern dominates in *V for Vendetta*. From a broad perspective, the ill-considered plan to exploit a viral outbreak in an effort to establish autocratic rule and to create a vaccine for the pathogen by recklessly experimenting on social undesirables generates the conditions requisite to the destruction of all involved, specifically by producing a veritable personification of justice and revenge who eliminates the perpetrators in a fashion symbolic of their crimes. Most of the principal malefactors are killed by an infusion of a lethal toxin, perhaps the same that they used to kill so many at Larkhill, St. Mary's, and the London Tube stations. Prothero, Lilliman, and Surridge are discovered amid their own vomit rather than their blood, and V actually shows Delia Surridge the syringe he uses to poison her. Creedy's and Sutler's respective deaths are perhaps more specific examples of the same pattern. Sutler's decision to order increasingly rigid prohibitions against his own population, culminating in martial law, has an effect antithetical to his intentions. The increasingly aggressive Fingermen inspire outrage and resistance rather than the expected pacification, even the subsequent martial law is not sufficient to keep the people in their homes on Guy Fawkes Day. Sutler's cruelty toward his subordinates ultimately places him under V's power. The belief that Sutler will use him as a scapegoat compels Creedy to surrender the Chancellor to their masked nemesis and even to perform the execution on his former leader. Thus V succeeds in turning the government against itself or compelling the ambitious to eliminate each other. Creedy's actions are motivated by the equivocal promise that V will surrender to him once Sutler has been killed. However, he fails to understand that while V may ultimately sacrifice himself for his cause, he has no intention of allowing Creedy to escape, not the man who first conceived the plot to unleash the St. Mary's virus on his own countrymen. Creedy's invention collapses upon his head when he discovers that V is sufficiently bullet-proof to overwhelm his armed guard.

More than anything else, McTeigue's film shares with *Hamlet* a preoccupation with the process of revenge, the latter work being the primary example of a sub-category of early modern drama — Revenge Tragedy — a subject explored memorably in Fredson Bowers' *Elizabethan Revenge Tragedy 1587–1642*. In this sub-group of early modern drama, the protagonist faces the necessity of exacting a retribution against a perpetrator, inevitably a person of elevated status — a Duke or a Monarch — who is not readily accessible but rather insulated from the direct access of the revenger. Thus the revenger's plans are delayed indefinitely, pending sufficient infiltration of the power structure. The motivations for the delay can be either objective or subjective. The external obstacles barring access are frequently substituted for the more profound deterrents, such as a moral reticence or a fear of punishment. The standard fare for the genre also includes a ghost, such as the spirit of Hamlet's father or the Spirit of Revenge in Kyd's *Spanish Tragedy*; a Machiavellian intriguer, as in *Hamlet*'s Claudius and Laertes or virtually any of the characters in Tourneur's *Revenger's Tragedy*; and "casual slaughter," a phrase borrowed from *Hamlet* to describe the proliferation of dead bodies that conclude the drama. Cyril Tourneur's Vindice consoles himself and his brother before their executions: "We die after a nest of Dukes" (*The Revenger's Tragedy*, V.iii.126).

The revenger is seldom satisfied with the mere execution of his antagonist, but seeks to damn his soul as well as torment his body, which, of course, explains Hamlet's failure to kill his uncle while the latter is praying; the revenger fears that Claudius is engaged in the cleansing of his soul and that a sudden death will be a guarantee of his salvation. The requisite damnation of the victim can also assume the form of physical or emotional torment. The revenger desires to the bring the subject to such a state of vexation that she or he will die either cursing and subsequently unrepentant or suffering great physical and emotional pain with a full awareness of the vendetta that has been exacted against her or him. Ambitioso and Supervacuo of *The Revenger's Tragedy* desire their elder brother, Lussurioso, to die cursing for his misdirected attempt on their father's life, and Titus Andronicus forces Tamora to eat her own children, who have been ground up and baked into a pie. The latter example illustrates the extravagance and spectacle of the revenger, who frequently goes so far in his efforts that he cannot outlive the apotheosis of his violent designs. Had he lived, Hamlet would have had to account for the deaths of Rosencrantz, Guildenstern, and Polonius, all of whom constitute the collateral damage in the revenge, and account for it by citing the commandments of his father's ghost; Kyd's Hieronomo would have had to explain the deaths of the heirs apparent of both Spain and Portugal; and Vindice would have to justify his murderous intrigue against the entire Ducal family.

The connection between the revenge tragedy tradition and a film entitled *V for Vendetta* is fairly obvious. Like the tragic heroes of early modern drama, V has lived with and plotted his revenge for a very long time — 14 years — and everything that he has done in the interval between outrage and punishment has been calculated to bring about the day of his triumph, nor does he have any intention of surviving the long awaited confrontation. V's loss of memory and identity during the Larkhill experiments and his subsequent assumption of the name V is a reminder of his commitment to revenge Valerie Page and himself against those responsible for the St. Mary's virus. Hamlet promises to "wipe away all trivial fond records" from the "table of ... [his] memory":

> All saws of books, all forms, all pressures past
> That youth and observation copied there,
> And thy commandment all alone shall live
> Within the book and volume of my brain,
> Unmix'd with baser matter [I.v.101–105].

V's memory has been erased, and only the charge of revenge is copied where recollections of childhood and identity building experiences were once written. However, he refuses to engage in Hamlet's self-denigration over lengthy delays; he pursues his objective with patience and meticulous planning. Hamlet's revenge is not so well plotted as V's either. The melancholy Dane finally surrenders to rashness and opportunism rather than careful preparation; he never manages to wipe away "the trivial and fond records," his fears, inhibitions, and scruples constantly hindering his project. V is Hamlet's ideal revenger, one who is not subject to the vicissitudes of "blood and judgment" but is resolute, unswerving in his intent, capable of carrying out his project without rage, pity, or soul killing vexation. V's lesson for Evey when he imprisons, tortures, and interrogates her constitutes a re-enactment of his own revelation: there are principles whose value transcends the value of one's life. Although he does not name those principles, one can assume he refers to self-respect, courage, and resolution, a resolution not to be defeated by cruelty and injustice. The remainder of Evey's life can then be committed to the unyielding pursuit of justice and revenge. He reminds her that she does not have to be consumed by hate; she can patiently await her vindication and live the remainder of her life on her own terms, free from the fear of fascist bullies.

V's revenge exceeds the mere execution of his antagonists. Had he sought only their deaths, he could have accomplished his task in relative safety and anonymity, but he wanted to taunt and torment the bullies, to demonstrate that in spite of their overactive national security apparatus, they are not secure, and this requires that they have a period of reflection, a full understanding of what they have done and what is to be done to them in retaliation. However, the early modern revenge tradition of damning the perpetrator's soul requires a makeover for a postmodern secular context. Since the fascist Sutler regime is predicated upon the triumph of hyper–masculinity, the appropriate degradation is to make the perpetrators buckle under their own fear, make them feel powerless like the many racial, ethnic, and gendered minorities that Norsefire deemed expendable. The soul-killing act is reducing the seemingly unassailable persecutors to tears and pleas, an act that annihilates their inordinate pride and righteous indignation. The destruction of the Norsefire ideology represented by the slogan "Strength through Unity ..." offers another dimension of secular damnation. V destroys the fabricated unity of the government by turning its cabinet members against each other. Creedy reduces Sutler to tears and pleas before he executes him in a summary fashion. Then V abolishes the spymaster's sense of smug invulnerability as he forces him to witness the systematic destruction of his bodyguards, rendering him vulnerable to V's brandished steel. Creedy surrenders to fear and disbelief just before his death. The same is true of other party members guilty of complicity in the Larkhill genocide, most of whom, like their leaders, are destroyed at the height of pride, except for Delia, who patiently accepts her much deserved death. She may be the only one who is tragic since she is the only one who has any insight, any understanding of the role she played in her own annihilation. Prothero and Lilliman are both killed in those acts that have "no relish of salvation," the former triumphing in his own public image and offering summary judgment of his subordinates and the latter enjoying the pedophilic pleasures of his bed.

V's actions may exceed the acceptability of violent revenge. The medieval tradition of revenge inherited by Shakespeare and the early modern playwrights held that private revenge in lieu of public justice was only acceptable when the passage to the law or public justice was obstructed, because the perpetrators were themselves responsible for the prosecution of crime or because their influence could hinder impeachment of the matter. Since the Norsefire Party is the prevailing and indeed the only power structure in the realm, V has no choice but to pursue a private vendetta. However, his actions may exceed what is acceptable to his audience, as was the case with the revengers of the early modern stage (Bowers 187–189). While the movie audience are certainly supportive of V over Sutler, Creedy, Prothero, and Lilliman, the death of Delia Surridge seems gratuitous, particularly since she experiences such compunction for her crimes and so patiently abides her own murder/assassination, nor is she arrogant and powerful like the other malefactors. While her death is certainly warranted considering the enormity of participation in genocide, it might have become V to temper justice with mercy in this case. The incarceration of Evey, while it seemed to have a positive effect on her personal growth, may also be construed as heavy-handed on the part of the revenger. While she may require a desperate cure for her fear, it is presumptuous of V to assume the role of pedant. The suffering that brings about her personal growth is also projected onto the macrocosm in the form of civil unrest. The death of the small girl in the Fawkesian mask follows V's encouragement, his call to arms, and although the death is primarily the fault of Sutler's cronies and policies, V must share some of the blame. He has arrogantly assumed the role of "physician of the state" who will unilaterally apply the painful curative, forcing the population to experience great tribulation and loss under the pretense of public good. While his actions might benefit the country in the long run, they will demand sacrifices that he has no mandate to offer. V's death is necessary at the end of the film, not just because it brings his antagonists under his power, but because it demonstrates that he is willing to make the same sacrifice that he has imposed on others.

The microscosm/macrocosm symbolic duality has a direct application to the Shakespearean and/or early modern intertext. Indeed, *V for Vendetta* shares this idea with both *Hamlet* and *Macbeth*. The political mythology from the early modern era, indeed from the Middle Ages, regarded the health of the land as an extension of and indivisible from the wellbeing of the King: if the King was sick, the land was sick; if the King was wicked, the land would suffer; if the King was decadent, the land decayed, as the King and the land were one. The image of the King as the head of the body politic constituted by both the population and the land itself is one of the many the mythical correspondences, the manifestations of divine order, outlined in E.M.W. Tillyard's aged but still useful text *The Elizabethan World Picture*. In *Hamlet*, the true king has died, and even before the revelation of his murder, the language of the drama suggests that the land, like the King's body, is in a state of advanced decay. We cannot forget such memorable lines as "This bodes some strange eruption to our state" (I.i.69); "My father's spirit in arms! All is not well" (I.iii.254); and "Something is rotten in the state of Denmark" (I.iv.89). Hamlet compares Denmark to a "dead dog" (II.ii.181) and the world to "a foul and pestilent congregation of vapors" (II.ii.303–304), and he describes the "convocation of politic worms" that consume the King's, the country's, and, most directly, Polonius' body (IV.iii.20). *Macbeth* contains a similar lamentation of the country's health, particularly from the Scottish rebels committed to the tyrant's overthrow, those who desire to "make med'cines" of their "great revenge" (Iv.iii.214). They grieve over their poor country as though it were a dying organism:

> Each new morn
> New widows howl, new orphans cry, new sorrows
> Strike heaven on the face, that it resounds
> As if it felt with Scotland and yell'd out
> Like a syllable of dolor [IV.iii.4–8].

Macduff adds, "Bleed, Bleed, poor country!" (IV.iii.31). The lamentations are followed by images of healing embodied in the virtues of England's King Edward:

> How he solicits heaven,
> Himself best knows; but strangely visited people,
> All swoll'n and ulcerous, pitiful to the eye,
> The mere despair of surgery, he cures,
> Hanging a golden stamp about their necks,
> Put on with holy prayers, and 'tis spoken,
> To the succeeding royalty he leaves
> The healing benediction [IV.iii.149–157].

Edward's piety and holiness are counterpoint to Macbeth's solicitation of hell in his pursuit of power. Macbeth spreads pestilence while Edward purges the air.

The power structure of England in *V for Vendetta* is represented as a single scrupulous and salubrious body with Sutler as the head and his cabinet the various faculties or the senses that inform the brain; however, the introduction of a single noxious element (the revenger) initiates the decline and destruction of the entire organism. Like Hamlet's "vicious mole in nature" from which the body "take[s] corruption" (I.iv.24, 35), V multiplies like cancer cells, bringing the body of the state in one year to the throes of death and simultaneous rebirth. In his public diagnosis of Sutler's England, V says that "there is something very wrong with this country," and he appoints himself physician of the state, prepared to purge the power structure and restore the country's health. His use of chemicals and syringes in the elimination of high ranking Norsefire Party members suggests that the political structure is diseased, requiring a medical resolution. The ailing, languorous, and defeated population is roused from its enfeebled state and revived by the infusion of subversive potential. From this angle, the subsequent imagery of the state warring with itself suggests health and vigor, a people animated by diversity, disagreement, intellect, and unrest, as well as a commitment to freedom of expression and dissent.

Richard III

V's theatrical posturing includes a reference to Shakespeare's *Richard III*, and here as elsewhere, the cinematic avenger extols hypocrisy and dissimulation. Based upon the "morality vice" figure of medieval drama, Richard, Duke of Gloucester, embodies villainy and unbridled ambition, but for the vice, ambition is often abstracted from any material goals; he foments and perpetuates chaos and misery just because he can, because he finds it entertaining to demonstrate the superiority of his wit and cunning, periodically pausing to gloat over his political trophies and to encourage the theatrical audience in its appreciation of his hijinks (Spivack 148, 167; Happé 27). In a similar meta-theatrical fashion, V draws attention to the artificiality of his dramatic posturing, once again consciously modeling his character and action on a Shakespearean paradigm or rather living one of Shakespeare's lives as it were. In confrontation with Bishop Lilliman, V quotes Shakespeare's usurping English King:

> And thus I clothe my naked villainy
> With odd old ends stolen forth of holy writ,
> And seem a saint, when most I play the devil [I.iii.335–337].

The passage is very similar in content to Polonius' "sugar[ing] over the devil." The "I" appears to allude, as one might expect, to the subject of the utterance, V himself, who experiences a moment of compunction but who follows his vindictive agenda in spite of his conscience, or more richly, it can be read as didactic utterance, a moral lesson for a man about to die, one assessing the content of his life and the probable fate of his soul.

In the latter of the two alternative significations, V becomes his victim, assuming his antagonist's part, reminding him of his hypocrisy. Lilliman has advanced within the Church hierarchy, arriving at Bishop because he was able to veil his "naked villainy" under a cloak of secrecy and feigned piety. Just in case he has forgotten the true nature of his cries, V has come to remind him of the past which cannot be forgiven and which cannot be evaded. V's quotation from Shakespeare is a response to Lilliman's solicitation of God's "mercy," and it reminds the Bishop that he has been doing the devil's work while dressed in the robes of a saint, that he has consciously manipulated and exploited religion, not out of love for God or a desire to minister to humanity, but as a means to wealth and political power. The "odd old ends stol'n forth of holy writ" do not imply a fervent adherence to scriptures or religious principles, but the assumption of a pious mask constructed through biblical references. The use of the word "stol'n" suggests that the Bishop's use of scriptures is profane, his actions incongruous with his words. Like Macbeth on whom the King's "titles/Hang loose about him like a giant's robe/Upon a dwarfish thief" (V.iii.21–22) and Claudius, "A cutpurse of the empire and the rule" who "from a shelf, the precious diadem stole,/And put it in his pocket" (III.iv.102–104), Bishop Lilliman lays claim to spiritual power that does not suit him; he is a usurper of God's justice and prerogative, who cynically undermines religion and pious action in the promotion of his own base appetites. The Bishop has the temerity to plead for God's mercy after having presided over genocide, after having repeatedly committed statutory rape, and after having to be pried off of his most recent victim.

The unwarranted piety noted in V's quotation from *Richard III* has a broader application to Sutler and his government. The portrait of the Norsefire Party is a satire of Christian Fundamentalist government which pays lip service to scripture even as its actions subvert the elementary principles of the religion, such as mercy, humility, compassion, charity, forgiveness, and righteousness. Sutler is described by Rookwood/V as "a deeply religious man and a member of the conservative party." As he gains power, his religion conceals a monumental political ambition, one that seeks to control every facet of the people's lives, forcing religious uniformity in the name of national unity and security. He believes that his ambitions for church rule justify the most rigorous application of martial law, as well as the inhumane treatment of outsiders and non-conformists in fiendish biomedical experiments. So completely have the British Chancellor and his government abandoned the tenets of their religion that one might assume they no longer have any devotional concern, save for the appearance of piety. Like Shakespeare's Richard III and the Machiavellian prototype, Sutler only feigns religion for the success and maintenance of his political ambition. Richard repeatedly feigns religious devotion in his lunge for power. When Buckingham fails to rally public support for the disinheritance of the nephews, thus paving Richard's way to the throne, the Dukes of Gloucester and Buckingham stage a pageant for the people, cynically highlighting Richard's piety and humility. Buckingham devises the pretense:

> And look you get a prayer-book in your hand,
> And stand between two churchmen, good my lord,
> For on the ground I'll make a holy descant;
> And be not easily won to our requests [III.vii.47–50)].

In full view of the population, Buckingham will plead with Richard to take the throne while the latter will repeatedly refuse the gesture on the grounds that he has no earthly ambitions. The dissimulation will continue until the populace itself urges him to relent and assume the crown.

Creedy and Sutler conspire in a fashion similar to Buckingham and Richard, devising an inhumane plan to slaughter the innocent — literally children — in an effort to gain political dominion. Before the murder of his nephews, Richard enjoyed considerable power, serving as the Lord Protector of the Prince in his minority, an office that was quasi-monarchical, the Protector ruling as King while he and the country await the Prince's maturity. Similarly, Sutler enjoyed substantial power in advance of the St. Mary's viral attack, already sufficiently influential to instigate the Larkhill research; however, he sought "complete and total hegemonic domination" and, like Richard, achieved the same through subterfuge. Even after Richard branded his nephews bastards and assumed the throne in his own right, he was concerned about the longevity of his rule, knowing that rebellion would eventually ensue on behalf of the Princes. Richard enlists a desperate malcontent whom "corrupting gold ... tempts unto a close exploit of death" (IV.ii.34–35), namely the murder of his royal nephews. His ruthlessness earns him absolute power for a time, but also inflames his enemies (and even some of his former allies) against him, resulting in his eventual overthrow. Sutler and Creedy devise the plan to unleash the St. Mary's virus on the English population and to direct the torrent of blame onto the innocent. The horror of a viral attack, particularly the attack upon the school children at St. Mary's, radicalizes the electorate and sweeps Norsefire and Sutler into power. When Rookwood meets with Finch and Dominic to reveal the insidious conspiracy behind Sutler's rise, he does so at the site of the St. Mary's Memorial in which a sculpture of children dancing in a ring is surrounded by obsidian walls engraved with the names of the dead, perhaps another subtle allusion to the bubonic plague, the ostensible origin of the children's game "Ring around the Rosy." Like Richard, Sutler and Creedy, whose names now suggest "subtle" and "creepy" or "sleazy," respectively, have climbed to power on the backs of murdered children.

While Buckingham will not be privy to Richard's designs upon the lives of the Princes, Creedy actually devises the plan to murder citizens for the advancement of Sutler's political ambitions. Nevertheless, the rifts between Richard/Buckingham and Sutler/Creedy have much in common. When Buckingham refuses to be privy to the elimination of potential rivals to the throne, the mistrustful Richard turns against him:

> The deep-revolving witty Buckinham
> No more shall be the neighbor to my counsels.
> Hath he so long held out with me untir'd
> And stops he now for breath [IV.ii.42–45].

When Richard refuses to give Buckingham the property of the dead King Edward IV, the same that he promised as a reward for loyalty, Buckingham, recognizing his own peril, elects to depart without delay:

> And is it thus? Repays he my deep service
> With such contempt? Made I him king for this?
> O, let me think on Hastings, and be gone
> To Brecknock, while my fearful head is on! [IV.iii.119–122].

Hastings had been summarily executed by Richard for opposing the Protector's claim to the throne. Seeing that the tides of favor are turning against him, Buckingham flees to the opposition, betraying his fellow conspirator. Just so, Creedy, recognizing that years of murderous service to the Chancellor no longer inspire the latter's gratitude, elects to cooperate with V in the apprehension and execution of his former leader and ally. Thinking that he will succeed as Chancellor, Creedy betrays and kills Sutler before the latter can turn against him. However, both Buckingham and Creedy are unable to save themselves. While the Duke is captured and executed by Richard, Creedy is deceived and killed by his nemesis, V.

The relationship between V and Evey bears some resemblance to that of Richard and Lady Anne. The latter match is perhaps one of the most improbable in the canons of Western literature. Richard succeeds in seducing Lady Anne as she follows her husband's corpse to burial, the very same husband whom Richard is blamed for killing. She repels Richard's amorous advances calling him "black magician," "foul devil," and even "hedgehog," but eventually capitulates to his protests of love, his specious claims that he murdered her husband for her love. Lady Anne's capitulation is near kin to exhaustion, with little or no affection. The match is made still more improbable by Richard's "foul deformities"—a hunchback, a withered arm, and uneven legs. Richard admits that "love forswore ... [him] in ... [his] mother's womb," that he was "cheat'd of feature by dissembling nature/Deform'd, unfinish'd, sent before ... [his] time/Into this breathing world, scarce half made up" (I.i.19–21). Indeed, he elects to pursue the crown out of jealousy and boredom as the males of the royal house, in the absence of war, "caper" in ladies' "chamber[s]/To the lascivious pleasing of a lute" (I.i.12–13). By his own estimation, Richard's deformities preclude him from finding love, so it seems rather incongruous when he manages to attain a wife even before the end of the act. Yet he has not found love, he and Lady Anne continue to despise each other until Richard has her murdered so that he can make a more politically advantageous match.

The resemblance between Richard's seduction of Lady Anne and V's bond with Evey lies primarily in the union of beauty and deformity. V has been so disfigured by the explosions at Larkhill that he will not allow himself to be seen without a mask, and indeed, neither Evey nor the audience ever get a clear look at his face. In the graphic novel, however, he does show his face to Delia Surridge, perhaps because he wants her to witness the enormity of her crimes against him. When Evey attempts to unmask him near the end of the film, he thwarts her efforts, explaining that the face beneath the mask is not his face. The theory of deformity that lies behind the representation of V is one indicative of the twentieth century, not the sixteenth. One objective of the film is to demonstrate V's humanity in spite of his actions and his appearance, while the narrative of *Richard III* demonstrates the usurping King's inhumanity, his inability to love or to place anyone ahead of his own ambitions. Richard's deformity is indicative of the early modern assumption that physical irregularity was an outward sign of an inward deformity, be it spiritual or mental. The grotesque body divulged the grotesque personality. Richard becomes progressively more cruel and violent until even his own mother, the Duchess of York, despises him and cannot abide his appearance. While initially Lady Anne may seem to overcome her revulsion to her second husband, perhaps entirely for pragmatic reasons, ultimately she does not triumph over her loathing. She dies despising him. In contrast, Evey is initially revolted by V's terrorist attacks and assassinations and still more by his lack of remorse, yet she eventually comes to understand and even support his rationale, this even after he has tortured her in order to teach her courage and resolution. They declare their love for each other as V lies dying on the tube station platform beside the explosive-laden train.

Macbeth, Hamlet, Richard III and the *V for Vendetta* film script share other common traits, specifically an emphasis on usurpation and the villain hero. In each of the above Shakespearean plays, a rightful ruler has been supplanted by an undeserving upstart who facilitates his own ascent through villainy and murder. Claudius has murdered his own brother, King Hamlet, married the widowed queen, and "popp'd in between the election" and his nephew's "hopes," all before the curtain rises; Macbeth murders the "gracious Duncan" for whose overthrow he can invent no reasonable motivation, resorting to "vaulting ambition"; Richard, Duke of Gloucester, embarks on a virtual campaign of murder to clear his way to the throne. He does not kill King Edward IV, but he does kill his brother Clarence, Hastings, and King Edward's heirs — the Princes — or all who would "impede him from the golden round." Each of the above Shakespearean plays involves a revenge for a base injury, a "blood revenge." Henry of Richmond, later King Henry VII, revenges the murders of his young cousins and indeed the entire Lancastrian House by killing Richard III at the Battle of Bosworth Field. Hamlet remains the classic Elizabethan revenger, who supplants his father's killer to his own peril; and Macbeth is overthrown by the father/husband of his most recent and most gratuitous murder victims and by Malcolm, the son of King Duncan, and the rightful heir to the Scottish throne.

The application of these recurring Shakespearean plot devices to *VfV* has a multiplicity of facets. The rule of England has been usurped by a tyrant more than a decade prior to the opening of the film. As in the dramas listed above, the crimes that facilitated the Sutler/Norsefire rise to power have been concealed, the occulted guilt kept even from many of those closest to power. The revelation of the crimes coincides with the revenger's efforts to supplant and murder the usurper. V must expose the crimes of the Sutler regime in order to solicit sufficient support for his revolution. In all cases, the tide of public sympathy turns against the usurper and aligns itself with the revenger's murderous plot: "Blood will have blood" (*Macbeth*, III.iv.123). V, whose makeshift name references vengeance, is motivated primarily by the maltreatment of social undesirables who had no political influence. The tyrant's hand is against the innocent in most of the above cases. Beyond the literal innocence of the St. Mary's school children, the victims at Larkhill were unoffending save insofar as they were inconsistent with the Norsefire demand for uniformity of race, sexuality, ethnicity, and religion. The other victims of the St. Mary's outbreak were simple commuters and consumers of public utilities. An idea central to tragedy that is often difficult to reproduce in a contemporary context is the idea that the injury of the tragic perpetrator is exacted against an entire nation in the body of the King. In *V for Vendetta*, this injury against the nation is embodied in the loss of hundreds of thousands of people as well as the loss of civil liberties and elective government.

V certainly conforms to the role of villain hero, masking himself as one of the most notorious terrorists of British history, destroying the symbol of British justice, the Old Bailey, occupying Jordan Tower, plotting to blow up Parliament, engaging in a program of assassinations, and torturing the film's heroine. Yet in spite of his abominable behavior, V is charged with a virtuous task of liberating the English from fear and trepidation. He was reborn in the fires of the Larkhill facilities, and his subsequent role has been to unleash fire and destruction; Evey was reborn in the downpour following her incarceration, and her objective is creation or reconstruction. This dichotomy dovetails nicely with Moore and Lloyd's construction of anarchy in the graphic novel, where the authors repeatedly cite the paradoxical marriage of destruction and creation inherent in the breakdown of civil authority and individual restraint:

> Anarchy wears two faces, both CREATOR and DESTROYER. Thus destroyers topple empires, make a canvas of clean rubble where creators can build a better world. Rubble once achieved makes further ruins' means irrelevant. Away with our explosives, then! Away with our destroyers! They have no place within our better world. But let us raise a toast to all of our bombers, all our bastards, most unlovely and most unforgivable [Moore and Lloyd 222].

The cinematic V's crimes, while largely justified, are too much to countenance by the end of the film. He has survived entirely for revenge, and surviving beyond the fulfillment of that objective cannot be countenanced, by him or anyone else. Revenge has animated him for over a decade, and he is incompatible with the restoration of an orderly and rehabilitated world. His phase of the reconstruction has passed.

Twelfth Night

The allusions to Shakespearean drama are not limited to the tragedies. *V for Vendetta* also brushes up against *Twelfth Night* and *Measure for Measure*. While the former is specifically referenced several times in the film, including a quotation from the Shakespearean text, the latter seems to contribute more to the plot, but each of the allusions revolves around the idea of disguise. V not only wears a mask himself, but distributes masks to others or perhaps, in some cases, makes others realize that they have been wearing masks all along.

Twelfth Night is representative of that sub-genre of Elizabethan drama known as the "saturnalian comedy," a name derived from the ancient Roman Carnivale. Much like the contemporary Mardi Gras, the Saturnalia, beginning on December 17, was a one week period of "general license" in which the citizenry drank and ate to excess, while flaunting their disrespect for civil authority. The festival, limited both spatially and temporally, acted as a pressure valve designed to avert civil unrest by providing an outlet for popular aggressions, the same that might otherwise manifest in sedition, riot or rebellion. The saturnalia, lupercalia, and carnivale all mitigated the misery of the people's daily lives, but at the end of the designated gala period, the people were expected to return to their roles as obedient social subjects (Gardiner 44–47). Mikail Bakhtin, in his influential work *Rabelais and His World,* has taught contemporary critics the relevance of the carnival formulation — specifically its inversion of hierarchy and authority — to literature and particularly the novel. The Twelfth Night festivities, beginning at Christmas and running until January 6th, the Feast of Epiphany, was one of the many appropriations of pagan holidays to the Christian religious calendar in order to facilitate the conversion of pagans to the new religion in the middle ages. The Twelfth Night festivities were a lengthy period of celebration in which participants exchanged gifts and attended theatrical productions, feasts, and masks (Bevington 393). The saturnalian comedy is one in which the spirit of celebration reigns. The characters wear masks, whether material, social, or psychological; they engage in gender bending; and they enjoy nothing so much as flaunting their contempt toward authority, usually represented by a killjoy who attempts to impede the spirit of carousing and who must be rejected from the space of carnival revels. The saturnalian comedy pits the forces of riot and liberty against the forces of restraint and inhibition. However, eventually, the revelers go too far in their celebrations and are prompted to return to normalcy.

The saturnalian structure of *Twelfth Night* is captured in the respective characters of Malvolio and Feste, moralist and clown, melancholy and sanguinary, respectively. This dualistic structure is embodied in the two noble households of the play as well: Duke Orsino's is quiet, orderly, and sober and Lady Olivia's riotous and indulgent. The respective heads of each household seem to be misplaced. Olivia's mournful and melancholy self-denial seem more fitted to Orsino's environment, while the Duke's love sickness might be more appropriate among the carnival revels of Olivia's estate. The truncated lives of both Orsino and Olivia are broadened upon the arrival of Viola, disguised as a castrato, Cesario. Seeking employment, Viola is charged with winning over Olivia on behalf of the Duke; however, the complication arises when Olivia falls for Viola, whom she believes is a man, Cesario, and one irresistibly indifferent to her charms. The result is a true love triangle in which Viola loves Orsino, who loves Olivia, who loves Viola. The confusion increases upon the arrival of Viola's twin brother, Sebastian, whom she thought drowned at sea.

It is the masking in Shakespeare's *Twelfth Night* and the gulling of the killjoy that has the most significant application to *V for Vendetta*. It is not only V who wears a mask, although one might say that he is the only person in the film who is never unmasked since each façade reveals another. As I have cited previously, Evey's cosmetics and, by extension, her feminine exterior and demeanor, are revealed to be disguises, archaic social constructs perpetuated to force women into a male's feminine ideal. Only after Evey embraces an alternative self, one beneath the cosmetic mask, is she able to live freely without fear. All of the perpetrators of the Larkhill genocide and the St. Mary's viral attack are wearing disguises, and V's task is to expose them. The prime movers in the Norsefire party are masquerading as righteous and courageous puritans, puffed up with power and arrogance. Sutler, Prothero, and Creedy, the same men who dealt out death so lavishly, are reduced to fears, tears, and trembling even as their final vaunts are still echoing in the air. Sutler weeps and begs to be spared as his pre-recorded message offers no quarter to those giving aid and comfort to the insidious enemy. Similarly, Prothero helplessly recoils in fear at V's approach, while simultaneously the polemicist broadcaster's final rant expresses his longing to spend time alone with V in order to show that "every gutless, freedom-hating terrorist is a goddamn coward." Creedy seems to show the most courage, but only so long as he is shielded by men with automatic weapons. Once his guard has been neutralized and he is under V's power, his eyes grow wild; his voice breaks; and his body recoils. Each of the politicians maintains a façade of respectability, adopting the demeanor of a public servant or the guardian of the public welfare, and yet they all climbed to power on a heap of dead Englishmen, the imperial way strewn with the bodies of rivals, undesirables, commuters, children, and quiet suburbanites. The masks of the doctor and priest are perhaps the most cynical and hypocritical. Brutality and intrigue are an open secret in politics. So long as only those of an alternate party or establishment or members of a reviled social faction are harmed, the populace will wink at the sleaziness of politicians, assuming that extortion, leverage, and double-cross are the necessary Machiavellian instruments of state. However, often to their great disappointment, people anticipate more of doctors and clergymen, both of whom are expected to show sincerity and compassion in ministering to the population, yet Stanton and Lilliman betray their respective offices as well as the public trust by condoning and participating in genocide and eugenics. Stanton and Lilliman minister to body and the soul respectively, and neither offers the expected comfort to the wretched. Following the destruction of Larkhill, Diana Stanton disappears into the disguise of Delia Surridge, and Lilliman begins his ambitious climb up the hierarchy of the Church, hiding his pedophilic longings behind a veneer of respectability and holiness. The apparatus of the Church is mobilized to conceal the Bishop's dark secret to all but his closest aides and the eavesdroppers in the secret service. Like the politicians, he conceals the victimization of children that coincides with his rise to power. He was charged with the protection of innocence, and yet he violated the same. This portion of the film is in all probability a direct allusion to the complicity of the Catholic Church in concealing pedophilic priests. While Surridge is the most sympathetic of the malefactors, she is probably guilty of the greatest betrayals (violating her oath as a doctor to "first do no harm") as her actions create the greatest harm. She manufactures the vaccine/antidote that permits the politicians to use the St. Mary's virus as a weapon. Only her repentance saves her from the complete odium that engulfs the other conspirators and her confessionary journal facilitates the revelation of the Larkhill crimes.

V is the Lord of Misrule who unmasks pretenders, inverts the hierarchy of power, and signals the beginning of revels. He reverses the power structure by exposing the clay feet of the titans of government, and his planned destruction of Parliament issues in the temporary suspension of discipline and rule. I say temporary because the re-emergence of a political structure seems unavoidable. Yet for a brief time, the people in the streets wearing Guy Fawkes masks are liberated from restraint, breaching the lines of the patriarchal military and clamoring for a front row seat at the fiery demolition of the symbol of British government — Westminster Hall. V's exposure of the hypocrisy and arrogance of the English establishment is parallel to the gulling of Malvolio, the only court gall, who has forgotten his place and has adopted pretenses of importance even toward those of superior rank, such as Sir Toby and Sir Andrew Aguecheek, both knights. Although he is but a steward, Malvolio presumes to marry Olivia and condescend to Toby. His punishment is to be labeled insane and subjected to the tender mercies of sixteenth century mental health practices — kept in a dark room and taunted. Indeed, Sutler's tearful pleas in the dark abandoned tube station are reminiscent of the wretchedness of Malvolio in Trevor Nunn's cinematic version of *Twelfth Night*.

Beaten, filthy, and wretched, Malvolio pleads with the disguised Feste, the very man responsible for his capture and from whom he can least expect release.

The male/female duality that is embodied in Viola/Cesario suggests a necessary capitulation of vulnerable femininity to a more secure and assured masculinity. Viola dares not move about the country of Illyria or seek employment in the Duke's household in her own person. Women alone are not safe. She is employed by Orsino, a man transported to the extremity of love and melancholy, mooning over his unobtainable object. Viola/Cesario is readily enlisted to win Orsino's suit for Olivia's affections. However, Viola can only act with the requisite freedom and confidence in the guise and person of a man. Similarly Evey's initial encounter with Fingermen suggests the vulnerability of unaccompanied women in the Sutler regime. She is brought under the protection of V, who, like Orsino, is lamenting over and pursuing revenge on behalf of an unobtainable lady, this time because the lady is dead. Evey is progressively masculinized via the brutal ministrations of V: her head shaved, her temperate disposition altered, her sartorial choices simplified, and her cosmetics removed. She is stripped of all feminine pretenses and becomes a revolutionary prepared to complete V's destructive agenda. When Evey has returned to V's gallery in advance of the November 5th demolition, the revenger quotes Viola from *Twelfth Night*:

> Conceal me what I am, and be my aid
> For such disguise and haply shall become
> The form of my intent [I.iii.53–55].

The passage reveals the moment in which Viola, disguised as a man, decides to serve the Duke: "I'll serve this duke/Thou shalt present me as a eunuch to him" (I.iii.55–56). V's quotation of the passage alludes to his appropriation of the angry masses via the delivery of Guy Fawkes masks. All those who wear the mask will serve to promote his agenda. However, the adoption of a particular guise and demeanor in the pursuit of justice can also be attributed to Evey, who at first contributes through her vulnerability and desperation (with Bishop Lilliman) and later through her strength (the destruction of the Houses of Parliament). Evey adopts the mask of a Larkhill medical subject and with it the fanatical commitment to social change.

Measure for Measure

While there are no direct quotations from Shakespeare's *Measure for Measure* that might encourage the cinematic audience to consider the extensive structural parallels between drama and film, the 1604 tragi-comedy nevertheless informs the plot of *V for Vendetta* perhaps more than any of the precedent Shakespearean texts. Both works include a conservative governmental crackdown upon sexual liberties, a pattern of reformation, an unmerciful and hypocritical puritan, a disguised reformer, and a preoccupation with evenhanded justice. However, while the Shakespearean text plucks comedy from the jaws of death, *V for Vendetta* follows tragic necessity to its lamentable yet hopeful conclusion.

Measure for Measure begins with a transfer of power from Duke Vincentio to Angelo, deputized to rule Vienna in the absence of the benevolent or excessively lenient nobleman. Ostensibly the Duke will travel to Moscow after first investing Angelo with the power "to enforce or qualify the laws" (I.i.66). He has "Lent him ... [his] terror, dress'd him with ... [his] love/And given his deputation all the organs/Of ...[his] own pow'r" (I.i.20–22). This action may not seem so portentous were it indeed true that the Duke was traveling to Moscow, but in fact, he intends to move among his own people, disguised as a friar to monitor events in his ostensible absence. He offers several explanations for his actions, none of which are entirely satisfactory, explaining to the complicit Friar Thomas that he wants to see the "strict statutes and most biting laws" (I.iii.19) enforced against sexual transgression, laws which he has ignored for fourteen years and which have subsequently become "more mock'd than fear'd" (I.iii.27). He values Angelo's reputation for abstinence and severity and believes him the proper man to "put transgression to't" without any aspersions of hypocrisy that may attend the Duke's own efforts to enforce the long neglected edicts of Vienna. Duke Vincentio explains that the law would be too terrifying if he were to enforce it himself, and he would incur the people's odium for suddenly exacting retribution for that of which he himself is guilty and in which he has encouraged them through longterm indifference. However, he offers an additional excuse and one that reveals a mistrust of Angelo:

> Lord Angelo is precise;
> Stands at a guard with envy; scarce confesses
> That his blood flows, or that his appetite

Is more to bread than stone. Hence shall we see,
If power change purpose, what our seemers be [I.iii.50–54].

Clearly the Duke is dubious of Angelo's virtue, and he wants to determine whether his ascetic replacement will take corruption when invested with absolute authority over a weak and wayward populace. The Duke adds that he is reluctant to enforce the law himself because he fears that the sudden imposition of rigor would be too frightening for those caught in their fleshly indiscretions.

It is difficult to believe that the Duke could have been more terrifying than the dreadful mask of judgment that Angelo puts on following his lord's ostensible departure. Angelo shuts down the red light district, putting the flesh trade out of business, and he arrests Claudio and Juliet, an unoffending couple, condemning the former to death for getting the latter pregnant — seemingly out of wedlock — and consigning the latter to a convent to live out her days repenting her indiscretion. Claudio enlists the assistance of his soon to be cloistered sister, Isabella, who is embarrassed to argue for mercy for a man guilty of a crime she abhors to name, even if the man is her own brother. Isabella, nevertheless, overcomes her reticence, but her pleas to lord Angelo have an unexpected result. The puritanical leader succumbs to the temptations of the flesh demanding that Isabella concede to his amorous advances in order to save her brother. Fortunately, the disguised Duke is privy to the conversation, offering Isabella an alternative solution in which she can appear to relent to save her brother but maintain her revered chastity.

The social milieu of McTeigue's *V for Vendetta* is not unlike that of Shakespeare's Vienna. The government of England has been usurped by an excessively rigid and conservative political party, headed by a fanatical puritan who imposes the most extreme punishments for minor offenses and who seems to be particularly rigorous toward sexual indiscretions. While Lord Angelo's justice is undercut by his own lust, Sutler's religious, ethical, and moral principles are negated through his unyielding violence and his callous sacrifice of the public health for the acquisition and maintenance of power. Along with racial and ethnic minorities, sexual diversity is singled out for the Larkhill atrocities. Diversity is construed as inimical to the maintenance of order within the society. Both Angelo and Sutler appear to be completely insensible to the hypocrisy of their self-righteousness and both may be construed as having become corrupted by power. The virtue of Angleo may have been sincere before he became the Duke's surrogate, but he cannot sustain that integrity after he is vested with absolute power. Sutler may also have been genuinely virtuous before the Delilah of absolute power tempted him to transgress the bounds of human decency. Until they face punishment for their criminality, both men become increasingly brazen in their respective hypocrisies and condemnations.

V finds an analogue in the disguised Duke of Shakespeare's play. As the Duke walks in secret among his people, tallying their transgressions and consoling the condemned, so V, disguised first by disfigurement then by a Guy Fawkes mask, moves in a shadow world between life and death, visiting those he has condemned, hearing their confessions (as in the case of Delia Surridge), and administering the appropriate punishment — annihilation. The Duke witnesses the weaknesses of Lord Angelo and of Vienna, where he has "seen corruption boil and bubble/'Till it o'er-run the stews" (V.i. 323–324), and his ostensible homecoming constitutes a *deus ex machina*; he returns like divine justice separating the damned from the saved, allowing Angelo and Lucio to condemn themselves by their own insinuations, and encouraging Isabella and Mariana to ennoble themselves through the mercy that they show the undeserving. Similarly, V has returned from his fourteen year retreat (the same period since Duke Vincentio enforced his laws) in which he prepared his revenge against those who victimized so many and ruled with impunity, redirecting the torrent of blame upon the innocent. However, unlike the Duke's program for rehabilitation, V's vendetta will include no mercy for violent transgressors.

The Duke's method of reformation includes making his subjects mindful of their imminent deaths so that they will repent for their indiscretions and live more charitable and virtuous lives subsequently. Acting as confessor to Claudio, who faces execution for impregnating Juliet, the Duke advises the condemned to "Be absolute for death. Either death or life/Shall thereby be the sweeter" (III.i.5–6). He allows the fate of Lord Angelo to be decided by Isabella, who believes that her brother has been executed in spite of her ostensible concession to Angelo's lechery. The Duke even urges Isabella to impose the law rigorously, reminding her that her brother has been unjustly executed by Angelo who is guilty of the same crime for which he condemned Claudio. Unaware that her brother lives in spite of Angelo's malice, Isabella chooses to spare his life on behalf of Mariana whose husband he will become. Thus Isabella's reformation includes the necessity of showing more mercy than either she or her antagonist has shown formerly. She becomes enraged at her brother when he pleads that she save him by capitulating to Angelo's lust, but the disguised Duke counsels her to patience and forgiveness:

> The hand that has made you fair hath made you good. The goodness
> that is cheap in beauty makes beauty brief in goodness; but grace
> being the soul of your complexion, shall keep the body of it ever fair
> [III.i.178–181].

He suggests that she is too easily swayed from her just cause and that a greater understanding of people's weaknesses would make her more beautiful than she is already. Isabella's triumph at the end of the play is realized in her ability to understand and forgive Angelo's moral frailty. She even allows others to believe that she has dishonored herself in the effort to save her brother. Lord Angelo and Lucio are both rehabilitated first through the belief that they will be summarily executed for their transgressions against the Duke and his laws and then through imposed marriages to women whom they have previously cast off. Angelo is too humiliated and overwrought with self-loathing to plead for his life, while Lucio protests to the bitter end: "Marrying a punk, my Lord, is pressing to death, whipping, and hanging" (V.i.527–528).

V engages in a similar plan for the reformation and punishment of his transgressors. He is not content to allow the perpetrators of the Larkhill genocide, the St. Mary's viral attacks, and the Norsefire fascism escape without a full accounting of their wickedness and a brief period of fear and repentance. Of course, the circumstances of the film differ from those of Shakespeare's play insofar as the transgressions in the former are unforgivable. V visits each of the condemned, pausing in his revenge only long enough to inspire fear and regret. He makes his identity known to each, reminding them that they have not escaped the villainies of their past and that they are about to pay for them with their lives. He becomes an analogue to divine justice, privy to all the secret murders that live only in the perpetrators' consciences and doling out the punishments that are appropriate to their crimes. Even those who attempt to fight back are quickly humbled. As in *Measure for Measure*, the malefactors do not repent for their actions until they face their own deaths. However, unlike those who died at Larkhill, the Norsefire villains have the luxury of knowing why they have to die. In each of V's assassinations, the victim is reduced from vaunting pride to abject humility almost instantaneously, with the single exception of Delia Surridge, the only target who shows moral courage and dignity in the face of death.

V also demonstrates that his harsh ministrations can be employed to the rehabilitation of the living. His maltreatment of Evey in the incarceration and torture episode is perpetrated for the same reason that Duke Vincentio allows Claudio, Angelo, and Lucio to believe that they are going to be executed. The Duke explains his motivations for refusing to tell Isabella that her brother still lives and, in so doing, offers a concise articulation of the virtues of hopelessness:

> She comes to know
> If yet her brother's pardon be come hither.
> But I will keep her ignorant of her good,
> To make her heavenly comforts of despair
> When it is least expected [IV.iii.107–111].

V's intention in the interrogation of Evey is to bring her to a certainty of death in order to eliminate the fear of loss, to demonstrate that some principles are more important than the individual life, to bring her "heavenly comforts of despair. He, however, does not manage to teach her the single most important of Duke Vincentio's lessons — forgiveness — save for himself. Instead he shapes a revolutionary from a pacifist. Claudio's renewed courage following the Duke's spiritual counsel could be representative of Evey's personal growth under interrogation:

> To sue to live, I find I seek to die,
> And, seeking death, find life. Let it come on [III.i.42–43].

Evey's appreciation for life is intensified by the recognition that death is inevitable and perhaps even imminent, that risk is necessary in order to make life worth living. Upon this parallel discovery, she leaves the protective shadow of V and begins her life anew sans fear or trepidation.

The moral rectitude of Shakespeare's Isabella is shared by Evey. Both women recognize that their idealism must be tempered to conform to the flawed environments in which they live. Isabella is scandalized by the carnal weaknesses of those around her and is so afraid of sex that she cannot even name it in order to plead effectively for her brother's pardon. She has to be persuaded by Lucio not to break off negotiations for Claudio prematurely because a part of her believes that her brother actually deserves to die for his apparent carnal weakness. Her outrage over Angelo's suggestion that she could save her brother by surrendering her chastity demonstrates her naïveté and idealism. She believes her brother would rather die than allow her to pollute herself and becomes hysterical when Claudio, in a moment of weakness, pleads with her to save him even at the cost of her chastity. However, by the end of the play, Isabella's priorities and values have changed so completely that she is willing to allow people to believe she has indeed sacrificed her virginity to save her brother, a significant blot upon her reputation and honor, and she becomes complicit in the subterfuge that brings Mariana to Angelo's bed. Thus she is willing to dissemble but not to dissipate. However, the most important manifestation of her transformation is her willingness to forgo the convent and wed Duke Vincentio.

Evey begins her association with V inadvertently, and she is highly critical of his actions for the first half of the film. While in the graphic novel her presence on the street the night of her first encounter with V and the Fingermen is the result of her trying to prostitute herself, the film script includes a more virtuous Evey; she is going to see a friend. Even after V saves her from the government agents, she is as frightened of him as she is of the now dead or disabled Fingermen, and for most of the film, her interaction with the revenger is punctuated by her expressions of disapproval. She is shocked that he would steal paintings from the Ministry of Objectionable Materials and real butter from a supply train bound for Chancellor Sutler, and she is so scandalized by his murder of Prothero that she tries to warn his next victim, Lilliman, even allowing herself to pose as an exploited child. However, the events at Gordon Tower also demonstrate that she, like Isabella, is struggling between will and will not. The Shakespearean heroine wants her brother to live, but does not want to do what is necessary to ensure that life. Similarly, Evey does not approve of V's actions, but she does know that he is correct in his negative assessment of the Norsefire regime. Against her better judgment, she rescues V from Dominic who has apprehended the revenger. Later, she is amazed at and regretful for her own behavior in defense of an apparent terrorist and murderer. Yet eventually she comes to identify with her captor, and not exclusively because of Stockholm syndrome, although the same may be a factor in her psychology. Her priorities are redirected toward V's agenda when she finally loses her fear of death and comes to terms with the treatment of her family at the hands of the Sutler government. Like Isabella, she allows herself to be identified with those qualities that unmake her, those qualities against which she has defined herself—her abject. Isabella is ostensibly a whore and Evey a terrorist. Thus both characters are liberated from a reductive self-image, one that reflects the oppressive conditions imposed upon them.

Although *Measure for Measure* comes dangerously close to tragedy, the central complication in the narrative revolves around the comic pretext of error and misdirection. Claudio faces execution and Juliet the convent because their marital bands have not been made public. The two were indeed married, but there had been no witnesses to their match, yet the conception of a child renders any betrothal a legitimate marriage. In his book length study of Jan Van Eyck's *The Arnolfini Marriage Portrait*, Edwin Hall defines the difference between wedding and betrothal beginning in the twelfth century canon law:

> canonists and theologians from the twelfth century on distinguished a betrothal from a wedding according to the tense used in expressing the consent to be married: the words of consent in the future tense, or *verba de futuro*, that characterized a betrothal were no more than a promise of future marriage, whereas words of consent in the present tense, or *verba de presenti*, created the indissoluble marriage bond. Words of future consent followed by sexual union were held to constitute consent in the present tense, and a presumptive marriage was the result [29].

When the Duke visits Juliet in her cloister, he determines that their "offenseful act/Was mutually committed" (II.iii.26–27); thus whether the betrothal was *de futuro* or *de presenti*, it was nevertheless rendered a legitimate marriage by virtue of the obvious consummation. However, the surrogate Duke refuses to acknowledge a legitimate marriage; thus Claudio will be executed for sleeping with his own wife. Moreover, Angelo had formerly made a *de futuro* match with Mariana, but it had been broken off before consummation when her family was unable to produce the requisite dowry. The bed trick that the Duke and Isabella play on Lord Angelo has the effect of rendering his *de futuro* match a legitimate and indissoluble marriage. When Lord Angelo then decides to proceed with the execution, his hypocrisy is twofold. He has perpetrated the same crime that he wrongly believes Claudio has committed—fornication; in reality, he has merely slept with his betrothed and made her his wife, an act for which he will face death upon the Duke's return. In his puritanical rush to "put transgression to it," Angelo willfully denies a legitimate match and an abiding and sincere love between Claudio and Juliet. Like Isabella bound for the convent, he denies the flesh, but even Isabella can imagine alternative pathways to the altar; her initial reaction to her brother's apparent transgression is a recommendation of marriage: "O, let him marry her" (I.iv.49). *Measure for Measure*'s theatrical negotiation between legitimate and illegitimate marriages and loves constitutes another parallel with *V for Vendetta*.

Like Angleo's remorseless government, the Norsefire regime is particularly preoccupied with punishing what it regards as sexual transgression, in this case, queer identities, and like the disguised Duke Vincentio, V has dedicated himself to revenging those punished by the puritanical government because he may or may not have been an equal participant in sexual novelties before the disfiguring accident at Larkhill. It broaches the question: Why is V selected to be interred at the Larkhill facility, which experimented on foreigners, Muslims, and homosexuals, particularly since we know that he does not belong to either of the first two categories? The back story of events in the internment camp is told partially from the perspective of a lesbian, Valerie Page, who struggles for many years to find love and acceptance, and after a few brief years of contentment and co-habitation, the (un)wedded bliss with her life partner Ruth is shattered by the intrusion of the fascist regime that abducts both, sending them to internment facilities where they die. Here the concentration camp may allude to the places of enclosure where the sexual potential of Shakespeare's Juliet, Isabella, and Mariana is directed and contained, namely in the convent and the moated grange respectively.

The inclusion of the thematic of sexual transgression in the film is partially indicative of the context in which Moore and Lloyd's graphic novel was produced, alluding to the moral panic over the connection between the gay community and the proliferation of HIV in the early 1980s, and obviates the irrationality of the time which blamed lesbians as well as gay men for the spread of the disease while common sense and all studies of infection demographics demonstrated that lesbians were the social group least likely to be seropositive. However, the inclusion of this aspect of the narrative also allows writer and director to comment on a more contemporary issue — that of gay marriage — and to take another swipe at George W. Bush's neo-conservatism, which abominates love while embracing violence and persecution, which claims to respect life while reviling the flesh and provoking and condoning the obscene massacre in Iraq. Moreover, the connection between the marital debate and the AIDS crisis may seek to demonstrate that Bush's "compassionate conservatism" is just as vicious and insensitive as Reagan's inhumane policies toward the poor and the afflicted. Shakespeare seeks to demonstrate that sins of the flesh are universal even among the most ostensibly pious members of society. Pompey asks if Angelo intends "to geld and splay all the youth of the city" (II.i.229–230) and then adds that if he does not, he, Angleo, will be forced to execute everyone. *V for Vendetta* offers a similar insight into the universality of carnality in the episode with Bishop Lilliman who is a pedophile and who is the single member of the Noresfire power structure who could be expected to show restraint.

Of course, the central tenet of Christ's teachings is that all humanity shares in sin, The Sermon on the Mount internalizing the laws of Moses, rendering the mere thought of sexual indiscretion morally indistinguishable from the act itself. The result is a scenario in which none can safely judge others since they are implicated in the same crimes that they condemn, and this idea is the source for the title of Shakespeare's *Measure for Measure*. Jesus urges his followers not to render judgment upon others unless they are certain that they can escape a similar scrutiny and condemnation:

> Judge not, that ye be not judged. For with what judgment ye judge, ye shall be judged: and with what measure ye mete, it shall be measure to you again. And why beholdest though the mote that is in thy brother's eye, but considerest not the beam that is in thine own eye? [*Matthew* 7:1–3].

The scriptural origin of Shakespeare's title initiates the theme of judgment within the drama where an arbitrator is urged to temper punishment with mercy, to create a reasonable balance where the law is neither scoffed at by transgressors nor inhumane in its rigorous and unyielding application. Angelo should have shown mercy to Claudio even before the ducal surrogate was implicated in the same crime, but even more so afterwards; thus he faces the same punishment as Claudio for the same crime. Several times, Angleo is asked to search his memory for those times when he may have been guilty of a similar offense so that he can practice the mercy that was formerly shown to him, but he cannot appreciate the analogy; he believes he has never demonstrated such weakness. He is too self-righteous to rule and must share in the universal iniquity of humanity before he has sufficient understanding of human imperfections, sufficient humility and compassion to discern those times when judgment should be mitigated. All others show mercy in the face of even greater iniquity. Isabella chooses lenity even after she believes her brother has been unjustly executed; Mariana pleads for Angelo's life even though he crudely broke their engagement when her family could not produce sufficient dowry, and Duke Vincentio commutes the death sentence of Lucio who slandered him, both transgressors are ultimately punished by being compelled to marry against their will, the only punishment that was reasonable in Claudio's apparent offence.

The rule of law under Adam Sutler's regime is as unmerciful as Lord Angelo's and for the same reason. Sutler is a self-righteous puritan who is elected to office on a law and order platform, whose rigidity is initially regarded as a necessity to redress the emergent conditions in his country, a proliferation of iniquity. However, the problems that he resolves are those of his own making — the threat of biological terrorism realized through his own inhumane actions and civil unrest resulting from the ultra conservative *zeitgeist* which he labored to create. Punishment without mercy is the hallmark of the Norsefire regime, even for those who have not transgressed. The narrative of the film emphasizes the Kafkaesque disconnect between crime and punishment. There is no relation between an individual's guilt and the fate that befalls him or her in Creedy's prisons. Even Finch complains of the disappearance of witnesses who are vital to uncovering the location and identity of V, the government's number one priority. In his final public broadcast, the same that plays during his own execution, Sutler offers no quarter to those who are believed to be in league with the enemy:

> Those caught tonight in violation of curfew will be considered in league with our enemy and will be prosecuted as a terrorist without leniency or exception.... Tonight I give you my most solemn vow that justice will be swift, it will be righteous, and it will be without mercy.

Even as those words are ringing in the air, Sutler is begging for his life, but V is no Duke Vincentio; V is the shadow of punishment and revenge conjured by the regime's own ruthlessness; he is the visitation of death. Most of V's VIP victims beg for a mercy that has been canceled and killed by their own judgments and their own inhumanity. Like Lord Angelo, the

Norsefire perpetrators are guilty of the very crimes which they seek to punish — civil disorder represented by the marauding and predatory Fingermen and terrorism embodied in the St Mary's viral attack — yet the hypocritical regime never pauses to contemplate its own mechanisms in the maintenance of order. Moreover, in the name of public safety, the Sutler government tyrannizes over and victimizes the very people it ostensibly seeks to protect. V is indeed merciless himself, as are all avengers, yet he does figure his own death into the equation of justice. He must die in order to restore the balance of punishment and mercy, and he leaves the final act of dissolution against the fascist government to Evey, recognizing that it may not be an appropriate and/or auspicious beginning for a new era of justice.

Conclusion

If space permitted and patience could be further taxed, many more Shakespearean thematics could be pursued in the interests of tracing *V for Vendetta's* intertext. These include but are not limited to V's meta-theatricality as well as the medieval literary traditions that were commonplace in the Shakespearean drama, such as the "mirror for magistrates," the *danse macabre*, and the *de cassibus* tradition. However, one thing is clear within the materials covered here: Shakespeare plays an important and often openly acknowledged role in shaping the plot, thematics, and characterization of the film. This English narrative is viewed through the Shakespearean lens, the most English of influences, demonstrating that a drama in English cannot avoid exploring its debt to the Shakespearean paradigm even inadvertently. Shakespeare is the English cipher and the uniquely English mythology; he shapes and elucidates the narrative, both fictional and historical; he is the ghost within the linguistic machine, defining usage through invention, analogy, and antithesis; he constructs our humanity through his memorable, engaging, and powerful characters, and he leaves just enough undefined to invite our lived and literary participation. Shakespeare is the shadow that skulks in the dim corners of our texts periodically popping forth only to recede into the darkness again or, by virtue of his powerful cultural/gravitational pull, inexorably drawing lighter narrative objects into his spin and depositing them in an entirely new dimension of meaning.

Eight

"Monuments of Unaging Intellect"
The Shadows in V's Gallery

In his poem "Sailing to Byzantium," William Butler Yeats imagines the ancient city of Byzantium as an aesthetic treasury where the relics and masterworks of the ancient world were preserved during the Dark Ages when Europeans were actively hostile toward classicism. The speaker of the poem develops a contrast between Byzantium and "That country," the latter ostensibly referring to Ireland, the country of the poet's origin. However, the variance between Byzantium and "that country" can also be defined by binary oppositions — youth/age and body/soul (or perhaps more appropriately body/mind). "That country" is "caught in the sensual music" celebrating the pleasures of the flesh, pursuing propagation via intense physical passion, yet in the midst of carnality and constant change, the participants neglect the "monuments of unaging intellect," or the productions of spiritual and intellectual pursuits. Those "caught" in the "sensual music" fail to recognize the transcendent, that which survives both the sagging and the decay of the flesh. "Old men" no longer preoccupied with the pursuit of sexual gratification should turn to lofty spiritual, intellectual, and aesthetic preoccupations in order to find purpose within their lives. They must embrace the transcendent life of the mind, both by imagining a fulfillment beyond the gratification of the primal appetites and by "studying" examples of the mind/spirit's "magnificence."

Byzantium is a border land or a transitional space between a collection of overdetermined antitheses, not least of which are mind and body.

Byzantium, where the riches of the ancients as well as two and a half millennia of Western culture are enclosed, sustained, gilded, and canonized, signifies the treasury of the West, but also the gateway to the East. This directional component implies a transition between youth (East) and age (West). Byzantium is a place of ecstasy, where the "sages" stand in "god's holy fire" and the speaker himself, swept up in the "gyre," is transformed into a visionary or a "monument of unaging intellect." The religious ecstasy of Byzantium replaces the sexual ecstasy of "That country" where old men can no longer dwell. Byzantium also evokes the unification of West and the Near East via Christianity. The third stanza of the poem, set in the church of Hagia Sophia (Holy Wisdom), reminds us that in Byzantium the Christian Church resides amid the Muslim call to prayer. Its placement in this marginal, even liminal, space, suggests the necessity of preservation, the boundaries of self and other so nearly transgressed that a strident effort to retain a sense of identity is requisite to its own preservation. This metaphor is continued in the contrast between Byzantium and "That country," the latter inimical to the former, thus necessitating that the former "clap its hands and sing and louder sing for every tatter in his mortal dress." The old man's identification with Byzantium is comprehensive; he longs to be swept into the "artifice of eternity," to escape time and mutability, becoming a golden bird, unchanging, who sings to the denizens of Byzantium and whose sight and insight encompasses a trans-historical vantage.

Yeats' poem is the key that unlocks the literal and figural treasury of *V for Vendetta* — The Shadow Gallery. The content of the gallery includes art, artifacts, performances, and music, most objects rescued from the vaults of the Ministry of Objectionable Materials. Thus just like the curators in Byzantium's treasury, V preserves his cultural heritage in a period of regressive and repressive philistinism, a dark age that includes the suppression of cultural artifacts representative of more open, creative, and progressive ages, particularly the societies that have formerly occupied that land which now harshly suppresses beauty, dissent, and intellectual pleasure. The Sutler regime is one adverse to the artistic temperament, and while we actually see him produce no painting, sculpture, music, or dance, V is, nevertheless, an artist, in all probability an actor. The gallery may suggest V's vicarious engagement with life. So horribly disfigured that he must wear a mask, V lives vicariously through those activities captured in the multitude of frames surrounding him. Unable to live life directly, like the Lady of Shalott or the old man in Yeat's poem, V must settle for aesthetic stimulation and the ecstasy of retribution and gore that defines his monomaniacal pursuit. The content of the shadow gallery can even be understood as the interior of V's mind, fraught with beauty, pleasure, rage, pain, and loss. From this perspective Evey's entrance into the shadow gallery would constitute a phantasmagoric journey to the interior of the revolutionary and vengeful consciousness together with its many passions, a journey to the center of the artistic temperament. Indeed the paintings and artifacts within the gallery often seem to be externalizing subjective states or offering analogues to characterization and exposition to narrative. This may well be homage to the origins of the narrative in the graphic novel format, one that requires evaluation of both the visual and linguistic stimulation and particularly one in which the creators sought to minimize the amount of dialogue, allowing the pictures to tell the story (Moore and Lloyd 273).

The Collection

The trans-historical content of V's gallery is analogous to that of Yeats' Byzantium. The content of the latter exists unchanging in the ancient archive of the mind or the collective unconsciousness, speaking to countless generations — aesthetes and philistines alike — preserving and subsequently disseminating the collective heritage of Western civilization. Byzantium is both memory and desire, looking forward and backward. It defines the present through study of the past and anticipation of the future. Thus each moment in time is a negotiation of before and after, a "multiverse" in which a multitude of micro- and macro-narrative universes coexist and interact. V waits, trapped between two worlds, obsessed with past pain and loss, his experiences propelling him toward his climactic and apocalyptic future in which birth and death, past and future, high and low, male and female, and good and bad meet in an instant. V, like the historical personage he mimics, has no time for the present represented in romantic desire. The *V for Vendetta* narrative begins with a story of loss, in which Guy Fawkes is hanged in full view of his lady. The idea continues into the *Monte Cristo* narrative, about which Evey observes that

Mercedes was pitiful because the faux-Count loved revenge more than he loved her, and the idea recurs a third time in the romantic attachment of V and Evey. She attempts to dissuade V from indulging his self-destructive compulsion to make war against the establishment, but like Evey, who eventually realizes that principles are sometimes more important than life, V must pursue his course in spite of the inevitability of his own annihilation. He must abandon her for revolution, and her consolation lies in her decision to complete the work for which he gave up his life.

The Shadow Gallery is a place of inspiration, repose, and preparation. V surrounds himself not only with objects of beauty, but with reminders of his monomaniacal pursuit. The artifacts contained within the refurbished tube station constitute a reminder of the glories of civilizations past. Within his display cases he includes artifacts from ancient Egypt, Greece, Rome, India, and China. East meets West within the collection, North meets South, and the present rubs shoulders with the cradle of civilization. The implicit universality of the artifacts generates a variety of potential significations, suggesting the trans-historical contest between oppression and liberation, between democracy and tyranny, or between progression and regression, a carnival of political contestation in which the forces of liberty are pitted against the forces of restraint with one or the other gaining the upper hand only briefly and only within a limited region of influence. Within the political spectrum of Moore and Lloyd's graphic novel, the contest rages between fascism and anarchy, an excess of control and restriction to counter a surplus of liberty. This ancient struggle places the events of *V for Vendetta* within a historical context, one that could signify either futility or necessity. Emphasizing the ubiquitous presence of a conflict can have the paradoxical impact either of making resistance irrelevant in the present with the knowledge that change is inevitable or of urging immediate engagement in the perennial struggle to make life tolerable through the acquisition or maintenance of civil liberties. The notion that perpetual warfare is not a danger but a safeguard is one of the ideas that *V for Vendetta* shares with the great British dystopia *1984* (Orwell). The process may also refer to the Christ/Anti-Christ historical dialectic of Yeats' "The Second Coming," one which emphasizes the relativity of value systems. But the allusions to the past have other pertinent qualities, reminding the audience of those civilizations which have not survived — the same represented by the gallery's physical relics. This angle suggests that England too could pass into history if it does not resurrect and safeguard its constitutional ideals. The Shadow Gallery parallels Byzantium's "monuments of unaging intellect," insofar as it operates as memorial to glorious civilizations of the past that have much to offer for the direction and purpose of the present and the future. These civilizations may have passed into history, but the records of their pleasures, struggles, successes, blunders, agonies and ideals are still accessible through the tomes and relics they left behind. We live in an accumulation of the past, and V has created one of its gathering houses.

Many or even most of the artifacts collected in the gallery were formerly on display in the numerous museums of contemporary London — The Tate, The Tate Modern, The National Gallery, The National Portrait Gallery, The Victoria and Albert Museum, and The British Museum — and while the objects arrived in V's possession via the appropriations of and from official government censors, the Ministry of Objectionable Materials, they nevertheless represent Britain's glorious and not too distant past, though one defunct well before the apocalyptic events that fueled the rise of Norsefire. I refer specifically to Britain's imperialistic ambitions of the eighteenth, nineteenth, and early twentieth centuries, the same that catalyzed the accumulation of artifacts within the British Museum(s). Having pursued, appropriated, purchased, and pilfered the valuable cultural artifacts of many of the world's great civilizations, the British have created an extraordinary collection of cultural treasures, a collection that acts as a reminder of a time when Britain's influence included global dominance. Evey's incredulity at V's willingness to purloin the objects that he displays in his home is quaintly naïve, since many of the artistic masterworks owned by the British people were attained under less than honorable circumstances. Witness the fate of the Elgin Marbles, which Lord Elgin, taking advantage of the Ottoman Turks' control of Greece, appropriated and removed to England in 1806. The marbles, many of which are presently housed in the British Museum, have been the object of multiple legal challenges, demanding their return to Athens.

The visual allusions to Britain's imperialistic past on display in V's home generate a gallery of significations. They suggest a time when England was open to the rest of the world, interacting freely and sometimes even liberally with neighbors near and far, a clear counterpoint to the nationalistic paranoia and xenophobia of *V for Vendetta*'s England.

London has always been an international city with merchants and immigrants from Europe and the rest of the world. Norsefire's policy seeks to extricate the country from international relations, even from its former colonies and other Anglophone nations. The country turns inward out of fear of extra-national threats and influences. Prothero is not welcoming of the food-laden American ship that seeks to trade for medical supplies, and he speaks contemptuously of "Muslims" and "foreigners," indicating that the country is well rid of them. V's appreciation for diverse cultures, a sentiment echoed in Gordon's own gallery, suggests an international England gone into hiding; he is a reminder of the time before the great paranoia inspired by the nuclear holocaust that preceded the opening of the narrative and the subsequent civil unrest, not to mention the St. Mary's viral attacks. V's obvious wealth suggests the duality of maintaining a free and open society or a liberal democracy; openness brings prosperity and danger, but perhaps more of the former than the latter.

The preservation of aesthetic treasures within what seems to be an underground bunker is in all probably an allusion to the safeguarding of national treasures during World War II's Battle for Britain. Works from many British museums were stored in tube stations and underground bunkers so that they could be protected from destruction by air raids and/or pillaging in the event of an invasion by the German army. While fascism spends its rage on the streets above, the artifacts of civilization, of creation rather than destruction, are safely preserved below, preserved for humanity from the philistinism of a historical Hitler or an imaginary Sutler, waiting for a social and cultural reawakening free from the threat of destruction and conquest. The imagery may also suggest one of the most despicable oversights in America's ill-considered campaign in Iraq: the military's philistine indifference to the priceless cultural artifacts of Baghdad's museums, artifacts from ancient Sumer, one of the oldest civilizations on earth. The museum was ransacked and the displays stolen or destroyed in the heady days following the fall Sadam's regime. Colin Powell defended the failure of the American forces to safeguard these materials (despite urgent and repeated appeals of the world art community), expressing feigned incredulity that the Iraqis would raid their own national treasures, a statement of transcendent naiveté, considering how quickly Americans would do the same following the collapse of our national law enforcement infrastructure. V embodies the aesthete whose aims and values exceed political expedience, focusing on the preservation of culture every bit as much as the restoration of government.

Within the gallery, yet another cultural binary collapses. While we have touched upon national/international, singular/diverse, democracy/ tyranny and domestic/foreign, we have yet to cite the fusion of high and low cultures, a process that is taking place at every level of the narrative and meta-narrative. Perhaps this union of the exalted and the base is related to the diachronic features of the displays. Mystified and obfuscated by the passage of time, cultural artifacts formerly indicative of popular culture can be transformed into high art or culture. This is the process undergone by Shakespeare's plays over the past four hundred years, which at the time of their initial production were one of the popular forms of entertainment, the early modern equivalent to cinema or television, but which progressively became associated with the moneyed and the cultured elite. The historical and linguistic knowledge requisite to the understanding and appreciation of Shakespeare became increasingly rare, largely limited to those with university educations. One might also consider the parallel historical odyssey of antiques; a toy which at the time of its creation and circulation would be of little worth, save for the brief period of distraction that it offers a child, may over a period as brief as fifty years assume a far greater significance, increasing in value, both economically and culturally, until one finds it displayed on the shelves of the finest homes for the purposes of nostalgia, decoration, or valuation. Similarly, V's shadow gallery displays many of the aesthetic masterworks of world civilization alongside a jukebox, butterfly shadowboxes, movie posters, contemporary furniture, and film projection equipment. V's taste ranges across the globe, the millennia, and the cultural hierarchies, his imagination unfettered by class distinctions. He is fond of both old and more recent movies, a high/low dichotomy also collapsed at the level of meta-narrative. The construction of *V for Vendetta*, the film, upon a 1934 movie classic *The Count of Monte Cristo*, starring Robert Donat, can be understood as an intertextual leveling of cultural source and influence, as well as a collapse of cinematic genre. McTeigue's film, an action flick aimed largely at adolescents, is founded upon a romantic film classic that even in its day may not have been of interest to teenagers, the principal consumers of cinema and particularly action cinema. When one also considers that the film is the translation of a graphic novel into cinematic narrative, the high/low binary is again transgressed. While the film does seek a youthful audience, it also adopts many narrative elements obviously aimed at a more educated adult audience. As they did with *The Matrix*, the Wachowski brothers sought to create a film that could appeal to multiple age groups by offering both visual and intellectual stimulation. The music of V's Jukebox serves as a counterpoint to the content of the gallery, and the other musical selections covered in the film suggest a mixing of genres and tastes. V and Evey listen to Julie London's and Arthur Hamilton's *Cry Me a River* (1953), a blues classic that at the time of its recording would have been considered a less important musical genre than *The 1812 Overture*, also featured in the film. To add to the eclecticism, the sound track includes a recording from the 1960s badboys, turned ghastly mainstream geriatric rockers, The Rolling Stones, specifically *Street Fighting Man*. There are also recordings from the contemporary alternative group Spiritualized, verbal and visual allusions to the 1970s punk rock phenomenon The Sex Pistols, as well as a selection of less memorable artists.

The Paintings

The objects that crowd the walls and corners of V's home are not selected at random. They participate in the narrative, commenting and interpreting, offering access to the characters' interiorities. They can be roughly, but not uniformly, categorized into those that comment on V's origins and aims, those that illustrate Evey's options, and those that silently interpret the social and historical milieu of the narrative's post-apocalyptic setting. While the paintings share the trans-historical dimension of the Shadow Gallery's statuary, offering selections from many artistic movements, there is a greater limitation on the chronology, the selections beginning with the early modern period or the Renaissance and ending with the late twentieth century postmodernism. The paintings are also less expansive in their geographical references. There are no identifiable examples of non–Western painting, as all works were selected from the traditional canon of European/American art, but the collection is nevertheless representative of a variety of aesthetic schools.

The rubric for the interpretation of the Shadow Gallery is passively captured in the prominent display of Jan Van Eyck's *Arnolfini Wedding*

Portrait, which insists upon the cautious and methodical analysis of visual details in order to generate an understanding of larger cultural and historical processes exterior to the canvas. The close analysis of van Eyck's canvas by art historians serves as a model for the interaction between the film audience and the carefully decorated set of V's dwelling. Van Eyck's panel offers a variety of enigmatic or iconographic details that invite interpretation, such as the chandelier with a single burning candle and the mirror with the "stations of the cross" and the reverse image of the betrothal scene, which reveals the presence of witnesses to the ceremony. The terrier, the bed, the hand gestures of the couple, the shoes and more have been the subject of scholarly speculation in the effort to crack the enigmatic code of this single moment frozen in time. Controversy has raged over the presumed pregnancy of the lady and the exact nature of the match that is being made within the clasped hands of the participants. The painting creates a meta-cinematic dimension within the film, teaching the audience how to read or analyze visual imagery, and while it is indeed true that only those who already know how to conduct such analysis may notice this feature, the van Eyck reference, nevertheless, signals that similar investigations of the Shadow Gallery may prove fruitful, encouragement which may be necessary since the film could easily be dismissed as an action flick without substantive intellectual content. The painting urges exploration between material objects, characterization, and context.

One might well assume that the visual stimuli within V's home are definitive of the person who selected it from the voluminous collections of England's priceless artifacts. One might assume that he opted to appropriate particular works because he connected with them intellectually or emotionally, or because he perceived them to be pertinent reminders of his pursuit of revenge. The first two paintings that the film audience sees when Evey emerges from V's bedroom are directly related to the revenger's origins and fortunes. The first is William Blake's *Elohim Creating Adam* (1795), a watercolor that is part of the permanent collection of the Tate Gallery in London. The image depicts the winged deity creating Adam from the primordial chaos. However, the depiction is not orthodox in its theology since Adam's lower torso emerges from the coils of a serpent. Elohim lays his hand upon Adam's head, no doubt transmitting the spark of life, and the newly created man assumes the demeanor of an ecstatic (mouth open, arms outstretched), dazzled and ravished by the divine spirit.

The serpent coils contradict the orthodox article of faith that Adam and Eve were created innocent with the free will to remain upright or to fall. Blake's Adam is clearly either already fallen or doomed to the same, entangled in the devil's coils even at birth. Blake may believe himself to be following Milton in this particularly heretical line. Blake was the inspiration for what became the satanic school of Milton criticism, the same that held Satan to be the hero of *Paradise Lost*. Scholarship on *Paradise Lost* has suggested that Milton's actual sympathies lie with the devil, the spirit of rebellion that counters tyranny; he has the admirable qualities of the epic hero — an indomitable will, a willingness to endure any measure of suffering to interdict and counter God's goodness (Grace 117–119; Fish 138). He sacrifices and spends himself in a hopeless cause, the underdog and the romantic hero who prefers death before domination. The belief that Adam and Eve were already fallen is derived from the self-defensive rumination of Milton's God at the beginning of Book III, where he strives, perhaps too stridently to demonstrate that the fate of Adam and Eve is not his fault even though he always knew that they would fall, a revelation that suggests they were fated to the same, since one cannot logically contradict divine will, design, or foreknowledge. Milton wrestles with this paradox: how can God create Adam and Eve, knowing that they will fall, while simultaneously suggesting that they have the free will to remain upright?

Blake's painting comments on the measure of inevitability of V's course in life. He was created flawed, either at birth or through the cruel ministration of the Larkhill staff. If V is coded as homosexual in spite of his affection for Evey and Valerie, an argument for which there is no small amount of supporting evidence, then the creation of Adam already fallen and destined for punishment could refer to the contemporary theory of the homosexual gene, the result of prenatal conditions that lie outside of the individual's control. From this perspective, the condemnation of alternative sexual identities by conservative Christians, such as Adam Sutler and the Norsefire regime, appears to be particularly irrational, unjust, and indefensible. The homosexual is punished for a difference that she or he cannot control or change. Even if V is not supposed to be gay, the painting may signify homosexuality irregardless since the motivation for his revenge is unquestionably the maltreatment of a lesbian movie star, Valerie Page, at the hands of the nationalistic and religious extremists. In addition, the painting does not have to refer to the neonatal condition of the action hero, but could refer to the moment when he was born as a revenger. Repeatedly, he refers to the conditions at Larkhill that created him — the inhuman experiments, the discovery of Valerie's autobiography, the subtle machination of the humble gardener in room V, and the devastating explosion and fire that disfigured him. He complains, "What was done to me created me," adding "What they did was monstrous," to which Evey replies, "And they created a monster." The forces that shaped his identity, or lack thereof, ignited the fires of their own immolation, manufacturing the opposition to and eventual destruction of their own power. The ecstatic qualities of Blake's Adam suggest V's remarkable prescience, the same that allows him to manipulate the despicable characters around him, those who are eventually "hoist upon their own petards."

The painting adjacent to Blake's creation of Adam and the second to be viewed when Evey emerges from V's bedroom is Andrea Mantegna's *St. Sebastian*, painted between 1457 and 1458 and one of the works of V's gallery that is not an appropriation from the permanent collection of any London museum, but is, instead, the property of the Kunsthistorisches Museum in Vienna. While Blake's painting comments upon the revenger's origin, the Mantegna image foretells his end. The St. Sebastian depicted in the shadow gallery of Moore and Lloyd's graphic novel is *The Martyrdom of St. Sebastian*, painted by Antonio and Piero del Pollaiuolo in 1475. The decision to swap paintings could be motivated by a variety of issues. From a practical standpoint, the alteration may be the result of the producer's inability to obtain permission to use the Pollaiuolo piece, or perhaps the work was on loan or in restoration at the time of the production. A more interesting explanation might be that the Mantegna piece was more appropriate aesthetically for the film narrative. The Mantegna canvas does seem pertinent to the melancholy ambiance of McTeigue's film. While a crowd of archers surrounds the figure of St. Sebastian in the Pollaiuolo piece, the martyred figure of Mantegna's canvas is struck full of holes and left to die alone. The solitary suffering of the martyred saint suggests the existential dread of V, who faces an awful task alone as well as a lonely and melancholy yet long awaited death. V lives only for revenge, and the companionship that he finds in Evey is an incidental and unlooked for boon, but one that is as much burden as benefit since passion for life can interfere with V's pursuit of revenge. Mantegna's painting captures the moments after the archers have gone; indeed the canvas is completely bereft of other people save for two men at a distance walking away from the site of the slaying. These men may be archers fleeing the scene, or they may be indifferent travelers ignorant of the momentous events that have transpired a short distance away. In addition, the figure of Sebastian is tied to a ruined classical arch and column, and stands amid the fragments of a ruined civilization. The pieces of broken statuary in the image include heads, feet, and torsos. Behind the figure, a broken frieze of a family leans against a fragmented wall.

The iconography of the painting that is useful in this analysis is abundant. The broken wall and the battered statuary suggest the decline or even destruction of culture and civilization, a cause for lamentation in *V for Vendetta*, a film that obsesses over the decline, degradation, and imminent destruction of the Western cultural heritage by the puritanical and philistine aesthetic of a cruel nationalistic regime. The fragments surrounding Sebastian are clearly classical in origin; thus their destruction implies the ill-considered purges of those antiquities of pagan origin by the overly zealous churchmen and faithful of the Middle Ages. The blacklisting and censorship of offensive materials under Sutler's regime is by implication equated to the Dark Ages; he is engaged in an art purge that will be reviled by subsequent, more progressive societies committed to preservation of the humanities. Moreover, the image of the saint himself signifies V's struggles at multiple levels. For example, Sebastian was executed because he defended two Christians — Marcellinus and Mark — who had been condemned by the Emperor Diolcetian, and thus he divulged his sympathies for the fledgling religion, an indiscretion that resulted in his execution (Kaye 89). Similarly, V, having survived the St. Mary's virus and escaped the Larkhill internment camp, risks his own safety by seeking revenge on behalf of those murdered in the genocidal medical programs. One might even argue from a provincial point of view that his obsession with vindicating Valerie Page suggests his clandestine sympathies for the homosexual cause. In other words, the decision to risk so much on behalf of a lesbian would, for many, code V as homosexual himself. While this alone is indeed a rash and even homophobic assumption, there is much additional evidence to support the association between V and gay men. As mentioned in a previous chapter, St. Sebastian is a gay icon, his ecstatic martyrdom sometimes even equated to the sado-masochistic (s/m) pleasures of a small portion of the gay male population (Kaye 87). However, even without the s/m potential, the image of the tortured, athletic, and semi-nude body is an object of camp veneration for gay men seeking spiritual role models for the social ostracism and discrimination that they faced and still face today. The arrows that puncture Sebastian's flesh can be understood as the "slings and arrows of outrageous fortune," to which the gay and lesbian communities are commonly subjected whether through defamation, discrimination, or assault. However, the image of the martyred saint has been considered too passive a demise for the post–Stonewall, socially activated gay, lesbian, bisexual, and transgendered (GLBT) communities (Kaye 98). Perhaps, V is then the rehabilitated martyr who does not passively allow his flesh to be punctured, but who instead annihilates his persecutors in large numbers before he succumbs to many bullet wounds.

St. Sebastian is identified as the patron saint of plague, an issue that has a particular relevance to *V for Vendetta* in which the government has unleashed a devastating virus upon its own population. V is the single subject of the Larkhill experiments to survive the pathogen, and from his blood is created the serum or vaccine that protects the remaining population from the disease. In the Mantegna canvas, the wreckage of the architectural structures, the twin figures receding in the distance, and the solitary image of the saint invoke the devastations of plague, including depopulation through death and flight as well as the solitary suffering and hopelessness of the afflicted. The arrows that pierce the hide of the Saint are indicative of the divine wrath traditionally associated with plague and of the boils or lesions that cover the bodies of plague victims (Kaye 89), and in the context of *V for Vendetta*, the equation between sickness and punishment evokes the political/religious firestorm of the early AIDS epidemic. However, V is a secular figure, and the revenge is leveled against those, such as Prothero, who cited "godlessness" as the cause of disease when the pathogen had a very human source, not in the iniquity of the afflicted but in the villainy of the ambitious. V is the patron saint of plague insofar as he punishes those who willfully unleashed the same on their countrymen, and he offers his own blood (both through his death and through his antibodies) in the salvation of the suffering Englishmen.

Mantegna's *St. Sebastian* shares with Blake's painting the ecstatic imagery of the mystic/religious tradition. The saint is punctured by an arrow entering his lower jaw and emerging through his forehead just between the eyes. The upward gaze of the figure and the serene expression suggest the contemplation or perhaps the invocation of heaven by the dying martyr. His faith assures his place beside the divine seat. The pair of paintings may evoke the raptures of birth and death or the bliss of creation and destruction, both moments illustrating humanity's union with a divine source. V's actions signal a beginning and an ending; when one political ideology falls, another enjoys its inception. Viewed from a non-secular perspective, the revelatory imagery of paintings may suggest the operation of a teleology, or the unfolding of a divine plan that favors democracy and justice. Here V is liberating the country from a hypocritical puritan and restoring it to a path sanctioned by divine predestination. More convincingly for a film that satirizes religious posturing within politics, the ecstatic insight suggests V's political ideals, not religion but secular humanism; they inspire a vision for humanity that cherishes human values. Thus V is a visionary and a revolutionary, and one bold enough to create his own moral and ethical priorities; he does not need to have them dictated by the overly rigorous interpretation of an ancient and increasingly inapplicable tome. V's vengeance against those who victimize and exploit humanity is merciless, while his compassion for non-violent human frailty seems boundless.

Another painting within the shadow gallery that seems to have a particular relevance to V's character is Francis Bacon's painting *Study of the Human Body*, which is featured in the movie room. The distorted image of a human torso displayed on a table with a garish red background suggests the postmodern fragmentation of the self that is widely apparent in the film — text and meta-text. V's physical condition, his lack of face and eyes, his scorched body have resulted in a physical dysphoria, an alienation from his own image, one that necessitates the creation of an identity that is forever shifting; he constructs a "face to meet the faces that he meets." His condition is indicative of the undifferentiated self of the Lacanian pre-mirror stage in which the infant has no sense of a unified subjectivity (Lee 25). The subject is merely a collection of disassociated physical functions. The fiction of a unified ego — the imaginary — is achieved when the subject sees him- or herself in the mirror in the company of the mother and begins to believe that he can achieve and maintain a condition of pleasure and completion (Ragland-Sullivan 275). The figure in Bacon's painting is somewhat undifferentiated, merely an abstraction of the human form and particularly that part associated with the lower bodily functions.

The image may suggest the revenger's disparate qualities, none of which add up to a whole, his degraded body image, his appreciation for aesthetic beauty, or his penchant for progressive or revolutionary politics. The gallery itself constitutes the pieces from which V, and by extension all of his countrymen, compose and construct a national, gendered, ethnic, intellectual, and economic self. The distorted faces of Bacon's other canvases may also be invoked by the presence of the *Study of the Human Body*. The artist's portraits invariably include a paint smear for a face or jumbled features, a technique that may allude to V's own burned visage which is too distorted to be countenanced. Moreover, Bacon's art is a combination of intense beauty and nightmarish imagery, a combination that would seem to capture the rhythms of V's own experience.

As mentioned previously, much of the pictorial art in V's home includes imagery of women in distress. Ironically, the gallery comments in more detail about Evey than it does about V. The three most prominent paintings in the gallery offer a series of traditional life options for women, all of which are negated by her revolutionary course. The first and most ostentatious piece is Titian's *Bacchus and Ariadne*, painted between 1520 and 1523, and another piece of the permanent collection at London's National Gallery. The content of the painting is based upon Catullus' *Carmino* and Ovid's *Ars Amatoria* (Hope 67). The daughter of King Minos, Ariadne assisted Theseus in his escape from the labyrinth, but the hero was not going to allow gratitude to dictate his actions. He abandoned Ariadne on the island of Naxos where she was discovered and consoled by Bacchus/Dionysius, the god of wine, drunken revelry, orgy, and fertility. Titian's canvas depicts a parade of Bacchus' riotous followers who discover the distraught Ariadne on the shore watching Theseus' ship. She is rescued from harm by Bacchus who leaps out of his leopard drawn chariot to save her from ravishment by the fawns, satyrs, and maenads in his train. Upon their marriage, Bacchus presented Ariadne with a golden crown which was transformed into a circle of stars at her death, a celestial anomaly that can be seen in the upper left corner of Titan's canvas. The scenario depicted in Titian's painting suggests Evey's peril at the beginning of the film; she is the imminent victim of ravishment by reckless and unprincipled strangers until V comes to her rescue. She like Aridane is on her own, the subject of betrayal by a potential lover, perhaps an allusion to V's mishandling of Evey in the interrogation scenes. Aside from that, he like Theseus has placed the lady in danger by roping her into his vendetta and forsaking her through his death. The vulnerability of Evey in the moment that she is accosted by the Fingermen and rescued by V is also captured in the painting; she is alone and inexperienced and is even initially fearful of her rescuer. Ariadne, agreeing to be Bacchus' wife, constitutes a surrender to intemperate sensuality and riotous living, and in this sense V has little in common with his mythological analogue, save for an appreciation of life's sensory pleasures. However, V's violent agenda is attuned to the cycle of death and rebirth symbolized by Bacchus/Dionysius, the fertility god. V's activities will destroy one culture and, in the process, (re)engender another, and like Bacchus, he will become attached to Evey.

The announcement of Prothero's death in the BTN broadcast evokes a frank conversation between V and Evey in which the latter discovers V's murderous resolution, and the emotions of the speakers are translated through the image of Titian's *Bacchus and Ariadne* which is visible in the background. As they talk, Evey's shock, incredulity, and apprehension are mirrored and elucidated by the canvas on which Ariadne attempts to flea the fearful onslaught of bacchanalian revelers. After having assisted an inconstant man who then abandoned her, Ariadne must have been relieved that Bacchus turned out to be generous and beneficent. Similarly Evey wants and even needs to trust V, but she is fearful that she has been inadvertently allied with a madman and perhaps even a betrayer. However, like Bacchus, who makes Ariadne immortal by placing her crown of stars in the sky, V will thrust Evey into history through her participation in his vindictive and revolutionary designs.

The next painting in the series, and the one that has been most frequently named in reviews of the film, is Waterhouse's *The Lady of Shalott*, which operates as an alternative function within the context of this chapter. Waterhouse's painting depicts a scene from the Tennyson poem of the same name, in which a lady, trapped in a tower, ceaselessly weaves a tapestry, but is unable to look directly out her window at the world she depicts in her art. She must observe the world through a mirror exclusively because there is a curse upon her through which she and her art will be destroyed if she ever interacts directly with the outside world. The lady, distracted by the passage of Lancelot on the road to Camelot, cannot forbear gazing out the window, an act for which she is punished with a lingering death.

Waterhouse's painting captures the moment when the Lady enters the boat that will carry her to Camelot in search of her Knight and of wholeness or happiness. Nevertheless, she dies before she reaches the port, and the clueless Lancelot remains ignorant of the role that he played in her destruction.

If Titian's work suggests the orgiastic or intemperate potential of the solitary female, the victim of male aggression, Waterhouse's painting implies the lady's deliberate isolation, one that allows her freedom to pursue her own destiny separately from that of men. The traditional roles of women in the three portraits — the virgin, whore, and wife — are deconstructed within the cinematic text. The Lady of Shalott's cloistered life is unfulfilling, and her sudden and self-destructive fascination with Lancelot suggests a self-annihilating need to attach herself to a man even if it means her death or the death of her art; the sexist implications, of course, suggest that women are not happy or fulfilled unless they are attached to a dominant male. The circumstances of the canvas capture the collateral impact of V's incidental encounter with Evey. She appears to be completely happy with the rhythms of her life until she twice encounters the revenger and is subsequently and inadvertently drawn into his destructive machinations. The Waterhouse canvas serves as an allegory of Evey's activation as a revolutionary. She abandons her safe and dull existence for a chance to participate in an action that is historic in its consequences. Her activation also includes an opportunity for love if not romance. She is apparently drawn to the potential for excitement represented by V.

The Waterhouse reference that implicitly equates V to the medieval knight who lures the Lady out of isolation and complacency may have some depth. The popular notion of the knight, particularly one of Lancelot's qualities, includes an ethical dimension, the knight committed to the prosecution of injustice and particularly to the protection of mistreated women. He wanders the realm searching for violations of chivalry and corrects the abuses through trial by combat. The knight's connection to V is not difficult to glean. The revenger seeks out and punishes injustice — as demonstrated in his serial murders of state officials as well as his rescue of Evey from the Fingermen — as a part of a larger commitment to the rehabilitation of the state and the return of England to a rational and just society, perhaps even a liberal democracy. Like the medieval knight, V prosecutes injustice by exchanging strokes with the foe. The justice system in England is corrupted; there can be no redress of grievances through the courts, a frustration illustrated in the destruction of the Old Bailey. V also shares Lancelot's romantic indiscretion, not that he sleeps with Evey (or anyone else for that matter), but that he allows himself to become romantically attached just before he is expected to sacrifice himself for honor and for the good of the nation. Beyond his connection to Evey, V's revenge is motivated by decision to obtain justice for another idealized lady — Valerie Page.

If the Titian canvas represents Evey's potential for sensuality and release and the Waterhouse the impulse toward isolation, chastity, and inhibition, then the third canvas in the prominent series — Van Eyck's *Arnolfini Wedding Portrait*— suggests a compromise between the preceding two, completing the sequence of traditional options for women — whore, virgin, and wife. The Van Eyck portrait alludes to wedded bliss and does so even if it only depicts a betrothal rather than a secret marital ritual as has been long conjectured (Hall 8). Indeed, the painting may be more relevant if it does indeed depict a betrothal ceremony since the two lovers, like the images on the side of the *Grecian Urn*, are frozen in time at a moment immediately prior to fulfillment, forever happy and fraught with anticipation, but never sated. V and Evey only dance and protest their love for each other; they are not even capable of meeting flesh to flesh since V cannot allow his to be countenanced. They are only romantic potential as he is, in effect, a dead thing resurrected to carry out his program of justice, after which he will disappear; however, spiritually they are united in a common goal at the conclusion of the film — the creation of fundamental political change. The van Eyck is even placed next to the juke box where V and Evey dance to Julie London's performance of "Cry Me a River," a song which continues the thematic of lost love. Evey would have the avenger quit his self-destructive pursuit and embrace love and romance, but he has a greater ambition to change the world. The reluctant lover, the audience of the song, believes love is too "plebeian," a term which suggests a political agenda, perhaps even a Marxist point of view, which keeps the lover from surrendering himself completely to his lady. Thus the song continues the thematic of women whose men care more about politics than love. The *Arnolfini Portrait* suggests a union between V and Evey, but not a marital bond, rather a bond of love and common purpose. Moreover, the passive lady in the betrothal image, who awaits the attentions of her man, is antithetical to Evey's more activated approach to the world. The image of the bed in the Van Eyck canvas and the potential pregnancy of the lady suggest that the role of the consort is procreation, a confinement to the domestic sphere. Evey, however, will not be so limited; she will join her partner in the revolution.

The Shadow Gallery contains other images that depict the fate of women who are destroyed because they inadvertently became engaged in politics. As mentioned previously, the images of Ophelia and Lady Jane Grey hang in V's dressing room. Delaroche's 1833 painting of *The Execution of Lady Jane Grey* hangs just above V's vanity. The image depicts the final moments of Jane's life, a young woman who was selected to become queen following the death of Edward VI so that the council and Jane's family could guarantee the continuation of a Protestant monarchy and also act as the power behind the throne. Jane was reluctant to assume the throne, and the refusal of the English people to accept her rule was immediately apparent. Jane stood sixth in the succession to the monarchy, as the eldest daughter of Henry VIII's eldest sister. Despite being crowned in London, she was rapidly overthrown and imprisoned by Mary Tudor. Lady Jane and her husband, Guilford Dudley, were not, however, executed until they were the focus of an insurrection that sought to overthrow Queen Mary. The image of Lady Jane on the scaffold awaiting execution suggests the peril of being swept up in political intrigue and rebellion. It is particularly pertinent to Evey's predicament insofar as both women had no intention of becoming embroiled in a struggle for power and yet their inadvertent involvement was tantamount to a death sentence. Evey is condemned by the Sutler power structure simply by virtue of her accidental association with a so-called terrorist, and no evidence vindicating her is sufficient to eradicate the initial assumption of her guilt and complicity. The briefest glimpse of a corner of Millais' *Ophelia* is sufficient to invoke the tragic tale of Shakespeare's heroine. Ophelia drowns because she is too mad to understand her perilous predicament, and her madness is the result of a conflict between her personal loyalties. Hamlet, the man she loves, kills her father and is sent away to England. Her sanity is tested by the conflict of duties represented by father and suitor. The dilemma carries into the plot of *V for Vendetta* insofar as it signals a conflict between Evey's loyalty toward V, a potential romantic interest, and a misguided patriotism that seeks to rescue the state and the lives of its commissioners while simultaneously vindicating her of suspicion of treason and terrorism. Like Lady Jane, Ophelia is caught up in court politics by virtue of her birth and is destroyed.

The presence of the Delaroche and Millais paintings in such close proximity to V's vanity suggest a *memento mori* (reminder of death) similar to the skull that is often included in depictions of the study of the medieval and early modern scholar. The skull serves as a reminder of the brevity and fragility of life, a reminder that the living must make the most of time, for death can ensue instantaneously. The *memento mori* was a particular reminder of the universality and sudden mortality associated with plague. The reminders of death in V's dressing room may seem out of place, but the time he spends there constitutes a rehabilitation of the damage done to him by plague, tyranny and discrimination. And it is the reminder that he must not only avenge himself and the mistreated Valerie Page but he must engage in life's pleasures while there is still time.

V for Vendetta: From Script to Film, Director James McTeigue comments on the multiple aesthetic choices made in the production process of the film:

> When Evey first comes out and listens to the jukebox, a large part of that is played against a Francis Bacon painting. It's called *Study of the Human Body*, which I thought was nice to have behind her, considering Bacon's painting is in some ways about confusion and distortion, and at that moment she's really confused, and events have been distorted [qtd. in Lamm and Bray 196].

Here, McTeigue acknowledges one instance in which the imagery in the gallery captures the mindset of the dramatis personae, and thus he draws attention to the same practice operating in other frames of the film, particularly in the shadow gallery scenes. One particular exchange between the revenger and his captive collaborator is played out against the backdrop of two unidentified portraits which offer perspective on the interiority of the characters. As Evey offers a plaintive account of the tragic death of her brother from the St. Mary's virus and the disappearance of her mother and father at the hands of Creedy's Fingermen, her image is framed by a painting of a female nude who attempts to cover herself with her arms, thus creating a exemplary image of exposure and vulnerability as well as youth and naiveté. Evey concludes her remarks with the revelation that she is afraid constantly and that she knows the Sutler government is corrupt, but she is too frightened to become involved in the impending insurrection. She exposes her deepest concerns and emotions to V, and in a manner of speaking, she lays herself bare to her protector/captor, an idea reiterated in the background imagery. The frequent cuts between Evey and V in the scene reveal a similar framing practice. The revenger is shadowed by the portrait of a noble bearded gentleman in the traditional red coat of the British military; however, the painting nevertheless appears to be either late nineteenth or early twentieth century. It could even be Czar Nicholas II, a visual allusion that might offer an interesting dimension to the film if one could be certain of the identity. Nevertheless, the formal aristocratic portrait accurately captures the formality, condescension, aloofness, and single-minded resolution of the revenger. While he is cordial, he is not warm, nor can he be dissuaded from his arduous and self-destructive course. He is hardened by suffering and ready to enact justice without compunction or mercy upon those who have injured him. The juxtaposition of the two paintings suggests the emotional and ideological rift between the two characters, one that can be understood as a contrast between youth and age, between emotion and reason, between passive and active, between innocence and experience. While Evey is laid bare, V is inaccessible to passion and pity, at least at this early portion of the film. Of course, his austerity is eventually softened by his acquaintance with Evey, as her naiveté is altered by the lessons in suffering and real politics that she accrues in V's faux-prison.

A similar instance in which sentiment and art are equated occurs after Evey is released from captivity. The growing recognition that she has been incarcerated, tortured, and interrogated by the man that she had come to believe was on her side is shadowed by an El Greco canvas, *A View of Toledo*, in which the pastoral imagery of the sleeping city is overshadowed by ominous storm clouds. Obviously, the placement of the canvas behind Evey captures her increasing hysteria, offering an almost playful postmodern literalization of the figure of speech, "gathering storm clouds" as it refers to an impending grief or rage. When the figurative clouds burst, the heroine is framed by an image of the *Venus D'Arles* (created in the 1st century A.D. and currently on display in Paris' Louvre), a classical statue of a semi-nude woman with breast exposed and arms extended in the gesture of embrace. The full-length statue suggests the protagonist's (Evey's) need for understanding, comfort, and compassion at that moment, and V offers a lengthy explanation of his motives for mistreating the woman he has come to love. He argues that he needed to toughen her up, to show her just how brutal the world can be, and to demonstrate that there are principles of greater value than life. The gathering storm of El Greco's painting becomes literalized in the downpour that follows when Evey emerges from the V's lair. The storm that initiates her regeneration suggests the paradoxical union of destruction and creation, both in the understanding of her future revolutionary endeavors and in the elucidation of *A View of Toledo;* the city will emerge from the threatening storm renewed by life-giving rain.

The faux movie posters created to celebrate the life of the fictional star, Valerie Page, are revered and even idolized by V, who creates an elaborate memorial to her in his home. When Evey declares V a "monster" created by the monstrous maltreatment of him, the revenger is positioned in front of a movie bill in which the word "murder" features prominently. In addition, at the center of V's shrine to the dead movie star is a poster from her most memorable performance — *The Salt Flats.* The title suggests sterility and desolation; the image on the poster places the actress' head and upper torso above the image of a desert waste land. The commentary offered by the simple movie ad is far reaching. In a planter in front of the poster, a huge collection of roses are in full bloom. The image of Valeria above the salt flats suggests her death, while the roses suggest the brevity and beauty of life as well as love and the hope for renewal. In effect, Valerie's shrine is another example of the iconography of women in distress that is so prominent within V's home. The desolation of the arid, arduous, and lifeless flats serves as an analogue for the slight rewards of revolutionary zeal. Valerie lived her life on her own terms and under the political circumstances, her resolution may be heroic and revolutionary, but her life was brief, infertile, and tragic. Evey may expect similar recompense if she elects to become engrossed in anti-establishment activities. The romantic attachment between V and Evey, which begins to flourish in the same scene, also becomes the subject of the aesthetic editorializing. The love between captor and captive is unattainable. V never even met Valerie Page, and, in addition, she was romantically inclined toward women, so any relation between them would have been impossible even if they had not been separated by death. The Valerie shrine, particularly *The Salt Flats,* poster completes the narrative of women's choices created by the paintings in the main room. Evey does not have to be ravished and possessed by a man (Titian), or pine after a man (Waterhouse), or enjoy wedded bliss with a man (Van Eyck); she can instead live her own life independent of men, as did Valerie, and while she may die childless and alone, she will have triumphed over low expectations and won fame and immortality through her own works. She will have become the subject of veneration and pride, a woman of great historical import.

The selections in the shadow gallery include at least two paintings that foreshadow the events to transpire on the 5th of November when V completes his revenge. Hanging above the Titian and Waterhouse paintings, and never clearly in focus, is John Singleton Copley's *Death of Major Peirson* (1782–1784), a piece from the Tate Collection. The canvas depicts a pitch battle between the British army and an invading French force in the streets of Saint Helier on the island of Jersey, 1781. Near the center of the canvas is the dying Peirson who, having fallen backward and having dropped his sword, is held in the arms of his comrades. The principal drama takes place directly beneath the Union Jack, which is the most prominent feature of the piece, emphasizing self-sacrifice in the pursuit of patriotic zeal. The image is created from the defender's perspective behind the British lines, and the chaos of battle rages all around the dying Major, tending to deemphasize the significance of his death. Since the eye of the viewer is always directed initially toward the flag, for a time the dying officer is swallowed up in the confusion of battle. Taken as a whole, the painting suggests that the overall struggle to repel invasion is of greater consequence than the death of any particular soldier, even one of elevated rank. The Copley painting foreshadows the death of V in the preliminary events of November 5. As V is the leader of the revolutionary assault upon the Norsefire regime, his death would seem to be fatal to the insurrection, but the movement becomes larger than the life of any one man. V will die quietly in advance of the revolution that he fomented, and he will be cradled in the arms by his confederate, who must immediately return to the fray and launch the most devastating strike against the power structure, the immolation of Parliament. The street conflict of Copley's painting predicts the confrontation between the legion of Guy Fawkes impersonators and the British military. However, unlike the Battle of Jersey, the combatants are not of separate nationalities, so once the executive branch of the government has been neutralized, the people are free to enjoy a perfect amity and a renewed commitment to social and institutional reform.

Another dimly viewed canvas within the shadows of V's gallery is Turner's *The Burning of the Houses of Parliament, 16th of October 1834* (1839), another work from the Tate collection. The image in watercolor can be vaguely discerned on the back wall of his television area. As the title of the painting indicates, the subject is the destruction of both Houses of Parliament by fire in the mid-nineteenth century. The fire was caused by an overloaded stove being used to dispose of a mass of accumulated wood. The conflagration of 1834 was the impetus for the construction of the current structure — The Palace of Westminster — the same which V seeks to destroy in McTeigue's film. Clearly, the painting serves as a daily reminder of his objectives. The vague outlines of Turner's paintings became the inspiration and impetus for Impressionist Art, particularly the opaque pastoral imagery of Monet. Taken together with the entire room of landscapes in V's residence, the content of Turner's watercolor may suggest the passage to a restored bucolic milieu, such as that celebrated by Impressionist painters and the Romantic poets of that same age. The yearning for a lapsed pastoral innocence can also be seen in the flashbacks to Valerie Page's life and particularly her movie career. The Romantics also lionized revolution, believing the French Revolution to be the great hope for the liberation of humanity from the tyranny, exploitation, and corruption of monarchy. The Romantics further venerated the alienated, self-destructive, and unsatisfied hero — subsequently named the Romantic Hero — a literary paradigm that they appropriated from Milton's *Paradise Lost*, and a classification into which V very clearly falls.

The collections in the Shadow Gallery include a multitude of other paintings, sculptures, and artifacts, including but not limited to Botticelli's *Birth of Venus* (1483), Van Gogh's *The Church at Auvers-sur-Orsay* (1890), and Giacometti's *Man Pointing* (1947). The careful attention paid to the artifacts within V's home ensures that there are indeed topical connections between the additional pieces of art and the content of V's life; after all, he is supposed to have chosen each piece from the vaults of the Ministry of Objectionable Materials, a process that validates two assumptions: there was a reason that the work was initially banned, and there was a reason that V chose to liberate each piece.

Conclusion

Political tyrannies that suppress and censor artistic expression seem to have a greater appreciation for the power of cultural artifacts than do liberal democracies, which usually put art on public display in spite of the socio-political message that the work may carry. While this may seem counter-intuitive and even paradoxical, the explanation lies in the fact that authoritarian state, by making art inaccessible, tacitly acknowledges the corrosive impact that it can have on the citizenry, and while it may be argued that liberal democracies permit the circulation of potentially corruptive art because they value freedom of expression more than law and order, there is also an element of disbelief that art — particularly traditional forms such as painting, sculpture, and literature — could impact any person so profoundly that they would be irrevocably damaged or become socially pernicious after having been exposed to it. The banning of art work at the whim of Sutler and his government suggests that they recognize the chaotic potential in the interaction between cultural artifacts and political discontents, and V's liberation of art from the government censors confirms their fears. The resurrection of the artifacts is equivalent to the resurrection of the past, and reverence for the aesthetic choices of a bygone age can suggest a discontentment with the present, a yearning for restoration of an idealized past. Certainly, V's collection suggests his veneration not only for the era in which each individual work was created, but also for the more recent period in which such artifacts circulated freely through public exhibitions and through the mass (re)production of cultural artifacts.

Intertexual theory argues that cultural references cannot avoid quoting other cultural references (Allen 5), each deriving meaning from the other and each altering in relationship with other. Culture is a network in which individual works are constantly contextualized and recontextualized, both through their usage and through the introduction of new cultural artifacts. For example, when Mary Shelley produced *Frankenstein* and/or Allen Ginsberg composed *Howl*, they added permanent footnotes or perhaps even rewrote portions of Milton's *Paradise Lost*. Similarly, V's accumulation of art is an homage to the recontextualizing of the past. He has selected works which comment upon his contemporary predicament as well as his private tribulations and objectives; a re-created past is resurrected as inspiration for the present and future. Painters such as Titian,

Waterhouse, Van Eyck, and Turner could not have anticipated the uses their art would serve, save, perhaps, in a broad assumption that it would slip the bonds of expectations.

The Shadow Gallery scenes serve as a meta-cinematic device offering an object lesson on the role that imagery and allusion play in the cinematic art form. Film too cannot avoid alluding to other films and other cultural processes; some of the references may be intentional, while others are the tricks of slippery language and imagery, and the Shadow Gallery obviates the (inadvertent) intersection of art forms taking place at the narrative level through the openness and allusiveness of the visual and auditory texts. *V for Vendetta* is not an independent and integrated text, but is constantly being punctured and occupied by external narrative features, many or most of which the reader creates in his or her apprehension of the text. Thus each reiteration of the *V for Vendetta* story is a re-creation. The film, like the "old men" of Yeats' poem, will occupy a place within the archive of history and civilization, speaking anew to each generation of what is "past, or passing or to come."

Nine

V for Virus

The Spectacle of the AIDS Avenger and the Biomedical Military Trope

In the past ten or fifteen years, the panic and uproar over the AIDS epidemic in the U.S. and Europe have slowly receded, thanks in no small part to a greater understanding of the disease and its specific modes of transmission, to more effective drug treatments that can prolong the life of the afflicted indefinitely, to a more coherent, compassionate, and energetic governmental response to the crisis, one which may have resulted from the recognition that the disease would be targeting all segments of the population, not merely gays, Haitians, and IV drug users, to a preoccupation with the illnesses more devastating effects elsewhere on the globe — Africa and Southeast Asia — and to the incremental reduction in the negative stigma associated with the affliction. Progressively in the mid-nineties, the epidemic seemed to become more manageable. We stopped hearing about the "innocent" victims whose suffering was far more pitiable than the tribulations of those who — through "reckless" and/or "perverse" behaviors — deserved to die. The mass protests over the government's failure to respond proportionately to the epidemic died down. People began to have hope for the future, for the containment of the virus at least within the industrialized world. The effort to "de-gay" the disease so that the governmental institutions as well as the heterosexual population would start taking the threat more seriously was so effective that gay/lesbian activists began trying to "re-gay" the disease to make sure that a proportionate number of resources were directed toward the population in the U.S. most heavily impacted — gay men (Vaid 74–78; Watney 145–147). At some point in the mid-nineties, gay men, even those who were already infected, began to have hope.

The past ten years have almost wiped away the awful memories of the rage, inhumanity, incharity, irrationality, panic, discrimination, hypocrisy, and grief of the 1980s health crisis, even for those of us awake and watching at the pandemic's monstrous birth. I remember walking through the Dallas airport on my way home from an academic conference in the mid-eighties and being solicited to sign a petition by a man standing beside a makeshift display table in the main terminal. He shouted across the atrium that my colleague and I should add our names to the list of those calling for the quarantine of gay men and the HIV infected, unless we (he added), have been "hanging out in gay bars." I cursed at him to the scandal of the solicitor, the security guards, and my traveling companion. I wondered at the time how anyone proposing so obscene a solution to a public health crisis could be so easily embarrassed by profanity. Perhaps I was the only person all day who told him what I really thought of his plan or perhaps the uncertainty of the times led him to believe that he was performing a valuable and just public service.

The irrational hatred and vituperation against gay men that followed in the wake of the AIDS epidemic was stunning in its verbal savagery and inhumanity because it forced governmental institutions to address a segment of the population regarded as beneath acknowledgment and consideration. Senator Jesse Helms managed to push through legislation that defined public health advertisements directed at the gay community as pornographic and obscene (Watney 42), and Thatcher's administration in Britain edited public health information directed at gay men because it appeared to condone an alternative lifestyle (Watney 238). The vituperation from the pulpit was unrelenting: gays and intravenous (IV) drug users were being punished by God with a horrible affliction for their transgressions against the "natural" sexual order, for their deconstruction of the simplistic gender duality, a belief which conveniently forgot that lesbians were the social group least likely to contract the virus. Of course this type of ignorance continues even into the first decade of the twenty-first century. A recent AIDS public service announcement aired in Mississippi included an infected white heterosexual woman expressing incredulity that she could be a victim even though she is not gay. Being a lesbian would have made her much more secure against the sexual transmission of the virus.

Those who believe that AIDS is God's punishment are part of an inglorious history of blaming the victims of an epidemic for their suffering and for the genesis of the disease that afflicts them, a practice which ascribes the origin and proliferation of disease to the victim's social position or ethnicity or to some other form of magical agency. Sociologist William A. Rushing reminds us that the bubonic plague was attributed to diverse causes: divine punishment, miasma, planetary alignment, and poisoning by Jews (139). The advent of syphilis in the 15th and 16th century inspired similar reactions. God was punishing Europeans for the presumptuousness of their geographical explorations, for "transgressing the God-given boundaries of human endeavor" (Gilman 100), and the "greater pox" was simultaneously blamed on Native Americans. The cholera epidemic in the early 19th century was attributed to the poor who were the most widely afflicted with the malady (Rushing 144).

AIDS also legitimized prejudices that already existed. This more contemporary scapegoating based on sexuality, race, and behavior is equally irrational, apocalyptic, and prophetic. Douglas Crimp in his introduction to *AIDS: Cultural Analysis/Cultural Activism*, quotes an anonymous surgeon on the subject: "We used to hate faggots on an emotional basis. Now we have a good reason" (8). Such a statement emerging from the same institutions charged with developing treatments for the newly emerged infection was unsettling to say the least. Moreover, HIV appeared at a time when there was a widespread belief that infectious diseases had been permanently eradicated. The last infectious disease had been polio in the 1950s, and its elimination had generated a conviction that contemporary medicine could and would develop cures and vaccines for any emergent ailments (Rushing 146). For several years after the emergence of AIDS, the viral origin of the ailment was yet unknown, and even after HIV was identified as the infectious agent, the virus proved to be baffling in its complexity and its ability to mutate, rendering vaccines elusive and/or ineffectual. Thus, demands for the quarantining of those who tested positive for the disease continued to issue from medical professionals (Watney 3, 12) and laymen alike, this even after the surgeon general, C. Everett Koop, confirmed that quarantines would be useless in the containment of the disease.

The voices of condemnation from the political and religious right were deafening. Preachers, politicians, and other demagogues sought to fill up the vacuum of legitimate explanations with traditional mythologies. Simon Watney, writing in 1986, describes the disease as a "*malade imaginaire* ... the viral personification of unorthodox deregulative desire, dressed up in ghoulish likeness of degeneracy" (11). He adds that "AIDS is invariably made to create a supplement of fantasy which both precedes and exceeds any actual medical issues" (14). Rightwing demagogue and former Reagan speech writer, Pat Buchanan, writing in 1983 explained that AIDS was "Nature fighting back.... The poor homosexuals — they have declared war on nature and now nature is exacting an awful retribution" (qtd. in Rushing 171). Jerry Falwell and the American Council of Christian Churches concurred in the "Wrath of God" explanation, the latter arguing that "God was 'spanking' gays for their sins" (Rushing 171). Even many of the so-called rational perspectives were incharitable and inaccurate in equal proportions. Watney quotes a Reagan speech writer's specious account of the origin of the disease: "There is one, only one, cause of the AIDS crisis, the willful refusal of homosexuals to cease indulging in the immoral, unnatural, unsanitary, unhealthy and suicidal practice of anal intercourse" (51).

Out of the terror and irrationality of that uncertain time emerged a multiplicity of conspiracy theories from the political right and left, some of which persist even to this day, and these colorful hypotheses serve as the back story of Moore and Lloyd's graphic novel *V for Vendetta* as well as the McTeigue and the Wachowski brothers' cinematic adaptation. From the political right, the conspiracies were relatively muted as most opted for the sanctimonious divine retribution explanation, one which conveniently explained away all anomalies (such as the fact that lesbians were the social profile most unlikely to contract the illness or that conversely babies were contracting it from their mothers in utero) with the added caveat that "God works in mysterious ways." Evidently AIDS babies were merely God's collateral damage. The secular conspiracy theories coming from the right were equally incharitable, revealing the level of suspicion and ignorance that came into play once the mainstream public was forced to address the subject of homosexuals and homosexuality. The image of the gay AIDS predator was born, a character so angered or addled by his or her condition that she or he sought to make the heterosexual world share in his or her suffering. G. Antonio, in *The AIDS Cover-up: The Real and Alarming Facts about AIDS*, argued that the government was intentionally falsifying the numbers of the afflicted in order to protect the gay community and that the latter was maliciously contaminating the "blood supply as a form of 'blood terrorism,'" and Representative Dannemayer imagined a similar criminal conspiracy, but this time the motivation for the insidious plot was to speed the response of the federal government to the epidemic (qtd. in Rushing 157). Perhaps the most well circulated story within the popular consciousness was the specious cautionary tale that deliberately blames the spread of the disease on women. Here the predator is a prostitute (sometimes not) who hooks up with a man at a night club. In the morning after a night of unprotected sex, the man finds his date gone and a message scrawled across the bathroom mirror, welcoming him to the community of AIDS afflicted (Treichler 43).

The insensitivity, mistrust, and even cruelty of leaders from the political, religious and medical establishments probably fueled the explosion of conspiracy theories from the left that sought to explain the presumed nefarious origins of the syndrome. In the social climate of the early to mid eighties, it was easier to believe that the clandestine apparatus of the American government could conceivably manufacture a devastating virus that had escaped the lab to create panic among the general population. After all, President Reagan did not even mention the word AIDS in public until 1987, and then only to encourage people to get tested (Treichler 57), at the time, a practice that created paranoia in the potentially infected, as it could lead to discrimination in housing, health care, and employment, not to mention the possibility of quarantines. In addition, the country was at the time still embroiled in the cold war, so the intentional creation of devastating pathogens for the purposes of biological warfare seemed more plausible. The open hostility toward and the separation of the afflicted into antithetical moral camps — the guilty and the innocent — also encouraged belief in spurious accounts of the pathogen's genesis. Such explanations were, in some ways, a means of fighting back, the afflicted turning "their tortures into horrid arms." Often the theories seemed specifically tailored to disburden members of a particular social group of the AIDS stigma, characterizing them as innocent victims of the disreputable machinations of the state's clandestine operations rather than the deserving and potentially malicious disseminators of infection.

Since there was initially a higher incidence of the disease among African Americans than among other ethnicities, a significant percentage of that population believed that the disease was a genocidal plot to decimate the black population in America (Rushing 158), a theory made easier to believe by the revelation of the Tuskegee experiment which was conducted between 1932 and 1972 on African American men and which came to light in the early 1990s. The subjects of the experiment had been refused treatment for syphilis (given placebos) in order to study the long term effects of the disease (Rushing 177). As Africa became increasingly blighted by AIDS, the theories expanded to encompass the post-colonial populations. AIDS became an "imperialist plot to destroy the Third World" (Treichler 319) or, in the conception of Louis Farrakhan, a pretext for the appropriation of Africa's wealth of "natural resources" by the avaricious Western nations (Rushing 157). Treichler cites the perspective of a Dominican prostitute who agrees with Farrakhan's assessment, arguing that AIDS did not exist but is an invention of the American government that seeks to decimate the poor, taking away the few possessions they still possess (103).

The rapid spread of AIDS through American cities fomented speculation on the part of the international community that the U.S. intentionally or inadvertently generated the disease, which emerged either from its weapons programs or its so-called immorality. Either way it was construed as payback for America's aggressive political and economic strategies abroad. The French initially blamed the pathogen on an "American pollutant," and the Soviets saw the disease as a manifestation of Western decadence (Treichler 29). Conversely, Americans assumed that patient zero was a Haitian who had been infected by an African (Gilman 103); for Westerners, Africa seems to be the presumptive origin of all unknown pathogens. The alternative theory is that the Haitian population became infected by a gay American tourist (Gilman 102), the blame still firmly placed among minorities.

Confronting the decimation of their communities, American gays and lesbians became radicalized in action and ideology. Suspicion of the motives and intentions of the American establishment was rampant. The organization ACTUP employed the "New Left" strategies of civil disobedience, protesting the glacial pace of new drug approvals as well as the prohibitive costs of the resulting treatments, staging "die-ins" to dramatize the government's indifference or irresolution when facing the imminent deaths of thousands of Americans, and disrupting public appearances of administration officials — in one instance blowing whistles throughout the speech of George H. W. Bush's Surgeon General at an international

AIDS conference. The more dignified "Names Project" sought to eulogize the dead by putting on public display a massive quilt, composed of six foot panels, each illustrating the unique life and interests of a person dead in the epidemic. "Queer Nation" sought through sundry means to illustrate the disenfranchised position of gays and lesbians by seizing public locales and transforming them, briefly, into in gay-friendly spaces.

The queer activism of the eighties and early nineties generated its share of hysterical theories explaining the nefarious origins and objectives of the HIV virus. Most prominent was the hypothesis that the political right wing (or the CIA) intentionally manufactured the disease to eliminate undesirables — gay men, blacks, and heroin addicts — but that the nefarious plot had backfired, infecting the general population. Another theory held that the establishment had created AIDS as a pretense to legitimize intrusions into the average citizen's private life (Treichler 319). While such speculations carry little credence, one issue that is difficult to deny is that the government was very slow in responding to the outbreak when they believed it would only impact undesirables. The Reagan administration did not offer a comprehensive plan for coping with the epidemic until 1987, five or six years into the epidemic (Treichler 57). When one considers the comparatively brief period necessary to respond to 9/11, the infamy of Reagan's inaction comes into view. The threat of AIDS to America and to humanity dwarfs that of global terrorism. The efforts of political and religious conservatives to re- or misdirect the resources for fighting the disease away from the communities most affected (such as manifest in the above cited Helms Amendment) demonstrate that the conservatives were willing to sacrifice as many lives as were necessary in order to avoid the appearance of encouraging or even tolerating homosexuality. The inactivity and indecision of the political right led author and activist Larry Kramer to accuse the Reagan administration of "intentionally killing gay men" by withholding funds for AIDS research. He later stated that "AIDS is our holocaust and Reagan our Hitler. New York is our Auschwitz" (qtd. in Rushing 57).

V for Vendetta

Hopefully, my subject has, after long prelude, come into view. The radicalized positions assumed by both sides of the political, social, and biomedical divide in the early AIDS epidemic are embedded in the narrative of *V for Vendetta*. In the introduction to the original DC Comic, Alan Moore summarizes the social and political milieu from which the graphic novel emerged, emphasizing the institutional homophobia and increasingly intrusive fascist tactics of Thatcher's conservative England:

> It's 1988, Margaret Thatcher is entering her third term of office and talking confidently of an unbroken Conservative leadership well into the next century. My youngest daughter is seven, and the tabloid press are circulating the idea of concentration camps for persons with AIDS. The new riot police wear black visors as do their horses, and their vans have rotating video cameras mounted on top. The government has expressed a desire to eradicate homosexuality, even as an abstract concept, and one can only speculate as to which minority group will be the next legislated against. I'm thinking of taking my family and getting out of this country soon [6].

At the same time, in the name of crime prevention, the British government was implementing the most extensive network of surveillance cameras (CCTV) in the free world, and the subsequent public outcry hailed the system as a profound intrusion in the people's private lives. Thatcher's government was finally toppled in the wake of mass protests over a proposed poll tax. Within this context, Moore and Lloyd's *V for Vendetta* becomes a protest against a gradual erosion of civil rights and against the increasingly fascist tactics of the British government. The dystopic England of the comic operates as a warning against the continued support of Thatcher's policies. For Moore, the glaring manifestation of creeping fascism is the intolerance and discrimination toward gays and lesbians and people with AIDS, and he particularly seems to see the practice as a slippery slope, potentially leading to reprisals against other minorities.

The viral narrative within both the graphic novel and the more recent film appropriates the discourse of the AIDS epidemic while it also employs the paranoia and plot devices of the conspiracy theories, literalizing the greatest fears and the most outlandish hypotheses, fulfilling an objective of a serial comic — to create caricatures for the purposes of social satire, here a warning against the continued maltreatment of a community that has the power to affect widespread contagion throughout the physical and national bodies. V becomes the embodiment of patient zero, the one individual who survived the fiendish government experiments, mounting a resistance to both the contagion and his persecutors among governmental officials. Deemed undesirable and dispensable, V is intentionally contaminated with a lethal pathogen under the assumption that he will die without incident or at least remain safely interred within the stone walls of the Larkhill facility. However, he survives, becomes stronger, and breaks out of his confines to exact a terrible revenge on those who considered him expendable. He is the artistic embodiment of the AIDS avenger who refuses to die, refuses to remain the subject of scientific study, refuses to brook his continued mistreatment, and refuses to observe the communal values that would deter him from spreading contagion liberally. He is Frankenstein's monster, breaching the confines of the laboratory to torment an unsympathetic public, the same who cannot countenance his visage, and returning "to plague the inventor."

The virus portrayed within the Wachowski/McTeigue film bears a striking resemblance to that of AIDS, both in the imagery and the discourse of the narrative. In her assessment of V's condition, Dr. Delia Surridge, formerly Diana Stanton, principal physician at the Larkhill facility, clearly alludes to the widely known symptoms of the patient with Acquired Immune Deficiency Syndrome, remarking that V "exhibits none of the immune system pathologies that the other subjects developed." She categorizes the affliction as a "blood" disease and adds that V has developed "several cellular anomalies in his blood" and the result is "the abnormal development of kinesthesia and reflexes." The latter symptom constitutes a departure from the well known HIV pathologies. In fact, it is antithetical to the expected human physical response to infection — "wasting," one of the final phases of the disease — the appetite is reduced and, simultaneously, the body is unable to retain or absorb nourishment; and the patient becomes increasingly thin and weak. V's enhanced physical responses could be an allusion to the use of anabolic steroids in the treatment of people with *Pneumocystis carinii pneumonia* (PCP), an ailment common among HIV infected persons (Feldman 99). However, in all probability, the extra-human physical response of the avenger is simply an ironic reversal of the expected prognosis for those infected with the virus, and the other subjects of the experiment fall prey to the predictable symptoms. The doctor remarks that they are "weak and pathetic" and expresses her contempt for them. Perhaps most revealing are the skin lesions figuring prominently on all of the patients, an obvious allusion to Kaposi's Sarcoma (KS), a rare skin cancer that appears on those who have weakened immune systems, particularly those suffering from HIV/AIDS (Feldman 34). While the Larkhill detainees are being processed the camera follows the movements of the as yet unidentifiable Valerie Page, who has lesions on her cheek, forehead, and neck.

There are also a variety of ways in which the St. Mary's virus deviates from HIV, changes necessary to create the kind of panic requisite to the political motives of the antagonists. In other words, the progress of the virus from infection to death must be sped up in order for the political conspiracy to be chronologically plausible. With HIV, those determined to be seropositive can remain asymptomatic for as long as ten years or more (Feldman 71). Even the most rapid progression of the disease requires months of incubation. The St. Mary's virus seems to kill with the rapidity of other, more potent pathogens such as Bubonic Plague, the Hantavirus, or Ebola; it can progress from infection to death in a matter of hours. Moreover, the St. Mary's virus, obviously an airborne pathogen, is more easily communicable than is HIV, which is actually quite difficult to contract, requiring exposure to infected blood or semen. HIV can survive only in the biological systems of some primates, principally humans. The intentional release of St. Mary's in population areas around Great Britain required that the virus be contagious rather than infectious. One of the release locations was "Three Waters" water treatment facility (perhaps an allusion to the Three Valley Water Treatment Facility that services many London boroughs). The spread of the virus via the water supply would require that the pathogen remain viable outside of the human host, and the release of the same in the London tube station would require that it be airborne. The imagery associated with St. Mary's school suggests that the virus may have been consumed through food. These departures from the common means of communicability associated with HIV may be exclusively for the purposes of narrative logic and experience, or a desire to keep the story from becoming too heavy-handed in its references to the contemporary pandemic. The spread of the illness could reflect theories that emerged during the early AIDS epidemic, before the transmissibility of the virus was determined. Centers for Disease Control teams converged upon the tiny towns of Belle Glade and South Bend, Florida where, for a brief time in the 1980s, the incidence of AIDS was the highest per capita of anywhere in the country. An article in the *Miami Herald* published in November of 1985 suggested that the virus may be transmitted by mosquitoes or may result from the degraded conditions in which the migrant workers who labored in the sugarcane fields lived. For a while the conjecture blamed the large number of migrant workers from the Caribbean, particularly Haitians. Finally, the determination was made that the cluster of AIDS cases were the result of heterosexual transmission exacerbated by the high incidence of intravenous drug use in the area. In addition, urban legends surfaced regarding nearby Clewiston which also had a high incidence of AIDS; here the theory was that the virus was being transmitted through the consumption of chicken, thus the warning "Don't eat the chicken in Clewiston" became current in Southwest Florida. However, the most likely explanation for the inconsistencies between HIV and the St. Mary's virus is that the latter seeks to evoke contemporary fears of biological terrorism following the World Trade Center catastrophe and the London Tube bombings, to give the narrative a more contemporary historical urgency.

The origin of the St. Mary's pathogen in the *V for Vendetta* narrative reflects conjectures regarding the AIDS epidemic in the early to mid-eighties. As cited above, there was a widespread belief within the national and international community that the AIDS virus was the production of the American biological weapons program, a bug that inadvertently or perhaps intentionally escaped the lab to decimate the communities of the socially reprobate (Rushing 158; Treichler 322). In his rant that opens the film, Prothero speaks contemptuously of the "former United States" who has sent England a shipment of food to exchange for much needed "medical supplies." In characteristic fashion, Prothero has no compassion for the "Ulcerated Sphincter of Asserica," arguing that America was once prosperous and blessed, but fell into a much deserved degradation. He explains that it "wasn't the plague they created," resulting in "the world's biggest leper colony," and it "wasn't the war they started"; "it was judgment" and "Godlessness." The Voice of London's ravings are reminiscent of the rhetoric of politicians and evangelical preachers who sought to blame the AIDS epidemic on sin. While the virus was yet unidentified, the illness was frequently referred to as WOGS ("the Wrath of God Syndrome"—Treichler 46)). With a familiar lack of compassion, Prothero recommends that the British ignore the suffering of America because the stigma of God's disfavor has fallen upon the former super power. The creation of an insulting translation for the familiar American acronym USA reveals the cruelty and childishness of those who choose to blame the victims of a disease for their suffering, but it also reveals the belief that anal sodomy is the source of infection; in his words, America is the "Ulcerated Sphincter of Asserica." And the British are free from further epidemic because they are armed with righteousness.

The allusion to the ravaging plague in America that has created "the world's biggest leper colony" generates some ambiguity within the conspiracy narrative of the film. Prospero himself is guilty of having infected healthy human beings in order to find a cure for the virus, subsequently allowing him to become very wealthy through his investments in pharmaceutical stocks, and he was in all probability complicit in the willful release of the virus onto the public in the push to consolidate power for the Norsefire party. His reward was not only extravagant wealth, but also advancement within the Sutler administration as spokesman or minister of propaganda. Considering the unreliability of his point of view, it is difficult for the reader to determine whether the American pathogen is actually the same that was released upon and subsequently cured by the British or whether it is an entirely different epidemic. Assuming that the authors/screenwriters would consider it confusing to introduce two separate plagues into a single narrative, we might conclude that the American food shipment was sent in exchange for a boatload of Prothero's pills. If this is the case then, the origin of the virus is the subject of dispute within the film. What then was the trajectory of the disease? Did the Americans create the virus intentionally or inadvertently and the British subsequently respond with the fiendish eugenic experiments to interdict the spread of the disease to their country? Or did the Sutler government create the pathogen for the purposes of power, with the Americans becoming the collateral damage of the British biomedical experiments? The latter seems counterintuitive but may actually be more interesting because it demonstrates the level of hypocrisy operating within the Sutler regime, and specifically within Prothero, one of the men primarily responsible for creating a pandemic and then blaming the victims of his villainy. The fact that the St. Mary's outbreak in Britain was eventually pinned on religious extremists reveals Prothero's willingness to implicate the innocent in his nefarious machinations.

The degradation of the afflicted within the Larkhill facility is reminiscent not only of the discourse of the early AIDS epidemic but also of fascism. Imagery associated with the experiments at the Larkhill Detention Facility creates a composite of three separate facets of the narrative's allusive structure: the internment camp at Guantanamo Bay, the Holocaust, and the AIDS epidemic. The film literalizes the fear of concentration camp like quarantines associated with the initial AIDS hysteria while creating a simultaneous swipe at the George W. Bush administration's suspension of civil rights and due process in the misdirected effort to interdict terrorism. The images of the Larkhill prisoners include bright orange prison garb and occasionally black hoods. The patients are bound and abused physically. Prothero repeatedly kicks a patient on the ground. These images allude to the public outcry in Britain over the opening of the Guantanamo detention facility and particularly the hooding, which is considered torture and is a violation of international treaty. Several prisoners are nude and hooded, perhaps alluding to the Abu Ghraib prison scandal. The assembly line processing of the prisoners/patients is, of course, a page ripped right out of a Nazi efficiency manual. But the most powerful allusion to the holocaust is the irreverent disposal of nude bodies which are shuttled through the hallways of the facility on dollies and then unceremoniously thrown into collective graves or ditches, where they are shown as a tangled mass of limbs and torsos covered in lime, among which the body of Valerie Page lies. In addition, the white tiled rooms in which the eugenics experiments are conducted are reminiscent of the notorious showers used for gassing Jews in the German concentration camps.

The dehumanization of the prisoner/patients continues with the images of the clear plastic cubicles in which some of the subjects are constrained. The implication is that the subjects are animals, perhaps chimps or vermin, kept in transparent boxes for observation. Of course, the ethnicity and sexuality of the prisoners is emphasized as well. One must remember that the people interred at Larkhill were described as "the usual undesirables." The inclusion of people with alternative sexual identities is embodied in the images of Valerie Page as the camera follows the prisoners through the process of unloading, orienting, shaving, infecting, wasting, dying, and burying. The inclusion of racial minorities is evident as well, clearly identifiable are people of African, Arabic, Asian, and Indian descent. Fundamental to the protocols of Nazi eugenic theory was the belief that people of Jewish, Slavic, and African descent were not fully human and did not have to be treated as such. This group of "sub-humans" also included homosexuals, gypsies, and communists. These racial, sexual, social, ideological misfits allude to the specious theories that AIDS was manufactured for the purposes of social control and for the elimination of the undesirables from the population of true patriots.

In *AIDS and the National Body*, Thomas Yingling, writing while he was himself battling the virus, described the contraction of the HIV as the erasure of subjectivity — "It is the disease that announces the end of identity" (15), and his editor Robyn Weigman summarizes his conclusions in Lacanian terms, "AIDS makes palpable — to the point of psychic crisis — the irreconcilability of the body's materiality and our imaginary relation to it" (2). While these characterizations address the effects of virus on subjectivity, McTeigue's film explores both the psychic and the physical representation of identity crisis. The process of de-humanizing the Larkhill detainees includes the shaving of their heads and the monochromatic sartorial choices of bright orange prison garb. The prisoners become progressively indistinguishable as evidenced in the processing of Valerie Page. Although the audience has not yet been introduced to Valerie when the film flashes back to imagery of the Larkhill patient/prisoners, the camera nevertheless follows her throughout the process as she mixes in and becomes progressively indistinguishable from the other inmates, culminating with her body being thrown into a lime filled pit. The audience's subsequent recognition of her individuality and her humanity via the notes delivered to the imprisoned Evey is more effective because had the audience members been familiar with her in advance of the processing scenes, they would not have been able to assess the activities of the facility as dispassionately as the narrative requires. The camp's procedures are, after all, offered from the point of view of Delia Surridge, the doctor who managed the experiment, and she cannot know whom she kills, nor can she as the physician become emotionally involved with her patients, particularly when her activities will have the inevitable effect of killing them. When Valerie is later identified through flashbacks to Delia's narrative, the true human impact of the research is emphasized. The patients/prisoners are no longer anonymous victims but multidimensional human beings whose loss impacts the culture — Valerie was a movie star. Here the text leads the audience through a process of humanizing the victims for which they formerly had little or no sympathy. This is representative of the anti–AIDS campaigns of the mid-eighties, the same which sought to demonstrate that the decimations of the virus within the gay community were having a detrimental impact upon the culture industry; those who were dying were not expendable after all. The honor role of luminaries dead from the disease began to appear in various media. These included Liberace, Rudolf Nureyev, and a multitude of others, but most important in the evolution of the public perception of the disease was the death of Rock Hudson who, like the fictional Valerie Page, created sympathy for the dying and, amazingly, in spite of his widely known sexual orientation, was able to convince the public that anyone could contract the disease, even heterosexual males, and regardless of lifestyle, wealth, fame, and sin quotient (Treichler 19).

The conspiracy plot within *V for Vendetta* offers a second approach to the rehabilitation of public perception in the fight against the deadly virus. As we know, V was the only patient to survive the Larkhill biomedical research, and ideally his cultivation and his victimization by a heartless nationalistic regime would under normal circumstances have been sufficient to generate sympathy for him; however, his violent agenda curtails the audience's ability to commiserate. The register of audience response is embodied in Evey's various condemnations of her torturer/benefactor. When V surreptitiously captures, inters, and tortures her, he argues that he has done so to save her from her own fear; however, his actions have an additional didactic goal, and one that he shares with anti–AIDS campaigns of the first decade of the epidemic. His incarceration of Evey is an emulation of his own treatment at the hands of the medical establishment as well as the covert wing of the Norsefire Party, the harsh lesson designed to elicit an identical experience and response to that of the Larkhill detainees. V is attempting to evoke Evey's empathy so that she will appreciate his remorselessness toward those against whom he pursues his revenge. However, within the AIDS discourse of the film the incarceration and torture constitutes an effort to share with the general public (here Evey) the indignities of living as an oppressed minority while simultaneously enduring the sickness and stigma of a devastating pathogen that threatens to wipe away an entire community while the political, medical, and religious establishments look on with what is at the best of times indifference and at the worst disgust and/or a sanctimonious appreciation of nature's/God's ironies. Evey's revelation is to be shared with the contemporary movie audience. When her head was shaved and she donned prison pajamas, she became one of the anonymous victims of the Larkhill atrocities as well as a person living with AIDS.

The AIDS Avenger and the Epidemic of Violence

Tales of the enraged and dying HIV infected person who deliberately strives to infect others were rampant in the first decade of the viral outbreak. These imaginary villains took on a variety of forms, including those who desired to share the infection out of revenge for their own suffering and social stigma, those who refused to curb their sexual appetites because they were dying and had nothing to lose, and those who were untested and unaware of their seropositivity and thus unwilling to adopt appropriate precautions against infecting others. One persistent rumor played upon the number of gay men working in food service, particularly as waiters, and imagined that they were deliberately infecting food to spread the virus to the heterosexual population. As cited above, another concern, this one offered by right wing conservatives, was that HIV positive gay men were intentionally donating blood to contaminate the nation's blood supply, either out of revenge or out of a desire to see the virus spread to the heterosexual population which would subsequently lead to a greater effort to develop treatments for the disease (Rushing 157). The HIV infected were portrayed as desperados willing to perpetrate a variety of villainies in order to survive. When figures were released regarding the high costs of treating people with HIV from infection to death, insurance companies feared that treating AIDS patients would overwhelm their resources, and for a time, many required testing before life insurance policies were written; however, eventually they settled into a practice of asking patients to declare their HIV status, evidently with the presumption that if the disease developed later they could argue that the policy had been issued under false pretenses. Generally speaking, there was a widespread concern that because AIDS was mostly affecting socially marginalized groups, there was a higher likelihood of fraud, villainy, and dishonesty from the infected populations.

The persistent rumors of the angry and vindictive AIDS patient suggest a guilty conscience on the part of the heterosexist establishment. After all, people do not pursue revenge against those who have done nothing wrong, save in instances of misdirection or misunderstanding. The reports of discrimination and mistreatment of people with AIDS (PWAs), coupled with a basic mistrust of minorities, were bound to lead to rumors of the blighted fighting back, particularly when, for so long, the blighted had no hope of a normal life, when spreading their infection liberally among the heterosexual population seemed both rational and justifiable, and when just such a irresponsible and villainous course of action seemed like a plausible means of survival. Within this line of thinking, the AIDS avenger was an embodiment of fate and/or justice; she or he was even a perverse kind of savior whose actions might affect a positive outcome in the social, political, and medical struggles of the afflicted.

V's campaign of terrorism and murder has both a personal and political motivation. He desires revenge for the mistreatment of himself and Valerie Page at the hands of the medical establishment and the ambitious Norsefire party, and he desires to unseat the politicians who established a fascist regime in England via the deliberate introduction of a pathogen into the body politic. His nefarious activities are simultaneously regarded as justifiable and deplorable, a spectrum of sentiments illustrated in Evey's ambivalence toward the revenger. V is not rash or irrational, but calm and deliberate in his pursuit of revenge because he is certain of the legitimacy of his cause, and thus he is unconflicted in its pursuit. Indeed, he is so comfortable with his violence that he begins to resemble an allegorical embodiment of fate or justice. He has in effect returned from the grave to torment his persecutors. Having defied all predictions of his death, he emerges from the flaming crucible of the Larkhill Detention Camp reborn in fire, an instrument of fate, destruction, and revenge. The iconographic image of the avenger in the conflagration is reiterated throughout the film, most memorably in its juxtaposition with Evey's parallel apotheosis in the rain. The conjunction of the two antithetical elements invites traditional, perhaps even clichéd readings, contrasting destruction and creation, male and female, and/or sterility and fertility — the two phases of revolution, the razing and the renewal.

The visitation of V to his adversaries constitutes a visitation of the grim reaper, even his costume suggests as much. He resembles the personification of death in Ingmar Bergman's film classic *The Seventh Seal* (a parallel that was developed in another chapter). V is the personification of a virus that escaped the lab to plague its inventors, the same who so callously infected others in the search for a cure that would render the agent ineffectual as a biological weapon. The first three subjects of his vendetta (Prothero, Bishop Lilliman, and Delia Surridge) are not killed by his swordplay, as are so many of the security forces in the film. They are instead poisoned by injection, a symbolic payment in kind for the willful exposure of medical subjects to a lethal pathogen. Ostensibly and ironically, the respective poisonings are perpetrated for similar reasons — to cure the state of undesirables. The experimental subjects at Larkhill were those considered expendable, whose elimination would, by some estimations, enhance the health of the national body; V, similarly, imagines himself the physician of the state, charged to purge the collective body, making way for a renewed and more compassionate political apparatus, the charge of which is left to Evey, and those who survive the great conflagration of Parliament.

The figurative return of the pathogen to claim its own maker constitutes a literalization of the specious theories accounting for the origin of the HIV virus. Like Frankenstein's monster, the virus could not be contained by the precautions and protocols of the medical and clandestine establishments who sought either to create a biological weapon to wage or deter war against the Soviet Bloc or to eliminate those individuals considered incompatible with American society. The Norsefire party sought to gain a multidimensional advantage from their medical experimentation: purging the state of undesirables, eliminating the pathogen as a threat to the national security when wielded by enemies, and enriching those who were invested in the resulting cure. The embodiment of death returning to claim those who unleashed a biological horror onto the world is the symbol of perfect justice: "with what measure ye meet, it shall be measured to ye." Thus V is not only death, but the image of the AIDS messiah who has come to save his people from persecution, to sweep away their enemies, and to reestablish compassion and tolerance as social and political principles.

The messianic imagery associated with V is both voluminous and heavy-handed. Mantegna's painting of a pierced and crucified St. Sebastian hangs on the wall of V's "Shadow Gallery," near the entrance to the avenger's bedroom, and is juxtaposed with William Blake's *Elohim Creating Adam*, the two together mythologizing V's beginning and end. The Adam figure in Blake's painting is being pulled from the tail of the serpent coiled around the tree of interdicted knowledge, implying humanity's origins in sin, born already fallen. The image of St. Sebastian suggests humanity's need for patience, courage, and salvation when facing martyrdom. The multiple piercings of the Saintly body foreshadow the bullet ridden torso of V at the end of the film when he has literally given his life in the process of revenging himself and others who suffered at the hands of the Sutler regime. In addition, St. Sebastian is considered the patron saint of those afflicted with plague; the arrows which pierce him are indicative of the buboes that appeared on the body of the victims of the Black Death. Moreover, in classical mythology, Apollo the archer was the deliverer of plague, the infliction of which was represented by the penetration of his arrows. Sebastian was a Roman soldier charged with the persecution of Christians; however, when it was discovered that he too was a Christian and that he had been showing mercy to those condemned by the Roman authority, he was executed. When the arrows were ineffectual in killing him, he was beaten to death (en.wikipedia.org/wiki/Sebastian). St. Sebastian's martyrdom parallels V's in a variety of ways, including but not limited to his self-sacrifice in defense of those who are persecuted. The inability to kill the Saint with airborne missiles is also indicative of V, who will not die from the bullets of Mr. Creedy's guards until he has successfully throttled the government agent with his own hands. In a particularly pertinent analogue, St. Sebastian is considered the intercessor or mediator between God and the Brazilian gay community, a similar role to that which the AIDS avenger plays in the subtext of the Wachowski brothers' screenplay.

Just as Saint Sebastian is believed to have saved Rome from the plague in 680 A.D. (en.wikipedia.org/wiki/Sebastian), V's blood literally generates the serum requisite to the salvation of humanity from the St. Mary's pathogen. The cure is derived from an agent in his blood that gave him an immunity to the virus. His blood, however, is exploited by the ambitious politicians and doctors in pursuit of wealth and power. Here, the political allegory becomes more complex, perhaps commenting on the exploitation of religion for the advancement of power and social control. In the early AIDS epidemic and even to this day, the HIV virus was often utilized for the purposes of consolidating political, spiritual, and financial power. Evangelical preachers mobilized the hateful sentiments of their congregations via the viral outbreak, maintaining HIV was God's wrath against the unrighteous and that the sin of social undesirables had become a threat to the entire population's health and salvation. Similarly politicians exploited the virus to foment hatred against social undesirables and consolidate their voting base who perceived the indifferent and inhumane policies of the Reagan administration toward PWAs as a program of viral containment, particularly the xenophobic prohibition against HIV infected foreigners traveling to the U.S. (Murphy 129–143). If V's blood, a secular source of salvation, is parallel to Christ's blood through their shared curative qualities, then the exploitation of V's blood in the stratagems of the Norsefire party may constitute an analogue to the same party's use of religion in consolidation of power. Sutler masquerades as a very religious man and builds his regime on the application and defense of moral values, and Prothero blames America's misfortunes — viral and otherwise — on "Godlessness."

However, beyond the curative qualities of V's blood, the avenger has very few Christ-like traits, unless one considers the duality of Christ predicted in both Old and New Testaments. The "suffering servant" of the Gospels will on the day of wrath return as the "Davidic conqueror" who drives iniquity before him. This Scriptural duality can account for the two lives of V — before and after the Larkhill conflagration. In his cell at the detention facility he was a quiet gardener who grew roses — Scarlet Carsons — but all along he is planning his liberation, his fiery apotheosis. After he has, in effect, been reborn from the flames, he initiates a lengthy program of punishing iniquity, razing the institutions of power, and initiating a social, spiritual, political, and cultural renewal. From this point of view, the respective elements associated with V and Evey may even suggest the two apocalyptic covenants of fire and water.

From the scriptural perspective, V's role as the AIDS savior/avenger may then be understood in two sharply opposing ways. It could be construed as a rehabilitative gesture essentially turning the tables on rightwing interpretations of the virus and those who live with it, suggesting that Christ's compassion and charity would be aligned with those afflicted and stigmatized by a ghastly pathogen regardless of the sexual orientation of the subject and that those who have borne such animosity toward the victims of plague will themselves suffer divine retribution. Perhaps more interestingly, V may constitute a parody of the salvation motif, a personification of the qualities most abhorred by the hysterical rightwing mindset that created such classic monsters as the AIDS predator. Thus V is not so much a Christ as an Anti-Christ, but not because he is evil; both film and graphic novel offer us a more complex personality in V than can be captured in our most superlative value terminology of "good" and "evil." In effect, the crimes perpetrated against the avenger have driven him "beyond good and evil." As an Anti-Christ, V literalizes the greatest fears of the Anti-AIDS/Anti-gay lobby of the 1980s. Desperation and rage have driven him beyond the pale of reason and patience, and he, now a mad killer, perhaps driven to murder by AIDS related dementia, remorselessly spreads death and mayhem in his destructive path. This representation however, is not a value judgment against V, but against the sanctimonious and short-sighted puritans who have driven an entire population to the brink of madness and despair and then expected them to patiently abide their own annihilation, adopting a sense of social responsibility toward the same countrymen who desired and, in the cinematic case, orchestrated their deaths. V acknowledges that the crimes against him created him, and this admission exposes the hypocrisy of the religious establishment who is charged with bringing people to God while simultaneously driving them away.

The Biomedical Military Metaphor

In her book *AIDS and the Body Politic*, Catherine Waldby analyzes the military imagery employed by the various social, political, religious, and medical authorities in their respective AIDS discourses, and specifically she demonstrates that the language is gender biased to the detriment of both women and gay men. The ideal body is coded as heterosexual male (10), while others are consigned to the status of immuno-compromised and radicalized bodies that constitute a threat to the collective organism, the body of state; the gay male form is a feminized body, one whose boundaries are porous because they are subject to penetration. Within the biomedical discourse, the body politic is represented in two radically different ways indicative of the microcosm/macrocosm binary so common in the language of literary allegory. The military metaphor permits the researchers to conceptualize the microcosmic activities of the immune system in the both the healthy and the HIV immuno-compromised bodies. In contrast, the same trope is also employed in the macrocosmic visualization of the collective body of state. Here the HIV infected individual is a single cancerous cell in the overarching organism that is the cultural body. Both of these metaphors are employed in *V for Vendetta*.

The post-apocalyptic English state is constructed as a single, highly efficient organism, actively eliminating all potential intrusions of disruptive bodies hazardous to the continued salubrious functioning of the establishment and the good order. The traditional representation of the administrative branch of government as the body's "head" is literalized in the language of *V for Vendetta*. Adam Sutler is, in a manner of speaking, the brain and perhaps nervous system of the governmental organism. He is continuously depicted as a giant head on a video screen to which the manager of each administrative subdivision reports and subsequently receives instructions coupled with harsh reprimands. The directors of the various departments are appropriately named, identified with the physical functions, or the senses, the human body's contact with the external world. Mr. Heyer is responsible for video surveillance of the population; thus he is appropriately nicknamed "the Eye." He reports on any disturbances of the peace within the body politic, monitoring citizen and governmental functionary alike. Mr. Etheridge is "the Ear," monitoring audio activity and providing the brain with quantitative data regarding the communications of the populace. In vehicles with powerful audio surveillance devices mounted on their roofs, his subordinates drive through quiet neighborhoods, collecting random samples of data from conversations within residences and communication networks. The appellation for Mr. Finch, the chief investigator within the law enforcement agency, is not terribly imaginative; he is identified as "the Nose," undoubtedly because of bloodhound associations common to the iconography of inspectors who sniff out crimes and criminals. Dascomb facilitates the body's "Voice," which is Prothero, thus both are associated with circulation of official (dis)information. Mr. Creedy is "the Finger." More prominent than the police, Creedy and his Fingermen are responsible for the interdiction of those bodies deemed incompatible with healthy and efficient ordering of the state. He curtails sedition and ideological impurity by abducting and eliminating those who are disruptive of the body politic's various systems.

The body of state is a radically nationalized body, the mind itself having become unhinged, savagely sexist, xenophobic, and homophobic, a condition resulting from extreme paranoia and fear of pollution. Even before the outbreaks of the St. Mary's virus, the country had begun to engage in a "Reclamation" which involved a radical redefining of citizenship and the application civil rights. In a fashion reminiscent of Nazi genocide and eugenics, the body politic began to purge itself of what was considered ethnic, racial, and sexual contagion — a literalizing of the expression "ethnic cleansing," or perhaps it is more akin to the idea of ethnic decontamination. The radicalized nationalistic consciousness defines itself through the creation of enemies or antagonists who signify all that should be excluded from the national body in the process of (re)defining the self. The existence of foreign, illicit, and/or depraved elements within the body is both an obstacle and an opportunity, the former insofar as the foreign organism must be eliminated in order to (re)gain a collective identity, and the latter insofar as the occasion for that cleansing of the system is itself the primary moment of self-definition. The subject is constructed via the continual creation and abjection of the "not self." The very existence of Creedy's clandestine service requires that a substantial portion of the population be retrograde to the coherent and healthy functioning of the state. In the event that all subversion were eliminated, the nationalistic systems would require the creation of newly demonized and interdicted populations. The role that racial and physical "purity" plays in the ideology of the Norsefire regime is glaringly apparent in the state slogan of the Sutler regime — "Strength Through Unity, Unity Through Faith" — and perhaps even more so in Moore and Lloyd's version — "Strength Through Purity, Purity Through Faith."

The inclusion of macro- and microcosmic visions of the social and political bodies generates a particularly rich biomedical trope within the subtext of the film. Here V becomes a literalization of the virus, which has colonized the body and redefined the identity, or perhaps more accurately, erased the identity. He can no longer remember who he is after his infection with the St. Mary's virus, and his emergence from the conflagration of the Larkhill facility emphasizes his facelessness; all character and identity have been burned away. Catherine Waldby argues that viral and bacterial contagions create an "ontological crisis" for those who become infected. The replication of the virus takes place within the host organism's own cells, which are appropriated by the foreign antigen and put to the task of betraying their own biological system. The virus becomes integrated into the body at the molecular and genetic levels, creating a human/viral hybrid, infected and infecting others both at the micro and macro levels (1). The progressive colonization and eventual destruction of the host organism is the inevitable culmination of the virus's activities. The role that V plays within the body politic creates an extensive allegory of the effects of a virus on a healthy system, with particular allusions to the impact of HIV and AIDS on the physical and the ideological bodies.

V's infiltration of the healthy system and his eventual revelation as a threat to order occurs after ten years of furtive activities in which the very powers threatened by his virulence remain ignorant of his existence, and yet he was corrupting and restructuring the body of state even before the Norsefire party came to power. The lengthy incubation of V's vendetta against the state has taken over ten years, a potential allusion to the prolonged period that the HIV compromised body requires in the progression from seropositive to symptomatic (Waldby 116–117). V explains that he spent more than ten years clearing and laying the tracks for the train that will eventually carry explosives to Westminster and the seat of government. Moreover, he harnesses the political body's own systems in his self-replication and his subversion of bodily functions. Indeed, he turns the powers of state against themselves, exploiting them to their own detriment. The replication of V the virus is literalized in the proliferation of masks, specifically Guy Fawkes masks. V's appearance suggests the weakening of the body's health, specifically its powers for interdicting and eliminating unhealthy foreign organisms. However, by the time he is identified and taken as a serious threat to the good order, he is already ubiquitous.

The replication of V via the distribution of masks is a literalization of the progressive spread of disease through the infected body. At the beginning of the film, there is only one viral cell within the body politic, but its recruitment of neophytes is energetic, overwhelming the body's defenses within one year of V's first appearance, from November 5th to November 5th. HIV infiltrates the tissue cells, co-opting the "natural gates and alleys of the body" for the distribution of the antigen throughout the lymphatic system. The imagery of McTeigue's *V for Vendetta* emphasizes the apparatus of transport employed in the manufacture and duplication of V's. The first example of the same is the surprising arrival of Guy Fawkes costumes and masks at the BTN news center prior to V's temporary takeover of the facility. However, prior to the first anniversary of the Old Bailey terrorist attack of November 5, the Fawkes masks have proliferated, arriving by boxcar and by lorry. Investigators Finch and Dominic estimate the distribution at hundreds of thousands prior to the attack on Parliament. If V masks signify viral cells, then the propagation of the former within the body politic suggests widespread contamination. Increasingly the Fawkesian masks begin to appear on the street obscuring the identities of those who are fomenting dissent within the social and political systems. After the summary execution of the little girl in the Fawkes mask who is spray painting V's on the Norsefire Party propaganda, the true allegiances of the formerly undisguised public are demonstrated. The citizens attack the Fingerman responsible for the infamy, and by the end of the film, the viral proselytes assume control of the streets, openly donning Fawkesian masks and overwhelming the defenses of the state.

The ability of the HIV to hide in plain sight mimicking healthy cells is one of its baffling and devastating anomalies. Waldby describes the virus's ability to mask itself:

> This failure to see is partly due to the protean and duplicitous "appearance" of the virus itself, which has a range of disguising and mimicking strategies. Once in the body it may for example "mimic certain molecules normally found on cells of uninfected individuals." The virus itself displays a high degree of biological variability, so that it can for example alter its viral envelope ... or, more simply, change its disguise [69].

Those individuals whose viral load has been reduced to zero through treatment are nevertheless assumed still infected with the virus hiding in what appears to be healthy cells. The behavior of the virus in this context creates a rich metaphor for subversion within the state; here malcontents committed to perpetrating sedition within the body politic appear to be obedient social subjects undermining the status quo even as they occupy elevated positions within the governmental apparatus. HIV's ability to disguise itself is embodied literally in V's propensity for masquerade. The opening images of the film reveal V primping in front of the mirror, and several times the camera returns to his dressing room. His disguises as Guy Fawkes, as interrogator and Fingerman in the torture scenes and as the long dead William Rookwood who reveals the insidious politics behind the St. Mary's viral outbreak constitute additional examples of his theatrical skills. He appears to be not only harmless but allied with the apparatus that would displace him. He also recruits Evey in his masking practices, enlisting her to impersonate an innocent school girl in order entrap Bishop Lilliman. Moreover, her own cosmetic rituals prior to socializing are visually equated to V's masking. The camera moves between V's and Evey's dressing room in the opening sequence of the film. For Evey, the most profound transformation follows her incarceration and torture, when her head is shaved. Her internal transformation becomes externalized, her altered character making her physically unrecognizable.

The effect of the infiltration of HIV into the human immune system has inspired a variety of blindness tropes in the language immunologists use to describe the disease. The virus, for example, has the capacity to make the immune system misrecognize itself and even eradicate healthy tissue (Waldby 69). The ability to turn the system against itself is one of V's most effective techniques. In the resolution of his attack upon the BTN network, the law enforcement misrecognizes BTN employees who have been disguised with Fawkesian masks in order to facilitate V's escape. He also effectively turns the various branches of the government against each other. Finch becomes progressively suspicious of the activities of both Sutler and Creedy whom he holds responsible for the country's worst terrorist attack, and Creedy becomes increasingly critical of Finch's allegiances since the inspector is unable to find V within the year allotted for his capture. The most dramatic compromise of the system's unity is embodied in the progressive hostility between Creedy and Sutler. Knowing he will be blamed for the failure to prevent V from blowing up parliament, Creedy turns his spy and security apparatus against the head of government, placing his own loyal operatives in charge of presidential security. Similarly, in order to save face with the English people following the failure to apprehend the terrorist V, Sutler plans to offer Creedy as a scapegoat. However, V's infiltration of the system allows him to predict the behavior of the two desperate men, and he succeeds in turning them against each other to their mutual destruction. He offers himself to Creedy if Creedy will hand over Sutler. The result is the death of all three men.

The long term effect of HIV on the immune system is another type of blindness or rather a loss of discernment. The human immune system is committed to the maintenance of the boundary between self and not self. Its job is to identify and eliminate intrusive "foreign antigens." This capacity has been dubbed the "biological nationality" (64). It is in describing this particular functioning of the immune system that Waldby recognizes the preponderance of bellicose imagery in the language of medicine:

> In biomilitary immunology the immune system cells regularly appear
> as the armed defenders of the vulnerable nation state body, where
> degrees of health are equated to degrees of mobilization [58].

That aspect of the immune system responsible for the identification and destruction of invading microorganisms is the T-cells, within which there is one subdivision known as "killer T-cell." This latter group is directed to the site of infection by the "T4 immune cells" which are consistently referred to as the "director[s] or commander[s] of the immune system" responsible for mobilization of the "armed defenders" (62). It is the T4 cell that is initially colonized by the virus, thus effectively undermining the system's ability to see and communicate. The killer T-cells can no longer recognize and subsequently eradicate the invading organisms. The national boundaries of the body state become compromised, literally opened up to invading armies or opportunistic infection. The self is overrun by the "not self" and the immune system betrays the politic body by refusing to preserve its borders:

> The consequence of this capitulation of the T-cells to the virus is in
> other words the eventual complete collapse of the self /other distinc-
> tion as it is figured in immunology. The body loses its biological
> national boundaries and is overtaken by foreign organisms because its
> standing army has been successfully infiltrated, perverted and demol-
> ished. Its dehierarchisation is equated with debilitating chaos and dis-
> solution, death by a kind of infectious entropy where the closed system
> is thrown open to a dangerous outside [Waldby 69–70].

The homicidal propensities and figural bigotry of the immune system which will not tolerate difference and diversity generates a rich metaphor for nationalistic politics and particularly that of the Norsefire fascist regime. The reclamation that took place in the recent past of the film was a nationalistic purging of those elements of the society considered troublesome to the salubrious functioning of the state. The events are reminiscent of speeches by Pat Buchanan and Pat Robertson at the 1992 Republican National Convention, particularly the former, which was organized around the refrain "Take back America." What followed was a list of those people who would be purged from the ailing system, who would be deemed America's "not self" in the process of racial, ethnic, gender, and social purification. Similarly, Prothero's infamous list of undesirables eliminated at the reclamation included "immigrants. Muslims. [and] homosexuals," who were shortly thereafter a "pestilence stricken multitude ... charioted to their wintry beds." The continued intolerance of the system is embodied in Creedy's Fingermen whose efficacy and brutality is reviled even by those who are allied with the system. The roving groups of Fingermen who patrol the streets looking for curfew violators and other petty criminals, against whom they are evidently given permission to perform summary executions, are suggestive of the "Killer T-Cells" directed by the surveillance portions of the governmental apparatus. The treatment of Gordon, who secretes a copy of the Holy Koran within his hiding space, is perhaps the most glaring example of the continued eradication of the "not self." The system operates against him with machine-like efficiency, oblivious to his celebrity and influence.

V's survival following the attempted eradication of undesirables indicates the biological system's inability to identify all of the viral cells in its effort to interdict HIV. A small portion of the antigen undermines the system's integrity and survives, hiding underground in the closed tube system of London. After the Saint Mary's viral attack on London commuters, the Sutler regime closed down the London tube network, ostensibly to deter further terrorism in a locale where Londoners have frequently been vulnerable to attack. (Irritated, I once asked a British policemen standing outside the Embankment station in Westminster why there were no garbage cans on the platform. He responded with no small amount of sarcasm, "Because people have a tendency to put bombs in them.") However, the real reason may be that they sought to cordon off an area that was difficult to monitor for subversive activities. Closing down this important urban transport creates a double entendre — shutting down the "underground" — an elimination of the train system and a euphemism for destroying the network of subversives who constitute a resistance to the power apparatus. The tubes within the biomedical metaphor of the body politic suggest the various transport system within the physical body, such as the circulatory, lymphatic, and nervous systems. Appropriating a space for himself in the abandoned network of tunnels, V has literally and figuratively made his home deep within the body's tissue where he hides, waiting for the opportunity to break forth, destroying the organism that has tormented and pursued him. He even uses the tunnels to deliver the death blow to the nerve center of the political collective — Westminster. His freedom of movement throughout the city is doubtlessly facilitated by the abandoned tunnels, and it is within this complex that he stages his final confrontation with Sutler and Creedy, subtly evoking in spatial terms the dark secrets of the national leaders, who are every bit as subversive as those they pursue.

In the progression of HIV disease, the lymphatic system becomes compromised by its own efficiency, and treatments sometimes include the suppression of the immune system long enough for it to recuperate. HIV uses the reproductive capacity of the T-Cells to replicate; by suppressing the production of these cells the duplication of the virus is curtailed. The figural militancy of the immune system operates to its own detriment; the homicidal and xenophobic T-Cells are compromised as they engage with the virus and are seduced into a "consensual but perverse [and ultimately destructive] union" (Waldby 68). Like HIV, the terrorist V breaks out after years of incubation, suddenly announcing his presence, appearing everywhere at once, a trope facilitated by his broadcast via the BTN takeover when he appears on every television screen in the nation. He then effectively disappears save for the traces of his presence illustrated by the red graffiti V's sprayed over the Norsefire propaganda posters. The population's progressive adoption of Guy Fawkes masks indicates the proliferation of the Viral V throughout the system as the government loses credibility because it is unable to stop terrorism. Finch describes the process in which the militancy of Norsefire leaders results in an even faster replication of cells, the increasing unrest within the body politic compelling Sutler to do "the only thing he knows how to do," which is to mobilize his armed forces against the civilian population, an action that results in an anti–Norsefire backlash, thus staging a spectacle of the power structure's impotence. Finch observes that the actions are all part of V's strategy to turn the various factions of government and population against each other and to his advantage.

The final simultaneous confrontations between V, Sutler, Creedy, Evey, and Finch, the dissident population of London and the armed forces suggest the final collapse of the system to chaos or more appropriately "anarchy," Moore and Lloyd's original topic. AIDS is a rich metaphor for revolution and anarchy within the body politic; "the closed system is thrown open to a dangerous outside" (Waldby 70), and any marauding adventurers can bustle in the resulting disorder. The anarchy is aided by the collapse of communication within the system. V destroys the head of government as well as the leader responsible for the direction of clandestine, security, and military forces. Evey, shortly thereafter, recruits to the revolutionary cause inspector Finch who permits her to destroy Parliament, silently conceding that there is indeed "something wrong with this country" and that its government must be destroyed in order to be reconstructed. The triumph of the unarmed population over the military forces guarding Parliament and Westminster results from the failure of communication between the varied branches of government. The armed forces merely await instructions from leaders who are already dead, leaders who have the ability to identify as enemies and direct lethal force against the civilians who constituted a threat to the good health of the nation. However, just as in the compromised immune system is rendered blind by the subversions of the virus, the order to interdict civil unrest never comes and the mass of Londoners are able to breach the defensive line. The ubiquitous presence of the Guy Fawkes masks among the protesters reveals both their alliance with V and, subsequently, their representation as viral or destructive cells. The allegorical significance of that episode is reinforced when the multitude remove their masks, and among the mass of humanity are many of the characters who died in the resistance to the collapsing regime. While superficially the return of these characters may be only an homage to the resistance fighters who died in the struggle against the fascist regime, the recurrence may also suggest the replication of the viral cells and the inability of the system to eliminate all subversive elements.

The rehabilitative quality of chaos or anarchy implied at the conclusion of the film seems counterintuitive, contrary to the good health of the body politic. After all, good health in biomedical discourse is equated to the orderly and savagely discriminatory immune system, filtering all invasive elements, all that do not work toward the unified national and biological identities:

> The normative ideal of health which circulates implicitly in AIDS discourse ... can be summarized as a seamless, impermeable, individuated body, a body inimical to infectious processes [Waldby 40].

Perhaps this is where the immunological metaphor of the "biological nationality" collapses, becoming incongruous with the priorities of the lived societies. The so-called xenophobia and bigotry of the immune system is not an adequate pattern for the complexity of contemporary societies. The effort to suppress potentially subversive elements within the political system, even before they have even been positively identified as inimical to peace and order, is fascist, a program for genocide, for racial, ethnic, moral, and ethical cleansing. Paradoxically, liberal democracy can be understood as a form of controlled chaos or anarchy, at least in the biological sense. The tolerance of difference and diversity within the political body is essential for a compassionate and decent society. Thus democracy is always going to have an element of danger and disorder, but it is a price worth paying for the coveted freedom of dissent, speech, and self-determination.

The anarchic breach of the military lines in the concluding images of *V for Vendetta* can also be understood as a counter-reclamation, the people taking back their government and their destinies from usurpers. Within the biomedical metaphor of the film, the triumphing over the bastions of fascist government may allude to PWAs' efforts to reclaim their lives and more importantly their public images in the wake of a devastating medical calamity. The metaphorical equation between AIDS and anarchy, AIDS and warfare, AIDS and sedition, AIDS and xenophobia, AIDS and divine wrath illustrates what Paula A. Treichler identified as an "epidemic of signification." The masses that faced down Sutler's military were maligned by the now dead chancellor, defined as complicit with the terrorist V just by virtue of their presence on the streets on the night of November 5. However, in the film's denouement, they reclaim the right to construct their own identities. In the first decade of the AIDS crisis, the people who suffered from the disease were too frequently identified as the disease itself:

> Gay masculinity has been so intensely medicalised and so closely associated with the AIDS epidemic that gay men are effectively treated by much of the public as if they themselves were the virus, the origins of infection [Waldby 12–13)].

The war upon AIDS became a war upon people with AIDS, who were construed as a corrosive and potentially debilitating segment of the body politic that, being removed, would reinstate a ante-lapsarian permissiveness in which unprotected and indiscriminate sex was once again safe sex. In its allegory of the early AIDS hysteria, the film effectively turns the tables on the religious and political right, revealing that the damned are those who failed to show compassion, courage, and humanity in the face of widespread suffering and death, who chose a medieval solution to a modern medical catastrophe, and the resulting pandemic can be blamed on these people who could not see past their prejudices in order to arm the public with information requisite to survival in a time of plague. The origins of the pandemic do not lie with those who first contracted it but with those who ignored it, and blame for the resulting chaos and the ubiquitous agonies of AIDS can be laid at their feet.

Conclusion

Of Shadow Texts

The "shadow text" can be construed as a simultaneous recreation and repudiation of the Platonic Ideal Forms, shadows cast on the wall of a cave for the benefit of benighted troglodytes. In this trope, the object carried before the fire, the same that cast the shadows in front of the bound observers, can be understood to signify either the primary or the second-ary text(s), the same with the shifting figures on the wall. If the puppets and puppeteers moving between the light source and the wall are the sec-ondary texts, then the shadows are primary created by the influence of antecedents, a distorted and refigured variation on an original that is sta-ble, but hidden. This, however, is too similar to a "metaphysics of pres-ence," a higher reality lying behind the shifting images, providing form and coherence, and hope for a revelation of truth when the subjects are once again united with the forms: the gum washed forever from their eyes. If the puppets are the immediate text — in this case *V for Vendetta* — the presumed interpretations, including source texts, play upon the wall, ephemeral shades cast in alternative directions simultaneously by multi-ple light sources — the fire and the diffuse light from the cave entrance. As the fire flickers, the shadows tremble, and the imagery shifts over time with the puppeteers progressing along the pathway before the fire. But here the model creates a stable and contained primary text that is merely subject to imperfect and discontinuous interpretations and speculation about ori-gins, and the handling of the puppets presupposes a puppet master whose intentions and perceptions are prioritized, even finalized, within the sys-tem of signification. The captives in the cave may have no closure in their apprehension of forms and concepts, but the puppeteers do, implying that the latter retain an absolute truth and understanding, a closure in the play of signifiers. Form suggests that the reflected text (or puppet) is stable, not subject to the cuts, biases, and reconfigurations of an all perceiving intellect. In this metaphor, the signifier would be stabilized within the mind of "God," thus initiating a return to the primitive myth of languages origins.

The fire itself may be the more appropriate signifier for the perceiver as it is the point of view creating the image. The image of the bound and passive audience on the floor of the cave is problematic. Here the model casts the author/creator as the final arbiter of meaning, retaining a consistent artistic point of view or significance that the audience/reader must get at. Intertextual theory makes the audience and the creator equal perceivers and interpreters; the author creator does not confer meaning but sets the signifiers at play and watches them multiply relations beyond intention, prediction, and control. If we cast the puppets as words and the images on the wall as the viewer's specific concepts, then we can come closer to post-structuralist linguistic theory and the intertext, but we must also place the fire within the equation. The shifting, swaying, waxing and waning fire constitutes the potential signifieds for a single signifier, the puppet, the material word or sound image. In this context the image on the wall is then the interplay of signifier and all of the potential signifieds from which the perceiver creates meaning consistent with context and disposition, but these concepts shift within the perceiver's scope (the movement of the figures across the pathway) until they disappear altogether from consciousness. The diffuse light from the mouth of the cave suggests that the concepts on the wall are always washed out by the second light source, possibly — depending on placement — creating concurrent images of the same object, the second light source facilitating the apprehension of the text's plurality.

The men bound in the cave call out the names of the passing shadows, suggesting a social dimension to the coupling of signifier and signified. Thus we can model the role of tradition or social repetition within Plato's figure. The voices can perpetuate a single interpretation or offer new perspectives on a familiar shadow. In this tortuous and unorthodox (and probably reductive) re-creation of Plato's cave allegory, I have sought to demonstrate that plurality resides even in the ancient figure advocating stability in abstract concepts. The voices echoing in the cave are legion; they may come to a consensus on naming, but that does not unify the various mental configurations of iconic figures and names. The troglodytes may agree on names; they may be able to predict the placement of shadows in the succession, but that does not mean that their respective concepts of the same concur. Nor can the creator or puppetmaster retain any control of the ephemeral artifact once it has been cast as a shadow on the wall.

Plato's cave seems to be a particularly apt metaphor for film, which is literally lights and shadows playing upon the wall for the benefit of a temporarily enthralled audience. While the projection of the image itself implies an intention to convey meaning to a second and third party, the *auteur* has little control over the reception of his shadows, however. The intertext intervenes in several places within this process of film creation, and here I once again model my idea within Plato's cave. Antecedent textuality can insert itself in the modeling of the puppets or in the angle of the light or the posture of the puppet master as he carries the figure in front of the fire. The intertext intercedes in the creative process, the artist driven by experiences and influences that are not even accessible to the conscious mind, and the intertext plays within the mind of the various audience members, all of whom have unique engagements with the world around them, and even if the artist could achieve a moment of transcendent creativity, producing an artifact completely unrelated to former experience, could break the bonds of history, culture, and nature, his or her work would ultimately be processed by minds still fettered to a tradition both personal and collective. The audience would be forced to vulgarize the ideal creative artifact through personal comparisons, just as the rattlesnake meat tastes like chicken.

Those who engage the *V for Vendetta* text (film or graphic novel) can appreciate or repudiate the work for a variety of reasons, some even paradoxical. The unthinking adolescent male will understand the film as escapist art, an action flick that delivers all of the requisite violence and excitement. The well-tutored (or should I say "Tudored") Englishman may perceive the narrative as a long awaited vindication of the 17th century counterculture hero/villain Guy Fawkes, along with an attendant acknowledgment that the historic struggles of Catholics against the English throne, since the mid sixteenth century, were justice not sedition. The Jewish audience would surely be engaged by the not so subtle allusions to and denunciation of Hitler, Nazism, and particularly the Holocaust. The

Muslim audience member may walk away from the film feeling exonerated by the narrative of the unprincipled Western government that scapegoats Muslims in an effort to hide its own grasping villainy or by the suggestion that under extreme duress violence is not terrorism but justice. The lettered audience may be hung up on the exploration of literary antecedents for the narrative, particularly the Shakespearean and Orwellian references which seem to have a wide-ranging appeal, and art scholars may perceive the film as a humanities lesson, not only on the necessity of preserving the artifacts that define culture and subjectivity, but also on the dynamic relationship between art and the culture that creates or apprehends it. Feminists will deplore the maltreatment of women by political orthodoxy on both right and left — Valerie Page persecuted by the right and Evey by the left. While the political right is unapologetic in its repression and repudiation of the feminine, the left ostensibly injures women for their own good. V tortures Evey to edify her, while the Sutler regime pursues her because she is antagonistic toward and antithetical to rightwing objectives. The Gay/Lesbian audience will not fail to recognize the cinematic repudiation of rightwing policies that deny same-sex couples their emotional and sexual attachments, and they can be expected to appreciate the condemnation of the inhumane, incharitable, irresponsible, neglectful, and perhaps even genocidal response of the American and British governments to the most devastating health crisis of the twentieth century.

This variety of potential responses is elicited by the viewing of a single film through the rose colored glasses of individual context and subjectivity. The narrative that initially seems unitary, spreads out like a Chinese folding fan, revealing a legion of alternate narrative ribs, all issuing from a common origin and bound by a unifying tissue of details, but also possessing their own unique trajectories. The above chapters constitute the arbitrary imposition of a variety of textual paradigms onto a single narrative, demonstrating the general relativity of readings derived from any one text, readings that compete with and shadow each other, tricks of the light, generated by the angle of observation. While the individual chapters within this study seem to be traditional source studies, the sheer number of simultaneous readings and interpretations divulge the intertextual play as well as the post-modern pastiche — the pieces of a fragmented culture pasted together to create a unified and pleasing secondary aesthetic object. In this sense, V's Shadow Gallery is a trope for a construction of the film, reappropriating and rearranging the pieces of a two thousand year old aesthetic and interpretive tradition in the doomed effort to create something new. Within the cinematic gallery, the audience views the diversity of images and ideas, selecting, processing, and constructing an entertainment of their own liking, one derived from preexisting images, patterns, ideas, and languages, an entertainment that is beyond their intention, control, or comprehension.

Like V's gallery, the film operates as microcosm, meta-text, or even manifesto for a stream of information that the post-modern audience is forced to process in the confrontation with their personal experiences. The film captures passions, histories, agendas, dogmas, traditions, discourses, and ideologies — a high cultural tutorial for the masses and a violent playground for intellectuals and aesthetes.

Bibliography

Alaya, Flavia M. "Tennyson's *The Lady of Shalott*: The Triumph of Art." *Victorian Poetry* 8 (1970): 273–289.

Allen, Graham. *Intertextuality*. London: Routledge, 2000.

Antonio, Gene. *The AIDS Cover–up: The Real and Alarming Facts about AIDS*. Fort Collins, CO: Ignatious Press, 1987.

Armstrong, Isobel. "*The Lady of Shalott*: Victorian Mythography and the Politics of Narcissism." In *The Sun Is God*. Ed. Barrie Bullen. Oxford: Oxford University Press, 1988.

Asquith, Clare. *Shadowplay: The Hidden Beliefs and Coded Politics of William Shakespeare*. New York: Public Affairs, 2005.

Bakhtin, Mikhail. *Rabelais and His World*. Trans. H. Isowolsky. Cambridge, MA: MIT Press, 1968.

Barthes, Roland. *Image-Music-Text*. Trans. Stephen Heath. London: Fontana, 1977.

_____. *S/Z: An Essay*. Trans. Richard Miller. New York: Hill and Wang, 1974.

Bergman, Ingmar. *The Seventh Seal. Four Screenplays by Ingmar Bergman*. Trans. Lars Malmstrom and David Kushner. New York: Simon and Schuster, 1960. 95–164.

Bevington, David, ed. *The Complete Works of Shakespeare*. 3rd ed. Dallas: Scott, Foresman, 1980.

Bloom, Harold. *Shakespeare: The Invention of the Human*. New York: Riverhead, 1998.

Botticelli, Sandro. *Birth of Venus*. Galleria Degli Uffizi, Florence.

Bowers, Fredson. *Elizabethan Revenge Tragedy 1587–1642*. Princeton: Princeton University Press, 1940.

Bradbury, Ray. *Fahrenheit 451*. New York: Ballantine, 1950.

Bray, R.S. *Armies of Pestilence: The Impact of Disease on History*. New York: Barnes & Noble, 1996.

Brazil. Dir. Terry Gilliam. Universal, 1985.

Buckley, Jerome. *Tennyson: The Growth of a Poet*. Cambridge, MA: Harvard University Press, 1960.

Budiansky, Stephen. *Her Majesty's Spy Master: Elizabeth I, Francis Walsingham, and the Birth of Modern Espionage*. New York: Plume, 2005.

Chadwick, Joseph. "A Blessing and a Curse: The Poetics of Privacy in Tennyson's *The Lady of Shalott*." In *Critical Essays on Alfred Lord Tennyson*. Ed. Herbert F Tucker. New York: G.K. Hall, 1993. 83–99.

Collinson, Patrick. "The Elizabethan Church and the New Religion." In *The Reign of Elizabeth I*. Ed. Christopher Haigh. Athens: University of Georgia Press, 1987. 169–194.

Connell, R.W. *Gender and Power*. Stanford, CA: Stanford University Press, 1987.

Copley, John Singleton. *Death of Major Peirson*. Tate Museum, London.

Count of Monte Cristo, The. Dir. Rowland V. Lee. United Artists, 1934.

Crimp, Douglas, ed. *AIDS: Cultural Analysis/Cultural Activism*. Cambridge, MA: MIT Press, 1993.

Culler, Dwight. *The Poetry of Tennyson*. New Haven, CT: Yale University Press, 1977.

Culler, Jonathan. *Ferdinand de Saussure*. Ithaca, NY: Cornell University Press, 1976.

Dante Alighieri. *The Divine Comedy*. New York: Everyman's Library, 1995.

Delaroche, Paul. *The Execution of Lady Jane Grey*. National Gallery, London.

Derrida, Jacques. *Of Grammatology*. Trans. Gayatri Chakravorty Spivak. Baltimore: Johns Hopkins University Press, 1974.

Dowling, William C. *Jameson, Althusser, Marx: An Introduction to the Political Unconscious*. London: Methuen, 1984.

Dumas, Alexandre. *The Count of Monte Cristo*. Trans. Lowell Bair. New York: Bantam, 1956.

Duvall, Raymond D., and Michael Stohl. "Governance by Terror." In *The Politics of Terrorism*. 3rd ed. Ed. Michael Stohl. New York: Marcel Dekker, 1988.

Feldman, Jaime L. *Plague Doctors: Responding to the AIDS Epidemic in France and America*. South Hadley, MA: Bergin & Garvey, 1995.

Fish, Stanley. *How Milton Works*. Cambridge, MA: Harvard University Press, 2001.

Foucault, Michel. *Discipline and Punish: The Birth of the Prison*. Trans Alan Sheridan. New York: Vintage, 1979.

Fraser, Antonia. *The Gunpowder Plot: Terror and Faith in 1605*. London: Weidenfeld & Nicolson, 1996.

Frieda, Leonie. *Catherine de Medici: Renaissance Queen of France*. New York: Harper, 2003.

Frodsham, John David. "The New Barbarians: Totalitarianism, Terror and the Left Intelligentsia in Orwell's 1984." *World Affairs* 147 (1984): 139–161.

Gardiner, Michael. *The Dialogics of Critique*. London: Routledge, 1992.

Giacometti, Alberto. *Man Pointing*. Tate Museum, London.

Gillies, Alexander. *Goethe's Faust: An Interpretation*. Oxford: Basil Blackwell, 1957.

Gilman, Sander L. "AIDS and Syphilis: The Iconography of Disease." In *AIDS: Cultural Analysis/Cultural Activism*. Ed. Douglas Crimp. Cambridge, MA: MIT Press, 1993. 87–108.

Ginsberg, Allen. *Howl and Other Poems*. San Francisco: City Lights Books, 1956.

Giroux, Henry. "Representations of the Unreal: Bush's Orwellian Newspeak." *Afterimage* 33 (2005). 18+.

Glassner, Barry. *The Culture of Fear: Why American Are Afraid of the Wrong Things....* New York: Basic Books, 1999.

Grace, William J. *Ideas in Milton*. Notre Dame, IN: University of Notre Dame Press, 1968.

Greco, El. *A View of Toledo*. Metropolitan Museum of Art, New York.

Greene, Brian. *The Elegant Universe*. New York: Vintage, 1999.

_____. *The Fabric of the Cosmos*. New York: Knopf, 2004.

Grunewald, Matthias. *The Crucifixion*. Musée d'Unterlinden, Colmar.

Goethe, Johann Wolfgang Von. *Faust, Part I*. London: Penguin, 2005.

Hall, Edwin. *The Arnolfini Betrothal: Medieval Marriage and the Enigma of Van Eyck's Double Portrait*. Berkeley: University of California Press, 1997.

Happé, Peter. "'The Vice' and the Popular Theatre, 1547–1580." In *Poetry and Drama 1570–1700: Essays in Honour of Harold F. Brooks*. Ed. Antony Coleman and Antony Hammond. New York: Methuen, 1981. 13–31.

Hogge, Alice. *God's Secret Agents*. New York: HarperCollins, 2005.

Hope, Charles. *Titian*. London: Chaucer Press, 1986.

Huxley, Aldous. *Brave New World*. New York: Perennial, 1932.

Iampolski, Mikhail. *The Memory of Tire-*

sias: Intertextuality and Film. Trans. Harsha Ram. Berkeley: University of California Press, 1998.

Idiocracy. Dir. Mike Judge. Twentieth Century–Fox, 2006.

Jackson, Richard. "The Discourses of Terrorism: Myths and Misconceptions: Richard Jackson Discusses the Nature of Terror and Questions the Likelihood of Success in the Present United States-Led War on It." *New Zealand International Review* 27 (2002): 1.

Joseph, Gerhard. "Victorian Weaving: The Alienation of Work into the Text in *The Lady of Shalott.*" *Victorian Newsletter* 71 (1987): 7–10.

Kaku, Michio. *Parallel Worlds.* New York: Anchor, 2005.

Kaye, Richard A. "Losing his religion: Saint Sebastian as Contemporary Gay Martyr." In *Outlooks: Lesbian and Gay Sexualities and Visual Cultures.* Ed. Peter Horne and Reina Lewis. London: Routledge, 1996. 86–108.

Kelly, Joh. *The Great Mortality.* New York: Harper, 2005.

Kristeva, Julia. *Desire in Language: A Semiotic Approach to Literature and Art.* New York: Columbia University Press, 1980.

Kyd, Thomas. *The Spanish Tragedy.* Ed. J.R. Mulryne. New York: Norton, 1985.

Lamm, Spencer, and Sharon Bray. *V for Vendetta: From Script to Film.* New York: Universal Publishing, 2006

Lee, Christopher. *1603: The Death of Elizabeth I and the Birth of the Stuart Era.* London: Review, 2003.

Lee, Jonathan Scott. *Jacques Lacan.* Amherst: University of Massachusetts Press, 1990.

MacCulloch, Diarmaid. *The Boy King: Edward VI and the Protestant Reformation.* New York: Palgrave, 1999.

Machiavelli, Niccolo. *The Prince.* New York: Norton, 1977.

Marlowe, Christopher. *Doctor Faustus.* Ed. Roma Gill. New York: Norton, 1989.

Martin, Robert Bernard. *Tennyson: The Unquiet Heart.* London: Oxford University Press, 1980.

Mattingly, Garrett. *The Armada.* Boston: Houghton Mifflin, 1959.

Millais, John Everett. *Ophelia.* Tate Museum, London.

Milton, John. *Paradise Lost.* In *John Milton: Complete Poems and Major Prose.* Ed. Merritt Y. Hughes. Indianapolis: Bobbs-Merrill, 1957.

Montrose, Louis A. "Professing the Renaissance: The Poetics and Politics of Culture." In *The New Historicism.* Ed. H. Aram Veeser. New York: Routledge, 1989.15–36.

Moore, Alan, and David Lloyd. *V for Vendetta.* New York: DC Comics, 1988.

Murphy, Timothy F. *Ethics in an Epidemic: AIDS, Morality and Culture.* Berkeley, CA: University of California Press, 1994.

Nacos, Brigette L. *Terrorism and Counterterrorism: Understanding Threats and Responses in the Post-911 World.* New York: Longman, 2006.

Nance, Gusta Barfield. "The Philosophy of Goethe's *Faust.*" In *Southwest Goethe Festival: A Collection of Nine Papers.* Ed. Gilbert J. Jordan. Dallas: University of Texas, 1949.

Nineteen Eighty-Four. Dir. Michael Radford. Atlantic, 1984.

Oliverio, Annamaria. "The State of Injustice: The Politics of Terrorism and the Production of Order." *International Journal of Comparative Sociology* 38 (1997): 48–63.

Orr, Mary. *Intertextuality: Debates and Contexts.* Cambridge, UK: Polity Press, 2003.

Orwell, George. *1984.* New York: Signet, 1950.

Peacock, Ronald. *Goethe's Major Plays.* Manchester, UK: Manchester University Press, 1959.

Perdue, William D. *Terrorism and the State: A Critique of Domination through Fear.* Westport, CT: Praeger, 1989.

Plamenatz, John. "In Search of Machiavelli's *Virtu.*" In *The Political Calculus.* Ed. Anthony Parel. Toronto: University of Toronto Press, 1972. 157–178.

Plato. *The Republic.* Trans. Richard W. Sterling and William C. Scott. New York: Norton, 1985.

Porton, Richard. "*V for Vendetta.*" *Cineaste* 31 (2006): 52–54.

Psomiades, Kathy Alexis. "*The Lady of Shalott* and the Critical Fortunes of Victorian Poetry." In *The Cambridge Companion to Victorian Poetry.* Ed. Joseph Bristow. Cambridge: Cambridge University Press, 2000.

Psycho. Dir. Alfred Hitchcock. Paramount, 1960.

Psycho. Dir. Gus Van Zant. MCA/Universal. 1998.

Ragland-Sullivan, Ellie. *Jacques Lacan and the Philosophy of Psychoanalysis.* Urbana, IL: University of Illinois Press, 1987.

Revengers Tragedy. Dir. Alex Cox. Fantoma, 2003.

Ruffo-Fiore, Silvia. *Niccolo Machiavelli.* Boston: Twayne, 1982.

Rushing, William A. *The AIDS Epidemic: Social Dimensions of and Infectious Disease.* San Francisco: Westview Press, 1995.

Scott, Walter. *Ivanhoe.* New York: Tor Classic, 2000.

Seventh Seal, The. Dir. Ingmar Bergman. Janus Films, 1958.

Shakespeare, William. *The Complete Works of Shakespeare.* Ed. David Bevington. 3rd ed. Dallas: Scott, Foresman, 1980.

Shannon, Edgar F. "Poetry as Vision: Sight and Insight in *The Lady of Shalott.*" *Victorian Poetry* 19 (1981): 207–223.

Shaw, W. David. *Tennyson's Style.* Ithaca, NY: Cornell University Press, 1976.

Shelley, Mary. *Frankenstein.* Ed. Johanna M. Smith. Boston: Bedford, 1992.

Shelley, Percy Bysshe. "Ode to the West Wind." In *Shelley's Poetry and Prose: Norton Critical Edition.* Ed. Donald H.

Reiman and Sharon B. Powers. New York: Norton, 1977. 221–223.

Smith, Elton Edward. *The Two Voices: A Tennyson Study.* Lincoln: University of Nebraska Press, 1964.

Somerset, Anne. *Elizabeth I.* New York: St. Martin's, 1991.

Spivack, Bernard. *Shakespeare and the Allegory of Evil: The History of Metaphor in Relation to His Major Villains.* New York: Columbia University Press, 1958.

Stohl, Michael. "Demystifying Terrorism: The Myths and Realities of Contemporary Political Terrorism." In *The Politics of Terrorism.* Ed. Michael Stohl. New York: Marcel Dekker, 1988. 1–27.

Stohl, Michael, ed. *The Politics of Terrorism.* New York: Marcel Dekker, 1988.

Targ, Harry R. "Societal Structure and Revolutionary Terrorism: A Preliminary Investigation." In *The Politics of Terrorism.* Ed. Michael Stohl. New York: Marcel Dekker, 1988. 127–152.

Tennyson, Alfred. "The Lady of Shalott." In *Tennyson's Poerry: Norton Critical Edition.* Ed. Robert W. Hill. New York: Norton, 1971. 13–17.

Tillyard, E.M.W. *The Elizabethan World Picture.* New York, Vintage, 1943.

Titian. *Bacchus and Ariadne.* National Gallery, London.

Tourneur, Cyril. *The Revenger's Tragedy.* Ed. Brian Gibbons. New York: Norton, 1967.

Townshend, Charles. *Terrorism: A Very Short Introduction.* Oxford, UK: Oxford University Press, 2002.

Treichler, Paula A. "AIDS, Homophobia, and Biomedical Discourse: An Epidemic of Signification." In *AIDS: Cultural Analysis/Cultural Activism.* Ed. Douglas Crimp. Cambridge, MA: MIT Press, 1993. 31–70.

Turner, Joseph Mallord William. *The Burning of the Houses of Parliament, 16th of October 1834.* Tate Museum, London.

Twelfth Night. Dir. Trevor Nunn. Free Line, 1996.

Vaid, Urvashi. *Virtual Equality: The Mainstreaming of Gay and Lesbian Liberation.* New York: Anchor, 1995.

Van Gogh, Vincent. *The Church at Auvers-sur-Orsay.* Musée de Jeu de Paume, Paris.

Varricchio, Mario. "Power of Images/Images of Power in *Brave New World* and *Nineteen Eighty-Four.*" *Utopian Studies* 10 (1999): 98+.

Venus D'Arles. Musée de Louvre, Paris.

V for Vendetta. Dir. James McTeigue. Warner Bros., 2005.

"V for Vendetta." *Wikipedia.* 8 Oct. 2006. http://www.refernce.com/browse/wiki/V_for_Vedetta_(film).

Waith, Eugene. "Manhood and Valor in Two Shakespearean Tragedies." *ELH* 30 (1950): 265–268.

Waldby, Catherine. *AIDS and the Body Politic: Biomedicine and Sexual Difference.* London: Routledge, 1996.

Waterhouse, John William. *The Lady of Shalott.* The Tate Museum, London.

Watney, Simon. *Practices of Freedom: Selected Writings on HIV/AIDS.* Durham, NC: Duke University Press, 1994.

Wheale, Nigel, ed. *Postmodern Arts: An Introductory Reader.* London: Routledge, 1995.

Weir, Alison. *Henry VIII: The King and Court.* New York: Ballantine, 2001.

Whittaker, David J. *Terrorism: Understanding the Global Threat.* London: Pearson Longman, 2006.

Yeats, William Butler. "Sailing to Byzantium." In *Selected Poems and Two Plays of William Butler Yeats.* Ed. M.L. Rosenthal. New York: Collier, 1962. 95–96.

Yingling, Thomas and Robyn Wiegman. *AIDS and the National Body.* Durham, NC: Duke University Press, 1997.

Index

235

Index

Index